It Takes a
Family

a cooperative approach
to lasting sobriety

Debra Jay

Foreword by Robert L. DuPont, MD

HAZELDEN®

Hazelden
Center City, Minnesota 55012
hazelden.org

ISBN: 978-1-61649-534-3; ebook 978-1-61649-562-6

Library of Congress Cataloging-in-Publication Data is on file with the Library
of Congress.

Structured Family Recovery™ is a trademark of Debra Jay. Having proprietary
rights makes it possible to protect its integrity and professionalism.

Editor's notes
The names, details, and circumstances may have been changed to protect the
privacy of those mentioned in this publication.

This publication is not intended as a substitute for the advice of health care
professionals.

Alcoholics Anonymous, AA, and the Big Book are registered trademarks of
Alcoholics Anonymous World Services, Inc.

18 17 16 15 14   1 2 3 4 5 6

Developmental editor: Sid Farrar
Production editor: Mindy Keskinen
Cover design by Kathi Dunn, Dunn + Associates
Interior design by Terri Kinne
Typesetting by Bookmobile Design & Digital Publisher Services

To Sara Critton Jay

*who saved her son
by intervening on his addiction,
making it possible for me
to meet him and marry him
ten years later.*

Thank you with all my heart.

A fine glass vase goes from treasure to trash the moment it is broken. Fortunately, something else happens to you and me. Pick up your pieces. Then, help me gather mine.

—VERA NAZARIAN, novelist

How can I know who I am until I see what I do? How can I know what I value until I see where I walk?

—KARL WEICK, psychologist and author

Contents

† The name Structured Family Recovery™ is a trademark of Debra Jay.

Foreword

"Houston, we have a problem!"

The problem presented in this impressive new book is not out in space, it is close to home. Today the expected outcome of addiction treatment is relapse. In fact, relapse is so common that it is a central element in the definition of addiction.

Of course relapse is common with many health problems: asthma, for example, or heart attacks. But addiction is different, because there is a way to manage this common disorder that reliably produces long-term recovery, not relapse. Over the past decade my colleagues and I conducted the first national study of this system of care management, the state Physician Health Programs. Begun four decades ago, these programs were pioneered by physicians, many of whom were themselves in recovery from addiction. The core strategy to these diverse programs holds the promise of greatly improving outcomes for addicts and their families. This strategy is called the "New Paradigm."

In this book, Debra Jay unlocks the secrets of this revolutionary approach to addiction. She adds a significant new dimension by focusing on the role of the family both in creating this system of care management and in making it work, long term. The author highlights an essential element of the approach as no one else has: the crucial role of the addict's family in this terribly painful family disease. She makes clear that the family has a role in the addiction, but then she carries this analysis to an entirely new level, showing that the family is a major beneficiary of the miracle of recovery and has the power to create a recovery milieu that serves as a powerful shield against relapse. Recovery is not just about the addict. It is accomplished with a team built around the family, others closest to the addicted person, and the greater recovering community.

This new approach, which she calls Structured Family Recovery™, has transformed the power of the New Paradigm for recovery used by commercial pilots, attorneys, and health professionals, bringing it into our homes and families. Structured Family Recovery provides a first-of-its-kind road map and, with it, good reason to expect success.

The key to this new approach is the long-term management of care, starting with an intervention to deliver the addict into treatment and recovery. The special role of addiction treatment is to help the addict understand what is wrong—the "disease concept" of addiction—and what to do about it. That path leads to recovery: "Go to meetings, work the program, and don't use alcohol or other drugs of abuse." After treatment, this approach monitors for relapse to any substance use, meeting any relapse with swift, certain, and serious consequences.

Successful recovery produces positive consequences as the result of adherence to the program. In addition, this approach manages overall compliance with the recovery plan, including daily or near-daily Twelve Step meetings. While treatment is a crucial part of this process for most addicts, the magic is not in the treatment; it is in the Twelve Step programs of Alcoholics Anonymous, Narcotics Anonymous, and Al-Anon. These entirely free and ubiquitous fellowships are everywhere in the United States. They are spreading rapidly around the world. I have many reasons to be proud of the United States, but one of the things I am most grateful for and proud of is the creation of these unique fellowships beginning in Akron, Ohio, in 1935.

How did Debra Jay come to this important new understanding? In addition to working with alcoholics, addicts, and their families for nearly twenty-five years, she is a child of such a family. Every day she lives the lessons and the rewards of her family's own struggle to survive this often fatal and relapsing disease. Addiction is a teacher, often a cruel, even pitiless teacher. The lessons to be learned by the family in the crucible of addiction are as precious as they are hard-won.

So fasten your seat belts for a space-age journey out of the chemical slavery of addiction, a journey that makes recovery, not relapse, the expected outcome of addiction treatment.

—Robert L. DuPont, MD
President, Institute for Behavior and Health, Inc.
First Director of the National Institute on Drug Abuse

Acknowledgments

This book is a product of the gift of working with families of alcoholics and addicts for over two decades. They reliably show tremendous love and perseverance in the face of a disease that ruthlessly changes their addicted loved ones, sometimes beyond recognition. To each of those families, thank you. You taught me much about our higher selves and have given me cause for ongoing hope.

Jane Dystel, my agent at Dystel & Goderich Literary Management, is my guiding light who readily gives of her depth of knowledge, steadiness of purpose, and great wisdom. But more importantly, everything she does is ultimately informed by her unwavering integrity and heart.

I thank Sid Farrar, my editor at Hazelden Publishing, who made this book possible by seeing the importance of the vision. It is a better book by his urging to write it for families who choose either to work with a professional or to proceed without one. He did much to improve this book in innumerable ways. For first-rate copyediting, a big thanks to Monica Frischkorn, and thanks to Mindy Keskinen for her excellent work as production editor.

I am indebted to Robert L. DuPont, MD, for agreeing to write the foreword of this book. He is a great mind in the field of addiction, and I have long admired his work. I especially thank him for being such a giving and warm person.

I am deeply grateful for the behavior design work I had the privilege of doing with B. J. Fogg, PhD, who has expanded my mind in amazing ways. His work at Stanford University on designing behavior for lasting change has added tremendous richness to this book. To use his favorite word, "Awesome!"

Several people close to my heart have helped make this a better book in deeply appreciated ways: Jim Balmer, Kevin Crowther, Jon

Erickson, Lori Forseth, Donna Greenbury, Philippe Malouf, Jerry Moe, Patrice Selby, Nancy Solak, and Angelica Stokes. All generously gave of themselves, and I thank them all.

Lastly, I thank my dear husband, Jeff Jay, who is my inspiration and my rock. My gratitude goes far deeper than words could ever reach. Without him, I could never do what I do.

• • •

A Note to the Reader

The words *alcoholic, addict, alcoholism, drug addiction,* and *addiction* are used interchangeably. They all represent the same disease. For the sake of simplicity in this book, I use *addict* to describe anyone addicted to mood-altering substances, whether the drug being used is alcohol or another addictive substance. Likewise, the word *addiction* is used to describe the disease of chemical dependency.

Using addict and addiction is not a perfect solution to our practice of ascribing multiple words to portray this one disease. Alcoholics generally don't like to be called addicts, and addicts generally don't like to be called alcoholics. Despite these differences, I think we can agree that addiction is an accurate description of the resulting problem, regardless of the drug being used.

I do not use *substance abuse* or *substance abuser,* because a person can be an abuser without suffering from the disease of addiction. I do not use the new popular diagnostic term *substance use disorder,* because it is better left to the lexicon of researchers. I think the term obscures the personal nature of this disease and its power. So I prefer the words we have long used, the ones that resonate with us in a deep and intimate way, because this disease infuses the whole of us and our families.

In this book I refer primarily to the two original Twelve Step groups. Alcoholics Anonymous (AA) was founded in the 1930s for people addicted to alcohol, and Al-Anon was launched some twenty years later for the families and friends of alcoholics and drug addicts. Narcotics Anonymous (NA) was formed in 1953 for those addicted to drugs other than alcohol. While AA is still dedicated to recovery from alcoholism, people with multiple addictions can go to AA meetings as long as they focus on alcohol or addiction in general. Today there are a great number of Twelve Step recovery groups for both addicts and their families, a list of which can be found at sobernation.com.

I do not list all relevant information and attributions, sources, publishers, and dates in the main text of the book. Attributions and sources are listed when necessary in the back of the book.

I've divided the book into four parts. Part I challenges how we've been taught to think about the disease of addiction and what it takes to create lasting sobriety. Much of this information is enlightening not only to families but to professionals as well. Part II is a guide for bringing the entire family together and setting them on a path of recovery that lasts. It puts in place the missing link needed for successful sobriety and for the rebuilding of family relationships. Part III provides the tools for putting Structured Family Recovery into motion. Part IV includes tools, checklists, and resources to help your family in recovery. Many of these tools, including the checklists, are also available as free downloadable PDFs at www.hazelden.org/web/go/ittakesafamily.

● ● ●

We Come Home Together

Structured Family Recovery is so simple, so obvious, it's a wonder it hasn't been done before. Often the truly simple is the most revolutionary.

Success doesn't come magically or accidentally. It is a result of what we do. The same can be said of failure. Usually it is a small change in one direction or the other that determines if we win or lose. Structured Family Recovery helps us make the correct choices and then steadily keeps us on course over time.

Jim Collins, author of *Good to Great*, writing of the most successful companies around the world, said, "In each of these dramatic, remarkable, good-to-great corporate transformations, we found the same thing: There was no miracle moment. Instead, a down-to-earth, pragmatic, committed-to-excellence process—a framework—kept each company, its leaders, and its people on track for the long haul."[1] He could as easily have been writing about Structured Family Recovery It is exactly that—*a specific process and framework*—that keeps families on track in their recovery for the long haul, with the power to keep addicts sober in great numbers and make our families not only good, but great

Up until now, families have been mostly left out of the recovery equation, which surely contributes to the ubiquitous nature of relapse. Structured Family Recovery starts with a family and ends with a family recovery team. We support sobriety by bringing together family and addict in a way that creates unity and mutual triumphs. Turning to social science, we learn what really creates change—*challenging the things we've been taught.* We apply discoveries of how the workings of the brain affect how we make real-time choices in life. We put it all together to create a family recovery program that is simple and smart.

Structured Family Recovery is a GPS system, a way of navigating through addiction and recovery using the elements we know work. It's about connectivity not isolation. It goes beyond patient-centered care to family-centered recovery. By working together, we create a different story and unshackle ourselves from the power of addiction.

The first section of this book provides a broad scope of knowledge on addiction, recovery, and change, so we can better understand what we're up against, what's required for sobriety, and how we can make change last. The second section of the book is the guide for Structured Family Recovery, putting into action the goals of achieving lasting sobriety and rebuilding family trust and respect.

There are many ways we find help, both for the addict and the family. Treatment and family programs dot the map of this great country, giving us any manner of assistance and head starts. But they don't keep alcoholics sober or drug addicts clean; they just begin the process. What keeps the addicted from going back to drink or drugs for the long haul is outside the domain of professionals. Programs for families, marvelous as they are brief, don't prepare us for the day we're again standing in the kitchen face-to-face with our addict, who has now relapsed. I recall the words of a woman who had just smelled alcohol on her recovering husband's breath: "What do I do now? I went to the family program! No one told me what I do now!"

Structured Family Recovery is not a response to crisis, but a safeguard against it. We do not stand alone in the kitchen. We stand with family and the entire recovery community. We come prepared for crisis, smoothing the waters with a family living in recovery, gliding forward steadily, with perseverance, over the ripples of turbulence, looking ahead, working for something better, saying farewell to our past ways as best we can. Imperfection is in us and all around us, but we can embrace it as the place where change begins.

Coming together takes the powerless and makes them powerful. Structured Family Recovery brings this power to the family and, in cooperation with the larger recovery community, stands firm in the face of addiction, which trespassed into our homes and multiplied itself into our lives. We crowd addiction out by building a family life brimming with togetherness and recovery, even though we may start out not knowing our way back to each other.

Rather than leaving families clueless in the dark, second-guessing, hoping and praying, we place family smack-dab in the center of recovery. This is when things begin to change. We can no longer leave lasting sobriety to chance, waiting around for the addicted person to figure out what it means to succeed. The cost to families is far too great, and sometimes we pay a price that is beyond what anyone can bear to pay.

Follow the book as it's written. The information builds on itself to move you forward. Not just with head knowledge, but in real ways to change the course of what's to come. Recovery is practical. It requires we take action. This book shows families the way into recovery with a step-by-step presentation of the Structured Family Recovery model. It's a place where the world begins to change, and it comes from the changes within us.

Families can engage in Structured Family Recovery on their own or work with an addiction therapist trained specifically to do this work. Whichever you choose, I have only one word for you: *commitment*. Family members must demonstrate to the addict, in deed, what this word means. Then along the way (usually not immediately noticed), recovery heals us, individually and together.

If we can trust just a bit, if not yet in each other, in the greater providence of good, and walk forward with only the barest of faith, we will find what we could not see before. Too few find their way alone. Let us bring family and the beloved addict together. It is in the "we" that we find an elegance in life that is as sweet as it is powerful.

We belong to one another. Nothing can change that, not estrangement, not even death. *Family* is defined by belonging. When we use the word *family,* it's for each of us to know what that word means—who it is we belong to and who belongs to us. We are born into families, marry into them, or choose them from people we love best. But family goes beyond love; it's primordial. It defines us. We are born with a deep need for knowing there are people who will always show up when we need them, stick with us through thick and thin, and love us at our best and worst.

As author and columnist Erma Bombeck once said, "We were a strange little band of characters trudging through life . . . inflicting pain and kissing to heal it in the same instant, loving, laughing, defending, and trying to figure out the common thread that bound us all together."[2]

This book is about addiction and family and lasting sobriety, and, ultimately, about working together to find that place where everyone is okay and safe and happy.

● ● ●

PART I

What We Need to Know

THIS SECTION IS WRITTEN to provide families with a knowledge base for Structured Family Recovery. It isn't information as usual, but clearly explains how to go about making the change we want, challenging what we're taught to believe, giving us a better way of thinking. There's an old saying, "Nothing changes when nothing changes." This section is not only about change, but the surprising ways lasting change works.

The information in this section isn't an optional read; it's very much needed before putting Structured Family Recovery into practice, which is covered in part II.

The Missing Element

We have a problem.

Fifty to 90 percent of alcoholics and addicts relapse in the first year after treatment.[3] In the face of such grim figures, it's easy to toss around blame. *Treatment doesn't work. The addict isn't doing what she should. Doctors are the new drug pushers.* But the truth lies elsewhere for the most part, and requires a new conversation.

Relapse is caused by underestimating what it takes to stay sober. Addicts, their families, and society commonly minimize what is required for successful recovery. Addicts can't simply think their way out of addiction. Recovery requires action. It's much more than leaving the drug behind, whether that drug is alcohol, cocaine, marijuana, heroin, methamphetamine, pain medications, or tranquilizers. Recovery is about changing behaviors, which leads to changes in thinking. It's about honesty and willingness and letting go of resentments. It's about taking a fearless look at one's self and the wrongs of the past. It's about cleaning house and making amends. Recovery is about more than abstinence; it's about becoming the kind of person who can engage in healthy relationships.

Abstinent without recovery, the addicted person is haunted by the past, suffers in the present, and can't see a promising future. The control centers in the brain are being depleted by the constant internal battle not to pick up a drink or a drug. Relationships with family are frayed and getting no better. For these addicts, relapse is usually just a matter of time.

An old adage says it best: "When a heavy drinker stops drinking, he feels better. When an alcoholic stops drinking, he feels worse." For alcoholics and addicts to begin enjoying life again, they need to work a rigorous Twelve Step program of recovery in groups such as Alcoholics Anonymous (AA) and Narcotics Anonymous (NA). These programs work because they treat the chronic nature of addiction that affects the mind, body, and spirit. There is no cure, only a daily reprieve that requires ongoing management. If we don't understand this basic tenet of success, we don't understand recovery.

When we believe treatment centers are the heart of recovery, we base our hopes and dreams on a flawed assumption. Treatment isn't recovery, and clinical teams don't know who will stay sober and who won't. Stellar patients drink on the flight home, and seemingly hopeless cases never drink again. Treatment staffs know what works, but no one knows who will follow directions and do what it takes to stay sober.

Recovery doesn't officially begin until treatment ends. It isn't dished out by doctors or teased out by therapists. It happens in a community and not just any community. It requires working a Twelve Step recovery program with other alcoholics and addicts. Recovery requires broad changes in how addicts live their lives, the kind of changes that would be tough work for anyone. They are attempting it with a brain so compromised by addiction that their brain scans look like Swiss cheese. With decision-making abilities impaired and emotions turbulent, it's no wonder so many don't get very far before they crumble and relapse.

The purpose of treatment is specific. It is designed to attend to the *acute* stage of this chronic illness. Involvement with patients is relatively short. A team of professionals administer to the most intense and severe symptoms, most notably the physical and emotional discomfort that comes with early abstinence. And many do an excellent job of it. But the score card we use to rate the success or failure of these facilities erroneously holds them responsible for patients' sobriety once they return home. Since addiction is a chronic disease, it must be managed by working a daily Twelve Step program. Treatment centers can only prepare patients to follow through with their ongoing recovery but can't do it for them. If addicts don't follow the directions for ongoing recovery, they are at high risk for relapse.

While not making direct promises of keeping people sober long-term, with some notable exceptions, treatment centers do so implicitly. Instead, professionals need to be very straightforward about what they can do, why it is important, and what they *can't* do.

This is exceedingly important because today we have so many treatment centers popping up across the country, trying out new strategies and protocols that will differentiate them from the pack but that aren't necessarily effective. This makes it difficult for families to evaluate treatment options. It's difficult to be smart consumers in a confusing arena.

The problem begins with the rubrics we're using—our scoring guide to evaluate the quality of treatment—which are flawed. *Treatment cannot be responsible for recovery outside the treatment program.* It can only be held responsible for its effectiveness at:

1. Medically detoxing and stabilizing patients, thoroughly assessing their needs, and setting treatment goals

2. Working with patients to break through denial at the deepest possible level, in a respectful and dignified manner, so they accept that they have a chronic disease that requires lifelong abstinence

3. Providing patients a recovery management plan that includes relapse prevention strategies and a clear understanding of how to work a Twelve Step recovery program when returning home (encouraging the patient to go to AA or NA meetings while in treatment and connecting the patient to a recovering person in his home area help accomplish this goal)

4. Inviting the family to attend the family program, and encouraging the children to attend a children's program if one is available

5. Developing aftercare recommendations designed to give an appropriate level of support that will increase the likelihood that patients will engage in recovery once they leave treatment

6. Engaging the family in the entire process, as appropriate.

There is also much talk about evidence-based treatment, but even though intentions are good, there are problems. *Evidence-based* doesn't necessarily mean the research is flawless, nor does it mean it is measuring the same outcome we should all be aiming for: lasting sobriety. Results depend on the quality of the research, the validity of the testing, replication over time by impartial researchers, and reviews by other researchers. Research bias—particularly the bias of what is actually published (mainly the positive results)—can lead to "proving" something is true when it is not true. Instead, we should be talking about "levels of evidence" and "quality of evidence."

According to Eric Topol, MD, cardiologist, geneticist, and researcher from the Cleveland Clinic, in his book *The Creative Destruction of Medicine,* "Consumers, unfortunately, are typically getting data from small, observational studies, published in obscure journals or not at all, in which there is no real control group or no randomization, and shaky end points."[4] He goes on to say that even very large-scale observational studies have produced faulty results, misleading the public more than once. Professionals are misled, too.

Dr. Topol has coined the word *litter-ature,* denoting that too much of the research is "littered with misleading and false-positive findings." We must be smart consumers of research, he says. "I don't want to be excessively negative, but the right assumption in reviewing any new data presented to consumers is to question it . . . consider the new finding null and void unless you are thoroughly convinced that the evidence is compelling." He is speaking of medical science, but results in the field of addiction and behavioral health are even more tenuous.

Misconceptions about treatment, leading to false expectations, coupled with the frustration of relapse, have families throwing up their hands and proclaiming, "Enough! Treatment doesn't work!" Once they reach this verdict, hopelessness can settle in, and the only question left is, "Now what?"

But what if I told you there was a group of addicted people who almost never relapse in the years following treatment? As a matter of fact, 78 percent never have a single relapse. Less than 15 percent have one relapse but not a second. And those with more than one relapse? A whopping 7 percent.[5] Not only that, but these folks are some of the most difficult addicts to treat. When I worked in inpatient treatment, having them assigned to our caseload would elicit groans of despair. "They're the worst patients!" because we knew our work just doubled.

But these patients are getting something other addicted loved ones aren't: a team who work with them for five years after treatment to make sure they build a solid program of recovery and make the prerequisite changes that lead to lasting sobriety. Because when alcoholics and addicts are left to their own devices—in spite of the universal cry that they can do it on their own—the odds are they'll be drinking and drugging again.

Author Stephen King, in his column for *Entertainment Weekly*, writes about just this point.

> Managing good sobriety without much help . . . is a trick very few druggies and alcoholics can manage. I know, because I'm both. Substance abusers lie about everything and usually do an awesome job of it. I once knew a coke-head who convinced his girlfriend the smell of freebase was mold in the plastic shower curtain of their apartment's bathroom. She believed him, he said, for five years (although he was probably lying about that, it was probably only three). . . . Go to one of those church-basement meetings where they drink coffee and talk about the Twelve Steps and you can hear similar stories on any night, and that's why the founders of this group emphasized complete honesty—what happened, what changed, what it's like now. . . . If my own career as a drunk both active and sober has convinced me of anything, it's convinced me of this: Addictive personalities do not prosper on their own. Without unvarnished, tough-love, truth-telling from their own kind—the voices that say, "You're lying about that, Freckles"—the addict has a tendency to fall back to his old ways.[6]

The problem is, of course, that most alcoholics and addicts coming out of treatment don't want to work a program of recovery that requires taking action. They're convinced they have changed with surprisingly little effort and in a remarkably short amount of time, and they often convince their poor gullible families of the same. These alcoholics and addicts think they have a better idea, which usually entails staying sober on their own with an easier, softer approach, one that eventually lands them back in the liquor store or crack house or doctor's office looking for a scrip.

This lack of compliance is repeatedly used by professionals and researchers as the reason AA or other Twelve Step programs don't work. Confusing an addict's compliance with a program's effectiveness is faulty analysis, either due to a lack of critical thinking or a degree of bias that leads to foregone conclusions. More accurately, the problem is one of compliance. It isn't that Twelve Step programs don't work—it is that alcoholics and addicts, for a complex set of reasons, have difficulty adhering to *anything* in a consistent manner—for reasons that are both purely human and that are central to the disease of addiction. Consider the struggles diabetics have trying to comply with their recovery programs—and they do not have to contend with the cognitive impairment we see in addicts. Research shows that among patients who only needed to take a medication to treat their illness, only 50 percent complied.[7] What it takes to recover from addiction is in another stratosphere from swallowing a pill.

But what if we, as families, could initiate a program with our loved ones that models the programs used by the recovery winners mentioned above—those people who almost never relapse? What if we could provide the missing element that makes it much tougher to relapse? Once we appropriately define the staff in treatment centers as the "first responders," not as providers of a stand-alone solution that does all the work for us, our expectations of treatment change. No doubt, treatment has a vital job to do, but it's not the only job to be done. Treatment centers can keep our alcoholics and addicts only so long, and then they come back home to us. This is when it takes all of us bonding together in recovery if we're to take our place among the winners. It most definitely takes a family.

Families and close friends have a tremendous amount of influence in an addict's life but usually don't know it. Too often, families not only don't understand their power, they often believe they are powerless. They often feel mistreated, disregarded, even hated.

The very people an alcoholic or addict needs most are the people he often fights against. He tries to appease family, only to break the promises he makes to them. Or he ignores those closest to him, pretending he simply doesn't care. The addiction not only punishes the people the addict cares about most, but it abuses him, too. He breaks promises to himself. He pretends none of the pain matters. And he begins losing everything he holds dear, yet he can't stop this downward spiral. He is typically filled with shame as he strikes out in anger. He doesn't understand what is happening inside himself. That is what it's like to live under the tyranny of addiction. However, a rigorous recovery program can reverse the insanity of this disease, making things better one day at a time.

● ● ●

2

Stick with the Winners

So who are the winners I referred to earlier, the ones who mostly never relapse in the first five years of recovery? They're doctors. And why are they selected to receive the exceptional support that safeguards them from relapse? Because no one can imagine opiate-addicted cardiologists or alcoholic neurosurgeons left to their own devices once they are discharged from treatment. If they are going to see patients, they must be sober.

Right about now I can hear people objecting, "Of course they stay sober. They're doctors. They know better than to relapse." But remember what I told you: *they are the toughest patients in treatment.* The belief that addicted doctors take direction well or commit to do what is required to stay sober is largely fictional. In truth, doctors are at even higher risk for relapse.

Let's put a doctor's risk for relapse into perspective by looking at something else they struggle with: hand washing. For the last thirty years there's been an ongoing effort to persuade doctors to wash their hands between seeing patients with little sustainable change. As a result, according to the Centers for Disease Control and Prevention, we spend $30 billion every year fighting infections in the United States, leading to the deaths of almost 100,000 people.[8] The fix? Soap and water. And yet, knowing this fact has not improved physicians' hygiene practices. So hospitals have been forced into action. They've trained hand-washing coaches and installed video cameras that send images halfway around the world so workers in India can monitor our doctors. They require doctors to wear radio-frequency ID chips that register each time they walk by a sink. Good hand-washers are rewarded with cash.

Another false belief is that success in sobriety is correlated with the fact that doctors have a medical license to lose. After all, retaining their privileges to practice medicine is a big motivator for staying sober. Most of us are concerned about loved ones who do not have the threat of losing a medical license looming over their heads. But our addicted family members have things they value, too. Things they do not want to lose. Topping the list is family, but they also value their jobs, friends, and reputation.

For most alcoholics and addicts, consequences in the distant future have little impact on what they do today. Whether it's someday losing a medical license or someday losing their family, the immediate pull of addiction has far greater power. The need to snort cocaine or shoot up heroin or drink a bottle of vodka today obliterates concerns about tomorrow. Whether or not a person is a doctor, the negative consequences that demand attention are the ones that happen right away, not in some far-off time. A drug court in Hawaii found that the future threat of a ten-year prison sentence was a poorer deterrent than being immediately sent to jail for three days upon failing a drug test.[9] Timing of a consequence is more effective than the size of a consequence.

Doctors entering treatment tend to be sicker than most, due to a seemingly inexhaustible supply of drugs and the ability to more easily hide their problems from others. People also look away and enable addicted doctors more than the average addict. Intervening on a doctor usually occurs only after the addiction is impossible to ignore. Consequently, addiction's progression is quite serious before most physicians find themselves in treatment. This makes their long-term successes all the more compelling. It appears they've found the Holy Grail of recovery.

Is there something we can learn from how doctors succeed in recovery that can help our loved ones? Before we answer this question, let's examine how the model of care for doctors is unique.

First, there is a high expectation for doctors to succeed. This is paired with the support required to make success possible. Too often, this is not the case among the general public. Treatment programs are clearly defined as acute care providers and only a first step in the recovery process. Once doctors are discharged from treatment, they engage in a second phase of care, which is designed to support long-term recovery. Called the Physician Health Program (PHP), this program provides five years of chronic care management. Doctors receive multilevel support with the flexibility to respond to changing needs over time. Even physicians who continue to struggle with sobriety longer than others are highly successful, because the program lasts long enough to give them the time to make it.

In 2007, researchers conducted the largest study to date on addicted physicians participating in five-year monitoring programs. Studying 904 addicted physicians who participated in sixteen different Physician Health Programs, the research showed that long-term recovery rates for these doctors were notable, not because they were physicians, but because they were highly engaged in PHP care management programs composed of what the program calls Eight Essential Elements.

Based on evidence and reasoning, these researchers also concluded that these same elements can be successfully used as a chronic care model for the general population of addicted people. They state, "On the basis of these findings, there is reason for renewed optimism for individuals with [addictions] and their families."[10]

It is helpful to remember that this is the *required* care for addicted doctors. It is well documented that these Eight Essential Elements, when applied simultaneously, work.

1. *Positive Rewards and Negative Consequences.* Establishing a clear understanding of rewards for positive behavior and consequences for negative behavior is key. Addiction is linked to unacceptable behaviors, and recovery is linked to desirable behaviors. These behaviors aren't about being good or bad, but about being sick or well. We know which behaviors precede relapse. Consequences, both negative and positive, must be meaningful, timely, and sustained if we expect them to have beneficial effects.

2. *Frequent Random Drug Testing.* Doctors are randomly drug tested for five years. They call daily to learn if they need to appear for testing. Relapse is linked to consequences that are predetermined and written on a signed document, so doctors clearly understand the cost of a relapse. Since there is no room for indecision, consequences are effective in producing changes in behaviors. Consequences are not synonymous with abuse or disrespect, but rather level-headed expectations properly linked to relapse behavior.

3. *Twelve Step Programs and the Abstinence Standard.* Doctors are actively referred to Twelve Step groups, not just passively encouraged to attend. It's known that Twelve Step programs are central to long-term sobriety, so showing up isn't left to chance. Additionally, doctors are enrolled in professionally led group therapy sessions designed for recovering physicians. Doctors are expected to abstain from all mood-altering substances not just their drug of choice.

4. *Viable Role Models and Recovery Mentors.* Doctors are paired with other recovering physicians who mentor them and provide recovery role models. These associations help doctors begin to identify positively with the recovery experience in Twelve Step programs. Mentors also build relationships with doctors' families and ask for input on progress. Newly recovering physicians receive feedback from their mentors and get report cards highlighting recovery strengths and recommendations for improvements.

5. *Modified Lifestyles.* Changes to doctors' lifestyles and professional lives position them for success in both recovery and work. For example, they may change their medical specialty or request outside monitoring of prescribing practices. Recovery-enhancing decisions are supported and encouraged.

6. *Active and Sustained Monitoring.* Designed to lay the groundwork for a lifetime of sobriety by ensuring early detection of relapse, doctors are monitored for at least five years after treatment. This extended period provides most doctors—even those who've

had one or more relapses—the level of support that eventually establishes solid recovery. What distinguishes Physician Health Programs from mainstream treatment is this extended time component that addresses the chronic nature of addiction.

7. *Active Management of Relapse.* When doctors relapse, the PHP process re-intervenes and re-evaluates. Rather than simply repeating the same past treatment experiences, a more intense, specialized treatment is recommended. The researchers explain, "The blend of support and accountability, alliance and toughness distinguishes Physician Health Programs from other interventions that seek but too often fall short of creating and sustaining these important ingredients."

8. *Continuing Care Approach.* Addiction is a chronic disease that needs to be managed on an ongoing basis just as we manage diabetes and other chronic illnesses. Lifelong recovery is achieved by managing the chronic nature of addiction appropriately. Physician Health Programs demonstrate this by sustaining therapeutic relationships with doctors for five years or more, and achieving high rates of lasting sobriety.

In the treatment field, we have long understood that each of these essential elements is effective for treating addiction. But Physician Health Programs are the first to demonstrate that implementing all eight elements into a single, long-term program is the formula for producing durable, lasting sobriety. Most alcoholics and addicts don't have access to this type of care management. Therefore, the chronic nature of their addiction isn't well managed and risk of relapse is high.

Doctors receive the gold standard of treatment. How can families and alcoholics convert these Eight Essential Elements into a model that they can implement into their daily lives?

• • •

3

How It All Started

William Duncan Silkworth, MD, was known as the little doctor who loved drunks. A Princeton graduate with a medical degree from New York University, he had a penchant for alcoholics. Even the most resistant drunks opened up to him and some wept. He spent his entire career working with alcoholics, more than 51,000 of them.

At a time when alcoholics were thought to deliberately bring devastation on themselves, Dr. Silkworth steadfastly believed in their intrinsic goodness. He was a man with special gifts, great devotion, and a deep understanding of alcoholism. Yet, with all his talents, Dr. Silkworth reported that only 2 percent of the alcoholics he saw achieved lasting sobriety. There was little hope for the truly addicted. These were times before Alcoholics Anonymous.

One of the drunks Dr. Silkworth treated was nearing death at age thirty-nine. His name was Bill Wilson. While hospitalized, Bill had a white light experience where he felt the presence of a Higher Power and had a spiritual awakening. Describing the episode to the doctor, Bill asked if he might be insane. Dr. Silkworth, having treated many alcoholics suffering from hallucinations, instinctively understood that what Bill had experienced was different. Rather than dismiss it as another drunk's crazy story, Dr. Silkworth told Bill, "I don't know what you've got, but hang on to it. You are not insane and you may have the answer to your problem."

Another doctor might have dismissed Bill's story as delusional, unwittingly dooming the future of Alcoholics Anonymous. But Dr. Silkworth encouraged Bill to take seriously the message he took from this experience: *You will stay sober only if you share your story with other alcoholics.* Bill's sudden understanding that he could stay sober by helping another alcoholic eventually led to Alcoholics Anonymous. To this day, it is the most dependable path to recovery with almost 115,000 meetings in 170 countries.

Sister Molly Monahan writes of Alcoholics Anonymous in her book *Seeds of Grace:*

> I once heard a Jesuit assert that when the history of twentieth-century American spirituality is written, Alcoholics Anonymous will be judged the most significant spiritual movement of the era. I am quite sure he was not a member of A.A. I am, and have been for over seventeen years. I am also a Roman Catholic nun, and have been for over forty years. I am inclined to agree with that Jesuit.[11]

Alcoholics Anonymous' spirituality leads some to erroneously claim it is a religious organization. As Bill Wilson wrote, "There is room for all shades of belief and nonbelief."[12] AA speaks of a Higher Power, but it is one of individual choosing. Atheists may find that power in nature and the Twelve Step program itself. For others, G-O-D stands for *group of drunks* or *good orderly direction.* Still others find their Higher Power through personal religious beliefs. Whatever the choosing, a Higher Power—a power greater than the self—is required for loosening the grip of addiction; willpower is not enough.

Bill Wilson, over the next months after leaving the hospital, shared his story with one alcoholic after another without a single success. Exasperated, he was ready to give up. It was his wife, Lois, who persuaded him to continue. "Bill," she said, "you are sober. That is miracle enough."

Lois' pivotal role, in this particular instance, is rarely mentioned in AA history. If she hadn't insisted Bill continue his work with other alcoholics, he may have called it quits, started drinking again, and died a hopeless alcoholic. But instead, *as a family member,* Lois helped change the course of history and probably saved her husband's life.

In 1935, Bill Wilson, six months sober, traveled from New York to Akron, Ohio, in hopes of jump-starting his career. When the business deal he was counting on fell through, Bill found himself alone, despondent, and with only ten dollars in his pocket. Rather than turning to the bar in the hotel lobby, he began searching for an alcoholic to help. He called a local minister, Dr. Walter F. Tunks, looking not for religion but another drunk.

Dr. Tunks gave Bill the names of ten people. Standing at a pay phone, it wasn't until he reached the last name on the list that Bill finally got a lead. A fellow gave him the name Henrietta Seiberling and her home phone number.

Now imagine this for just a moment. Bill, a complete stranger, calling person after person, announcing himself as "a rum hound from New York who's found a way to keep alcoholics sober," is given a name— Seiberling—he knows from his successful days on Wall Street. This, he knew, was the family name of the founder of Goodyear Tire. It must be his wife, Bill reasoned, and momentarily felt too embarrassed to call.

But a voice inside Bill's head said, "You better call the lady."

As it turned out, Henrietta was the daughter-in-law of Frank Augustus Seiberling, who was indeed founder of The Goodyear Tire & Rubber Company. Henrietta, with three small children at home, told Bill, "You come right out here."

Henrietta said later that her first thought was to put this man from New York together with an alcoholic surgeon and physician in town, Dr. Robert Smith. Bob Smith was losing everything to drink and desperately wanted to get sober. He had long before confided in her about his alcoholism. "Henrietta, I don't understand it. Nobody understands it. Some doctor had written a book about it, but he doesn't understand it. I don't like the stuff. I don't want to drink."

Henrietta picked up the phone and called Dr. Smith's wife. "Anne," she said, "I've found a man who can help Bob. You must bring him right over."

Anne was uncomfortable admitting, on this Saturday afternoon, that Bob was passed out drunk in his bed. It was only through Henrietta's dogged insistence that Anne confessed the truth.

"Bring him over for dinner tomorrow night at five," Henrietta said. It would be Mother's Day, 1935.

Dr. Bob, even though he had desperately wanted to quit drinking, did what alcoholics have always done when help is offered. He firmly declined. He wasn't moved by the promise of this man who claimed to sober up alcoholics. Bob eventually relented, but only because of his deep respect for Henrietta. He also knew she wasn't a person who took no for an answer. So he agreed, saying to his wife, Anne, "Only fifteen minutes. Let's make it snappy."

The meeting between Bill and Bob stretched out to six hours, one alcoholic talking to another alcoholic. Although Bill didn't know it at the time, Bob would be his first success story; he and Dr. Bob, as he was affectionately called, would go on to tell their stories to other alcoholics who would tell their stories to yet others, laying the foundation for the AA program that has brought hope to alcoholics around the globe.

However, Alcoholics Anonymous didn't begin simply with two alcoholics finding each other and getting together for a talk. It began with a friend and a spouse putting two alcoholics together, one of them objecting mightily. In other words, Alcoholics Anonymous began with a family intervention.

This story is important for all people who love an alcoholic or addict. We've been taught to step aside. We're told that alcoholics and addicts must feel ready to get sober before any good can come from anything. But Dr. Bob didn't feel ready to meet with Bill. The meeting with Bill happened irrespective of Bob's feelings of readiness. If Anne and Henrietta had waited for Bob to take the lead, Alcoholics Anonymous may never have formed.

A few years later, after Alcoholics Anonymous proved successful at keeping alcoholics sober, Dr. Silkworth was asked to contribute to the writings of the book *Alcoholics Anonymous,* more commonly known as the Big Book. In a chapter titled "The Doctor's Opinion," he wrote:

> If any feel that as psychiatrists directing a hospital for alcoholics we appear somewhat sentimental, let them stand with us a while on the firing line, see the tragedies, the

despairing wives, the little children; let the solving of these problems become a part of their daily work, and even of their sleeping moments, and the most cynical will not wonder that we have accepted and encouraged this movement.[13]

Even in these earliest times, recovery was understood as a family affair. Lois Wilson and Anne Smith, the wives of Bill and Bob, played crucial roles in the formation of Alcoholics Anonymous. As Lois told writer William Borchert, "I used to think my life really began the day I met Bill. I guess I was as addicted to him as he was to alcohol. Then he got sober—and I got well."[14]

Lois suffered through seventeen years of Bill's drinking, financial ruin, the loss of her family home, days when Bill wouldn't dress or bathe, and frequent hospitalizations. Eventually, she watched Bill almost die. Once Bill found sobriety and met Dr. Bob, Lois' life initially became worse not better. "I guess I thought once he stopped drinking, everything would go back to what it was like before—happy and loving," she said.

In 1959, Lois Wilson began Al-Anon, a Twelve Step program to help families and friends of alcoholics. By doing so, she gave the people who loved an alcoholic a path to hope, happiness, and peace of mind.

A member of Al-Anon writes about family recovery:

> I am sorry for families who have not taken refuge in the Al-Anon program. . . . When an alcoholic finds (A.A.), he often grows so fast that we must learn to grow with him or the relationship may be in danger. For this is a family disease. It needs a family answer. In order to achieve real unity, the whole family needs to practice the A.A. and Al-Anon principles, each in his individual way.[15]

• • •

4

Introducing Structured Family Recovery

Structured Family Recovery takes family members off the sidelines and puts them in the game. It's often said that recovery isn't a spectator sport. We can no longer afford to squander one of the best resources in the lives of most addicts—*family.* In early recovery, a time when a united front is crucial, families can make the difference between success and failure.

As families, our efforts to help the addict can be hindered by misconceptions. What we believe about addiction and recovery are often myths. The newly recovering person is not only misled by faulty ideas but further hampered by a propensity for dismissing the advice of treatment providers. Once a family engages in Structured Family Recovery, this is of little matter, because the process is designed to set the entire family on the right course.

Building on what we know about what works for doctors, Structured Family Recovery can bring a similar recovery management program to families using the Eight Essential Elements from the Physician Health Programs as a springboard. Structured Family Recovery is a framework. It's a simple process that gets results. It's easy for any size family group to participate in, and team members can begin before an addicted loved one goes to treatment, while he's in treatment, or after he's completed treatment. The addicted person isn't involved from the outset but is invited to join the recovery team at the appropriate time.

Structured Family Recovery gives renewed purpose to a family that's been fractured by the emotional and financial upheavals caused by addiction. Sharing a common goal—sobriety that lasts—naturally draws families together again. A higher calling unites us. Pulling together, we accomplish more than any one person can. In all areas of achievement, from sports to business to science, those who succeed stand up to congratulate the members of their teams: the mentors, coaches, supporters, cheerleaders, and experts. Similarly, families in recovery need teams built for success.

Structured Family Recovery is a program of action. It is therapeutic, but it isn't therapy. It supports Twelve Step recovery for alcoholics, addicts, and family members. Like Physician Health Programs, it supports ongoing recovery but is designed so that every member of the family contributes to preventing relapse, healing the whole family, and building trust. Through structure and accountability, a new outlook emerges. Everyone participating in a recovery program changes, not only each individual but the very grain of family life. Broken relationships start to mend, and the love we have for one another begins to reveal itself.

Structured Family Recovery starts with a decision to dedicate one hour a week to a family meeting. Since meetings happen via conference calls, it doesn't matter where you live, if you are home or traveling, in your pajamas, or walking in the park. People don't have to drive to designated meeting spots, find childcare, or figure out how to include family members who live out of town. If the addict is in residential treatment or a sober house, he can still participate. Each meeting is as close as your telephone.

Structured Family Recovery isn't punitive or judgmental. No one is telling anyone else what they think about them or what they should do. Instead, they talk about themselves and their own strengths, limitations, and needs. By focusing on themselves rather than on everyone else, they regain manageability in their lives. Everyone learns where to find their power and what they are powerless over. With time, everyone can begin to forgive and eventually can trust. There are bumps in the road, to be sure, but together, as a family, they work through them.

The Williams family decided to participate in Structured Family

Recovery when their mom was in treatment for the third time. All four children were grown with families of their own, and Mom and Dad were empty nesters. Mom's relapse with alcohol and oxycodone, an opiate pain medication, went largely unnoticed by the kids who were busy with their own lives. Dad didn't want to burden the children with news of yet another relapse, so he tried to manage the problem on his own.

Eventually, their mom found it hard to get enough pills to satisfy the demands of her addiction. Law enforcement had begun cracking down on the doctors who were making it easy for her to get prescription painkillers. This is when things changed measurably. She was forced to buy what she could on the streets. Some days, when nothing else was available, she bought heroin. An upper-middle-class housewife and grandmother turned street junkie once the doctor's office—the socially acceptable supplier of her drug—was shut down.

Soon it was impossible to hide her problem. Dad still didn't mention anything, but the children were terrified by how incapacitated their mother had become. At a granddaughter's birthday party, she was barely able to speak and repeatedly nodded out at the dinner table. Finally, her daughter broke the code of silence and demanded something be done, and they implemented a structured family intervention.

Once Mom was admitted into a residential treatment program, her children began to discuss the seriousness of their mother's addiction and how it was ripping the family apart. They knew if she relapsed again, she would die.

Addiction had taken its toll on everyone. There was too much secret-keeping, infighting, and general chaos. The adult children didn't get along most of the time, periodically stopped talking to one another, and dreaded celebrating holidays. They were frustrated by their father's passive approach to their mother's addiction and blamed him for allowing it to go on. Even the grandchildren were pulled into the family drama. Something had to change.

A family decision to participate in Structured Family Recovery felt like a leap of faith, because nobody fully understood the idea of family recovery or why it was necessary. They only knew that they needed to do something more than they had done in the past, hoping it would help their mother in her struggle to stay sober. Empowered by the success of the intervention, the adult children called their father asking him to get involved, too.

Because family relations were fractured due to many years of coping with their mother's addiction, they unanimously decided they needed to work with a counselor trained in Structured Family Recovery. Most of the family resided in Chicago, but one brother lived in Indianapolis and a sister was a flight attendant who was often not home. Since weekly meetings with the counselor were on conference calls, everyone could participate. Nobody knew what to expect, but the counselor reassured them, explaining that their mother also felt nervous and questioning of being in treatment and away from home.

The weekly meeting is at the heart of Structured Family Recovery. Everyone reviews their past week, determining what worked well for them and what didn't. Then members of the team discuss what they want to do in the week ahead. The counselor offers support and guidance to keep everyone moving in a beneficial direction. Everyone creates small, workable goals that produce big change over time. No one worries about being perfect. As a matter of fact, the Williams family chose "Progress not perfection" as their family slogan.

They made a pact to follow the directions and do whatever was required, just as they expected their mother to do in treatment. The counselor began educating them about recovery and how it worked. Everyone found a weekly Al-Anon meeting to attend, began reading recovery literature written for families, and completed simple assignments. Soon they began to see the power of small changes and the effectiveness of working as a group.

Halfway into treatment, they received a call from their mother saying she'd packed her bags and was leaving treatment. The family momentarily panicked and went headlong into a chaotic state. As they described it, "Everyone started freaking out. We fell right back into our old ways of coping, which was helping no one." But then they realized they weren't alone anymore. They quickly called their Structured Family Recovery counselor and then their mother's counselor. The family experienced firsthand how easily they could mobilize their team. Family and professionals, working in tandem, put a plan together. They scripted the best way to talk with their mother to help her make a better decision. A conference call with the family, the treatment counselor, and their mother made it possible for everyone to participate in dignified and respectful problem solving. In less than thirty minutes, their mother agreed to follow all the professional recommendations and stay in treatment. The power of the group was more powerful than the pull of her addiction. The treatment team agreed that none of them individually could have persuaded her to stay without help from the family team.

Before their mother was discharged from the residential treatment program, they invited her to participate in one of their Structured Family Recovery conference calls. They explained what they had been doing for themselves and invited her to join the family team. She readily agreed. Later, a counselor in the treatment center told the family how proud their mom was that the entire family was part of the recovery experience. She shared what happened in group therapy, smiling from ear to ear.

Today, the family has been engaged in weekly Structured Family Recovery meetings for over fifteen months. Mom is sober a year and three months and actively involved in her Twelve Step recovery program. The entire family knows the language of recovery, because they attend weekly Twelve Step meetings for families of alcoholics and addicts. While everything isn't perfect, the family is back together. They've begun having fun again, getting together on weekends for dinner and board games. They've even taken some short skiing trips together and are planning a family cruise. Grandchildren are at the grandparents' for overnighters. Everybody talks to everybody else.

The dad recently said, "I have to be honest. When we started this, I resented it. I thought, it's one more thing I have to do every week. But now, I see my wife sober, and I'm so proud of her. And I hear what comes out of my kids' mouths during our meetings, and I'm amazed. I think to myself, did I raise these wonderful children?"

Structured Family Recovery transforms recovery into a journey the family takes together. Ultimately, it gives families back the most important thing of all—each other.

A Shared Gift

On a lovely summer afternoon several years ago, my phone rang. The woman on the other end spoke with a most genteel Southern accent and informed me she was from Mississippi. She was calling for a friend who had concerns about her daughter. After we talked about the problem, she paused and said: "My daddy's been in recovery over twenty-five years. He was a successful man around town, but at home his alcoholism was bad. Now, with all this sobriety behind him, our relationship is as sweet and clear as moonlight through the pines."

After another pause, she added, "What a lot of people don't know about me is that every morning when I wake up, the first thing I do is thank God for the disease of alcoholism.

"You see, if my daddy hadn't been an alcoholic, we would never have belonged to a family in recovery." Recovery, she said, made them better and happier than they ever could have been without it.

Family involvement isn't just about motivating the addict to accept treatment. That's just the beginning. We need a systemic solution—healing the entire family not just one person. Family recovery requires refocusing on our own actions for the purpose of rooting out the ways addiction has changed our behaviors and the ways we relate to one another. Family recovery is defined by an unwavering belief in the integrity of our family and the process of healing.

When the disease of addiction is active, it's common for alcoholics to lie about everything. But what is not commonly recognized is how dishonest the rest of the family becomes. We lie to protect the addict and to spare ourselves from embarrassment or loss. We make promises and then don't keep them. "I'm not going to put up with this for another minute," we pledge. But we do, often for years, even decades. We do whatever it takes to survive. The addict is doing the same thing.

Alcoholics and addicts don't ask to get sick. They take a drink, maybe a drug, and somewhere down the line, the drink or drug takes them. They can't see it happening and neither can we, until things get much, much worse. We loved each other before things got bad; then we mix up the illness with the person and aren't so sure anymore. It's hard to feel love when we're consumed with anger, fear, and resentment. We think this is something our loved one is doing to us, and we can't understand why they don't stop.

Addicts can be just as puzzled. Still wanting to be the good guy, most create endless rules around drinking and using, and are astonished at their inability to maintain them. But their brain is in a negative, downward spiral. With everyone in the family unhappy with them, they can become filled with anger, fear, and resentment, too. Once they get sober, they might still smart from the stinging words they suffered from fed-up family members when they were using. Meanwhile, the family, who has also suffered their own hurt due to their loved one's addiction, can't believe the addict is angry with them. Nobody seems to understand that they've all been reacting to the effects of a disease that disrupts the brain and the spirit.

Addiction turns us into adversaries; Structured Family Recovery brings us back together. Moving toward the solution in unison, we create a sublime kind of accountability. We all become accountable in partnership. Accountability isn't just about the addict, it's about the entire family. That's when a new sense of harmony begins to emerge.

By the time addicts are discharged from treatment, their brains have been drug-free for weeks or months. They've worked through some acute emotional, psychological, and spiritual problems. Their bodies usually feel much healthier, and they look better. It's easy to believe they're fixed. We might even say, "It's up to you now."

As soon as we're lulled into that trap, we must remember the doctors we talked about earlier as the model for Structured Family Recovery. No one trusts the neurosurgeon to achieve lasting sobriety alone. So neither should we expect it of the schoolteacher, lawyer, waitress, homemaker, student, executive, or retiree. No matter how great they look when they walk out the door of the treatment center, no matter what they say, no matter what we believe, they are not cured. It's a chronic disease, and the road to long-term recovery starts now.

Recovery means something specific. There is a goal. Most alcoholics, addicts, and their families, when asked, say the goal is sobriety. Once the addict is clean and sober, they reason that all will be well. But the absence of alcohol or other drugs doesn't mend lives or families. This comes as a shock to many. Although sobriety is essential, recovery is much more than sobriety. It concerns itself with the way alcoholics and families live their lives *together*.

When families get involved in recovery, they find a new and vital integrity. People learn to say what they mean and do what they say. Each person strives to admit when they are wrong, forgive others for their shortcomings, and honor the progress everyone is making as a group. Truth is not used as a weapon and love is not used as an excuse for inaction. With everyone in recovery, the family—which now includes the addict on this shared journey—begins to feel safe.

Recovery is accomplished just one day at a time, but it radically alters our future. Most families who have successfully put Structured Family Recovery into practice say they are better than they ever were. A twenty-seven-year-old son said of Structured Family Recovery, "In the past ten years, my mother relapsed multiple times. As a family, we all stood outside the circle, passing judgment and pointing fingers. Now we're all inside the circle, holding hands, doing recovery together."

With recovery, we begin to see each other's goodness more clearly. We struggle and celebrate together. Life still throws its curve balls, but we are better at handling them and less likely to fall into blame. The good news is that we don't have to find our way blindly. We know what works.

As they say in recovery circles, "It works if you work it." Structured Family Recovery helps families work it. By doing so, we experience a spiritual shift. It's no longer "me against you and you against me." We are family, and we stand together.

. . .

A Misunderstood Disease

It's a commonly held belief that addiction as a disease is a relatively new concept, but this understanding was established well before the founding of AA, dating back to Greek and Roman philosophers. In the early sixth century BCE, it was noted that mental disorders can come from compulsive drinking. Nearly two thousand years ago, Roman writers Pliny and Seneca described symptoms closely resembling current observations of alcoholism: character defects, loss of memory, the shakes, antisocial behavior, swollen liver, insomnia, and untimely death. Seneca wrote that it destroys the mind with tragic consequences, using Marc Antony as an example of a great figure taken down by alcohol.[16]

The word *alcoholism* was coined in 1849 by a Swedish physician, and it eventually became the commonly accepted name for addiction to alcohol and eventually replaced the term *inebriety*, which was popular well into the early twentieth century. An article published by *Scientific American* in 1877, titled "Inebriety as a Disease," differentiates between drunkenness as a vice and drunkenness as a disease: "The man who drinks for pleasure, it holds, may look for benefits in the counsel of others or in his own strength of will; but he who drinks because he cannot help it, being led by an irresistible impulse, is a sick man, and needs a physician not a temperance pledge."[17]

In an 1885 issue of the same journal, the topic was again addressed, concluding that "to refrain from alcoholic indulgence is obviously not always within the voluntary power of the . . . inebriate."[18]

By the mid-nineteenth century, the idea of addiction as a distinct disease, not just a form of insanity, reached international recognition. J. Edward Turner, a physician specializing in the treatment of inebriety, described it as hereditary, a disease that could be passed down to off-spring. Treatment, he said, required complete abstinence.[19]

During this period, many who studied and treated addiction undertook the task of educating medical professionals, lawmakers, clergy, and the general public in hopes of changing the ways alcoholics and addicts were treated. The preface for a paper written in 1885 by Isaiah De Zouche, MD, reads, "Much misapprehension exists as to the nature of Inebriety, which has led to mistaken treatment of the inebriate by his friends, and to his wrongful punishment by the law."[20]

These same advocates would surely be shocked if they could see how many of these old beliefs still exist in the twenty-first century. Even with the success of AA after the publication of the Big Book in 1939 and the eventual confirmation in 1954 by the American Medical Association of Dr. Silkworth's ground-breaking case for alcoholism as a disease in his "Doctor's Opinion" that opens the Big Book, we continue battling misguided notions that addiction is caused by a deficit of character or loss of willpower. Media outlets commonly use the word *lifestyle* as a euphemism for addiction, as if it were a preferred choice. Even with recent research showing that addiction has a neurological basis and is a brain disease, many physicians still believe alcoholism is at least partially chosen by its victims. In many societies, including the United States, alcoholics and addicts are more likely to be punished than to be treated. As a result, families often still approach addiction as a moral failing rather than a chronic illness. Addiction remains the most misunderstood disease.

One of the great puzzlers for many is the question of how putting intoxicants into one's body could possibly be a disease. After all, most people who use mood-altering substances don't become addicted.

There are many examples of conditions triggered by environmental substances entering the body, most commonly allergic diseases. Hay fever is triggered when allergens such as pollen are inhaled by individuals with sensitized immune systems. Yet others breathe the same pollen with no adverse reaction. Likewise, food allergies are caused when the body mistakenly identifies a protein as an enemy and begins fighting against it. While most people have no problem eating foods such as dairy, soy, shellfish, fruits, vegetables, and nuts, those who are allergic experience symptoms ranging from mild (itchy mouth, hives, hoarse voice) to severe (anaphylactic shock, loss of consciousness, death). There is no cure.

Some newborn babies test positive for a mutated gene that results in an inability to break down amino acids in proteins. The disease is called phenylketonuria, and the simple act of consuming proteins causes mental retardation. By maintaining a low-protein diet, these babies grow into healthy adults. The warning "phenylketonurics: contains phenylalanine" is printed on certain food labels—such as diet sodas—to alert people with this disorder. It's through abstinence that these children avoid triggering the disease.

Addiction to mood-altering substances also requires consuming something from the environment. Some people metabolize intoxicants differently, setting off what Dr. Silkworth called an allergy of the body and an obsession of the mind that condemns one to die.[21] Since he wrote those words, sophisticated genetic research has shown that addiction isn't a learned behavior but an inherited disease, like so many others caused by our differences in genetic coding. To activate it, we just need to add alcohol or other drugs from our environment. As Mehmet Oz, MD, said, "Your genetics load the gun. Your lifestyle pulls the trigger."[22] In a drinking and drugging society, many triggers are unwittingly pulled.

The Genetics of Addiction

The concept of alcoholism as an inherited disease is time-honored, but it ultimately required scientific study to determine whether children *learn* to be alcoholics or *inherit* the disease through genetics. Research over the last seventy-five years has consistently found a genetic link to addiction. It's estimated that 50 to 65 percent of the risk is inherited. The remaining threat is supplied by the environment.[23]

Going back to the 1920s, answers to the question of genetics stem from twin and adoption studies conducted in Sweden. Twin studies determined whether genetics played a role in alcoholism by studying identical and fraternal twins. Identical twins have the same genes, so if one is alcoholic, the other is likely to be alcoholic, too. Fraternal twins are the same as any other sibling pair; they have some genes that are identical and other genes that are different, so their predisposition toward alcoholism is less likely to match.

However, if the cause is environmental, genetic makeup isn't relevant. In other words, the probability of twins matching each other's propensity toward alcoholism wouldn't vary between identical and fraternal twins. The determining factor would instead be similar environmental experiences. After decades of studying twins, researchers found significant differences between identical and fraternal twins, indicating that genes, not environment, play the deciding role.

Twins have also been studied to determine if genetics play a role in addiction to drugs other than alcohol. Outcomes show an inherited susceptibility to cocaine, heroin, other opiates, and marijuana addiction. Harvard Medical School used twin studies to determine if a predisposition exists for the enjoyment of marijuana. Researchers found a genetic link that determines whether getting high on marijuana is a pleasant or unpleasant experience. This supports the idea that people may be genetically wired to prefer the effects of one drug over another. We've long talked about an addict's *drug of choice,* the one he or she likes best.

Adoption studies provide even greater clarity to the question of genetics. Researchers in the 1920s began studying people born of alcoholic parents who were adopted at birth by nonalcoholic parents. These studies are most effective at separating the influences of nurture and nature. If the environment is responsible for addiction, those raised by nonalcoholic parents will show a low incidence of alcoholism. The results, however, support heredity. Babies born of alcoholic parents, but raised by nonalcoholics, are four times more likely to be alcoholic than babies born of nonalcoholic parents and adopted into nonalcoholic homes.

A Swedish research team combined adoption and identical twin studies, following the lives of twins adopted into separate homes. Even though each twin in a pair was raised by a different family, they had the same propensity for alcoholism. Again, nature, not nurture, was the deciding factor.

Animal studies also offer insight into the genetics of addiction. Genetically altered strains of rats have been engineered to either prefer or avoid alcohol. Alcohol-preferring rats choose alcohol over water, whereas, alcohol-avoiding rats don't drink alcohol even when deprived of water. Both sets of rats pass their preferences to their offspring.

Parents of alcoholics and addicts don't always have the disease themselves. Many people in an alcoholic lineage don't inherit the genes or never drink enough to activate them. Genetic heredity may originate elsewhere, from a grandparent or other ancestors. Sometimes it's difficult to track addiction in a family because of family secrets. *Grandpa had bouts of illness that kept him in his room, not alcoholism.* In other families, heavy drinking, abusing pills, or smoking pot is the norm, so alcoholism isn't viewed as abnormal.

There is no reliable biological testing for a genetic propensity toward addiction due to the complexity of genetic factors. Addiction isn't caused by one gene, but by multiple gene variants that can change from family to family. According to geneticists, alcoholism is one of the most complex genetically based diseases to study.

Children with a genetic predisposition to addiction who are born into heavily drinking families are more likely to model drinking behaviors, thereby activating the disease. However, when children grow into adulthood choosing to abstain from alcohol and other drugs, the disease never manifests itself. Many people decide not to drink precisely because alcohol is so problematic in their families. Others go headlong into substance abuse. Children who detest a parent's alcoholism will often begin drinking and drugging in their teenage years, believing they know better than Mom or Dad to become addicted.

There are, of course, many gray areas when it comes to addiction. The onset of addiction doesn't occur in the same way for each person. The amounts and duration of a drug needed for triggering the disease vary widely. Some people report being addicted from their first try at drinking or drugging. Others experience a slower progression, drinking fairly normally for several years before crossing the line into full-blown addiction. Some drugs have a shorter addiction cycle than others, such as heroin, meth, and crack cocaine.

Other people have periodic problems with addiction. For example, a young woman may show signs of alcoholism but quits using all substances while raising her children. Years later, perhaps when her last child is graduating from high school, she decides to take a glass of wine, and the disease is activated once again. In many such cases, people report that the addiction is worse than it was when they left off, as if it had been progressing all the while. The ability to stop is no longer within their control, and negative consequences quickly mount.

An example of the power of genetics is clear in the case of a forty-year-old wife and mother. Having witnessed the destructive nature of alcoholism in her grandfather's life and the toll it took on his eight children, she was vehemently anti-alcohol and never took a drink. In her late thirties, she was in a skiing accident and sustained a severe back injury. During her treatment, she was given powerful pain medications and quickly became addicted. Over time, she began visiting several doctors for multiple prescriptions and taking more than twenty pills a day. She spent much of her days in bed, and her husband and children believed it was due to her back pain not an addiction to painkillers. Eventually she lost interest in family activities, stopped making meals and cleaning house, became irritated when her children invited friends over, and grew increasingly unreasonable and argumentative. When her husband became suspicious of the pills, finding bottles hidden in drawers and closets, she accused him of not caring about her suffering. A woman who had never before taken a sip of an alcoholic beverage became a full-blown addict when a pain medication was prescribed for a legitimate purpose. It activated her genetic coding.

Our beliefs as a society are informed primarily by the concept that everyone should drink (or use other "recreational" drugs) responsibly. Drinking and, to a lesser degree, the use of other drugs such as marijuana are often encouraged in some circles. Marijuana is legal in some states, and doctors prescribe a host of mood-altering medications. Alcohol isn't even considered a drug by many, and those people who don't drink are sometimes viewed with a degree of suspicion. In some social settings, people try to goad non-drinkers into drinking. *Come on, have a drink and join in on the fun!*

Everyone using intoxicants is expected to follow certain norms, but these social rules are generally vague and malleable, so it's not always clear when someone has initially crossed the line. In a drinking culture, it requires considerable progression of the disease before alcoholics and addicts are seen as rule-breakers. Once identified as such, they're expected to shape up or risk the contempt of their families and contemporaries. They may try to follow the rules, but the disease continues onward, making it increasingly difficult. Even those closest to them simply don't understand.

Addiction as a disease may be part of our vernacular, but it's our emotional reactions that betray our true beliefs. People who are addicted continue to be stigmatized and blamed. They are frequently portrayed as *self*-destructive, and addiction is seen as something they are doing to themselves. In truth, many alcoholics and other drug addicts fight fiercely against the pull of addiction. They win some battles, even abstaining for various periods of time. When they fall off the wagon, families interpret their return to drinking or drugging as a choice or a failure, not as a symptom of a disease. The very thing that is destroying their lives has an irresistible pull that few can resist. In fact, the addict's brain is the major contributor to that loss of control.

Understanding that our loved ones do not choose to become addicted makes it easier for us to let go of our anger and replace it with compassion. In the words of Nelson Mandela, "Our human compassion binds us the one to another—not in pity or patronizingly, but as human beings who have learnt how to turn our common suffering into hope for the future."[24]

A Changed Brain

As addiction progresses, it's easy for families to see the decline of their loved one's state of mind. Personality is more explosive and less stable.

Negativity extends beyond active drinking and drugging. In all their undoing, addicts often stand in judgment of everybody and everything. *The treatment team knows nothing. My family is plotting against me. I'm being brainwashed.*

Regardless of the ongoing destruction caused by addiction, many alcoholics and addicts are stubbornly opposed to any help, most notably Alcoholics Anonymous or other Twelve Step programs. The resistance and denial that characterize the way alcoholics and addicts think can drive their families crazy. What causes this? It's most likely what seems to the addict to be the life-threatening prospect of having to give up their drugs. The addicted brain holds many of the answers to what is behind this irrational idea.

In the past, we could only study brains of alcoholics and addicts by autopsy on cadavers, many of whom were alcoholic men who died living on the streets. It was difficult to know if brain abnormalities were caused by addiction, disease, or malnutrition. Today, modern science has advanced in neurotechnology, allowing us to look into brains of living, breathing people. We can see how substances change the structure and functioning of the brain. Researchers assign tasks to addicts and then take images of their brains to understand how they operate in the realm of thought and higher-order activities. Today, addicted brains can be compared to non-addicted, healthy brains.

The most popular technology for brain imaging is the fMRI, or functional magnetic resonance imaging. It differs from an MRI, which takes snapshots, by creating movies of brains in real time. Scientists can now observe brains while they are *functioning,* thus the *f* in fMRI. Researchers aren't just interested in what makes a brain light up but in higher-level questions: How does an addicted brain make decisions, complete tasks, switch strategies, or process information?

One of the world's authorities on the neurobiology of addicted brains, George Koob, PhD, is a leader in the study of *reward systems* and *anti-reward systems* of the brain. These two systems give us the capacity to feel both good and bad. When brains are properly balanced, our moods aren't too high or too low. Alcoholics and addicts change the balance of their brains as they impulsively use mood-altering substances to boost their reward systems.

In the beginning, addicts are filled with great anticipation of their next high, because it feels so good to use the drug. Just thinking about it creates excitability. Emotional rewards spike far beyond what is normal, driving addicts to repeatedly stimulate the brain's reward center. Nothing else can compete—food, family, friends all drop in value. The addict's brain is preoccupied with one overriding thought: *When can I get high again?*

But then something interesting happens. Repeated substance abuse begins to deplete the reward system. No amount of alcohol or other drugs achieves the same high, because the reward circuitry is desensitized. At this point, the anti-reward system—which brings on adverse emotions—becomes dominant. Now, without alcohol or other drugs in their systems, addicts feel miserable. The brain is only producing emotional lows. More drugs are required to escape the darkness of the anti-reward brain. This is when the compulsion to drink takes over. The addict needs the drug just to feel normal.

By this time, addicts are now living in an ongoing negative emotional state caused by a decrease in the reward functioning of the brain and an increase in anti-reward functioning. This negativity is a hallmark of addiction. Alcoholics and addicts become chronically malcontent. When family members attempt to help them get treatment, addicts don't feel gratitude. They're suspicious of the motives of others. During periods of abstinence, they become irritable, restless, and obsessed with getting their hands on alcohol or other drugs. Anxiety and depression become the new norm.

The unrelenting stress addicts experience at this stage of addiction can be intolerable. There is no relief until alcohol or other drugs hit the brain. Even then, an addict no longer gets a great high but instead achieves something closer to emotional stability. The alcohol or other drug is primarily helping the addict find a way back to normalcy and equilibrium in the world. Drinking or drugging is now experienced as a *need* rather than a *want*. A need is a necessity that must be fulfilled, such as breathing and eating. So even though an addict may feel guilty, may be sorry, or may promise to never do it again, he cannot regain control *consistently*. The drink or the drug isn't his problem; it's his solution.

Harry Haroutunian, MD, physician director at the Betty Ford Center, describes his personal experience with this phenomenon in his book *Being Sober.*

I remember the day Nancy Reagan suggested that everyone "just say no" to drugs. And I tried. I tried to say no and failed miserably. I felt different and apart from the norm. It made me think of myself as a broken person who could not live in a society ruled by dignity and courage. No matter how hard I tried, I could never just say no; I felt shame.

When I learned that the area of the brain affected by this fatal disease is the same area from which emanates my heartbeat, my next breath, and all my vital functions, I finally understood I could no more say no to that next drink than I could say no to that next breath.[25]

Decision making and the higher functioning of the brain are compromised by addiction, too. This is something Alcoholics Anonymous has long understood, but science ignored until fairly recently. With brain imaging capabilities, researchers now observe how the prefrontal cortex—the thinking brain—is disrupted, making it difficult for addicts to change their behavior even in the face of punishment. Family members are dumbfounded by loved ones who continue to drink and drug even while under the threat of losing children and jobs, going to jail, being evicted. Understanding that an addicted brain functions in much the same way as an injured brain provides some insights.

The prefrontal cortex is the CEO of the brain. It's largely responsible for our success or failure in life. When we think of ourselves—who we are—it is this part of the brain that gives us our sense of identity. It regulates behaviors, makes choices between right and wrong, takes in and processes information, and controls social interaction. It makes decisions on how we should behave—what actions to take and what actions to avoid. It is primarily responsible for our intelligence and personality, and it allows us to plan ahead and create strategies. It helps us focus so we can set goals, pay attention to the world around us, and learn. Active memory—the ability to keep in mind recent events or bring to mind information from long ago—originates here. It is through the prefrontal cortex that we feel empathy for one another.

When this part of the brain is damaged or disrupted, the whole brain can be thrown off. Personalities can be altered, turning a mild-mannered person into someone who is aggressive or reckless. Or an extrovert may become self-absorbed and filled with self-pity. Morals and ethics are affected, diminishing the ability to differentiate between right and wrong. Chronic lateness and procrastination are symptoms. Emotional distress, loss of self-control, and socially inappropriate behaviors are other consequences. Planning, reasoning, and problem solving are diminished. Ultimately, addicts lose the ability to consider the long-term consequences of their drug use and, without regard for harm or punishment, make decisions based on immediate gratification.

Families, witnessing these changes, often interpret them as a refusal to accept personal responsibility. The two most common questions posed by families are: "Can't she see what she's doing to herself?" and "When is he going to learn?" It isn't understood that addiction erodes an addict's ability to act responsibly. In other words, it is becoming increasingly difficult for an addict to make good decisions. The ability to switch strategies when things are going badly is disappearing. Addicts keep doing the same things over and over, expecting different results. This is the definition of *insanity* commonly held in Alcoholics Anonymous circles.

The emotional brain, known as the *limbic system,* is also changed by addiction. This ancient part of the brain is responsible for motivation, learning, emotion, and memory. It is highly interconnected with the brain's pleasure center, and controls mood and attitude. Our ability to bond with others is centered here. The limbic system filters how we see external events through our internal events, or what is called *emotional coloring.* In other words, how we see the world is largely determined by how we feel. The seat of our spirituality, our passions, desires, and joy for living emanate largely from this area of the brain. The limbic system sets the emotional tone for everything about life: ideas, memories, emotions, and dreams.

When addiction causes disturbances in the limbic system, alcoholics and addicts become highly sensitive—especially to criticism—and increasingly malcontent. They experience mood swings and irritability. The limbic system floods the brain with negative emotions like depression and aggression, which, in turn, feed self-centeredness and paranoia.

Addicts become increasingly isolated emotionally and, sometimes, physically. Enthusiasm for living wanes, because, as social animals, we need a healthy limbic system to ensure our survival in the world.

Intellect is valued in our society more than emotional health. But neurologists tell us that we are not *thinking* machines that *feel;* we are *feeling* machines that *think.* Our thoughts and emotions don't operate separately but are interactive, one always influencing the other. When our emotional brain is not working well neither is our thinking brain. It cannot properly engage in problem solving, decision making, or planning.

To understand the addicted brain further, it is important to examine another function of the brain: the capacity for self-control. Until late in their addiction, alcoholics and other drug addicts commonly believe they can stop drinking or using on their own, and prove themselves right time and time again. The problem, however, is staying stopped. Alcoholics, addicts, and their families view these periods of self-control as proof that quitting is within their power if they want it badly enough. The return to drinking and drugging is attributed to weakness of character or a stubborn refusal to do the right thing. But it is neither. Self-control is a limited cognitive resource. In other words, we only have so much available; when it's used up, we lose control.

The implication of self-control as a finite resource supports two important concepts that we'll develop more in the next chapter: 1) Motivation doesn't produce long-term changes in behavior, and 2) Alcoholics need the right level of support to succeed over time.

In short, self-control only works for a limited time. When circumstances require sustained self-control, there is eventually a breakdown. Therefore, when we overvalue motivation and undervalue support, we get relapse.

Researchers Mark Muraven and Roy Baumeister, at Case Western Reserve University, explain:

> Exerting self-control may consume self-control strength, reducing the amount of strength available for subsequent self-control efforts. Coping with stress, regulating negative affect, and resisting temptations require self-control,

and after such self-control efforts, subsequent attempts at self-control are more likely to fail. Continuous self-control efforts, such as vigilance, also degrade over time. . . . It is concluded that the executive component of the self—in particular, inhibition—relies on a limited, consumable resource.[26]

Forty years of research have shown that only 15 percent of dieters kept weight off for three years or more. Among those who were successful, a high percentage participated in ongoing group support. Presumably, they didn't deplete reserves of self-control—or what some would call willpower—because they also relied on outside help.

One of the practical applications of this research is its value in helping addicts and their families understand why self-control isn't a reliable solution for overcoming addiction. The researchers at Case Western Reserve University noted that "addiction counselors may find it useful to realize that addictive and relapse patterns are hardest to overcome when the person is subjected to depleted resources—including depletion by factors that seemingly have little or nothing to do with the addiction itself."[27]

We know that addicts experience escalating negative consequences in many areas of their lives before they receive treatment. They have problems with their jobs, relationships, finances, health. They sometimes exhibit co-occurring disorders such as depression, anxiety, and PTSD, or sexual, spending, and gambling compulsions. Varying degrees of self-control are applied to these problems in an attempt to overcome them.

But since the brain's capacity to control and change behavior is limited, this strenuous overuse of self-control depletes the reserves, making it difficult to exert control in areas of life unrelated to addiction. In other words, there is a growing sense of unmanageability in life generally. Families often experience this as promises made and promises broken. The addict believes his promises when making them but no longer can muster enough resolve to follow through consistently. As the disease progresses, it requires greater amounts of self-control using a brain that is "running on empty."

We create the perfect recipe for relapse when we expect addicts to exert self-control over drinking and drugging, with the added burden of an impaired thinking brain and emotional brain, and no proper support. Many try and fail multiple times. Repeated relapse creates hopelessness because the addict believes he is incapable of staying sober, and the family gives up.

Many people continue to define addiction as *drinking or using too much,* and the solution is simple: *drink or use less.* But addiction is a complex disease, and recovery is highly challenging. Brain imaging has helped us understand how an addicted brain is changed. But addiction also causes a spiritual sickness that prevents the addict from reaching out for help, making it all the more difficult to get well.

Alcoholics and other drug addicts might be able to quit for periods of time, but they don't know how to live every single day sober. Without a program of recovery, the disease makes abstinence a grim existence. The brain is impaired and exhausted. It's no wonder so many fail. Twelve Step recovery programs that include practicing the Steps and attending meetings, coupled with establishing mutual trust and support with loved ones, exercise the mind and spirit in a particular way that for millions of alcoholics and addicts has resulted in contented, lasting sobriety. The brain heals, and addicts remember how to love life again. As a recovering alcoholic wrote in the Big Book of Alcoholics Anonymous:

> When I had been in A.A. only a short while, an oldtimer told me something that has affected my life ever since. "A.A. does not teach us how to handle our drinking," he said. "It teaches us how to handle sobriety." . . . God willing, we members of A.A. may never again have to deal with drinking, but we have to deal with sobriety every day.[28]

• • •

Motivation Isn't the Answer

Before AA founders Bill Wilson and Dr. Bob Smith ever met, both men were highly motivated to stop drinking and had tried many times. Alcoholism was incrementally destroying every aspect of their lives. Bill Wilson lost a successful career, fell into financial ruin, and almost died by age thirty-nine. Dr. Bob once said, "Well, I can't conceive of any living human who really wanted to do something as badly as I think I do, who could be such a total failure." Motivation to quit helped both men leave alcohol alone for various periods of time, but lasting sobriety eluded them. Even after experiencing the benefits of being alcohol-free, they always returned to the drink. Family members were dumbstruck and unable to fathom why.

Where recovery from addiction is concerned, motivation isn't correlated with long-term success. Its value is in the short term to get us going, but long-term change requires something more. We're taught to believe in the power of motivation, but the evidence of its limitations is all around us. Sit in an airport and watch people walk by. Americans are increasingly overweight and out-of-shape. How many people, do you suppose, are highly motivated to lose weight and begin a regular exercise program? How many succeed?

By reviewing articles and reports on dieting—something many of us are personally familiar with—it's easy to see that motivation isn't linked to long-term success. A small minority of dieters keep off the weight they lost. They lose weight in the short term, then gain it all back. These results lead people to believe that diets don't work. Experts now emphasize lifestyle change as the answer, but this hasn't resulted in the slimming of a nation or a reduction of health problems either.

Danish researchers Ayyad and Andersen reviewed 900 scientific articles on dieting to determine its value. The first thing they learned was that 883 of the articles they were evaluating were based on unreliable research. Of the studies published over the last thirty years, only 2 percent were considered worthy of review, which is a cautionary tale in and of itself. Of the remaining studies—seventeen in all—only 15 percent of the dieters maintained their weight loss over a three-year period. The most successful dieters, as it turns out, were participating in group therapy.[29] Evidently, the power of the group works for more people than just alcoholics.

What researchers found is that diets actually do work. It is people who fail. And when they do, they tend to blame their failures on inadequate motivation or insufficient willpower.

We're Often Wrong about How We Change

Jeni Cross, PhD, professor of sociology at Colorado State University and national public speaker, says that our greatest adversary to change isn't that change is hard but that our beliefs about how we create change are wrong. Dr. Cross points to three common misconceptions.[30]

The first myth claims that education will change behavior. It presumes that people who aren't motivated to make change simply don't know any better. By educating them, we motivate them to take action. But education is a poor predictor of changes in behavior. When it comes to addiction, it has long been assumed by many that educating addicts on ways that addiction damages the body, brain, and family life is enough to motivate them to stay sober. But if education alone changed people, we would have stamped out addiction long ago.

The second myth claims that we need to change attitudes before we can change behavior. Sociologists tell us we have it backwards. Forty years of research prove repeatedly that it is a change in behavior that changes attitude. Families often say, "She'll never go to AA. She hates

AA." The belief is that until she changes her attitude, she won't change her behavior. But we cannot depend on attitudes to change behavior or predict them. A change in attitude—*Okay, I guess AA is a good program for alcoholics*—doesn't mean she will attend meetings. And disliking AA doesn't mean she won't attend.

A mother called about her alcoholic son who had just landed in treatment for the fourth time. "He won't go to AA. He's tried it, and he doesn't like it." That didn't leave many options, other than a miracle or death, so we suggested he work with a recovery mentor who could re-introduce him to AA in a more promising way. After a few days of work-ing with the mentor, the son's attitude changed completely. He loved AA. He was introduced to great people and enjoyed their company, both learning from them and having fun again. He listened to how others overcame addiction and felt understood for the first time. He began to believe he could succeed by following the AA program. His recovery mentor didn't try to change his attitude. By helping him change his be-havior, everything else fell into place.

One of the secrets to changing behavior, according to social scien-tists, is setting up *behavioral expectations*. The recovery mentor, in this case, set a behavioral expectation: "We are going to AA meetings to-gether." The alcoholic wasn't given an option. He could have said no to mentoring, but it would have meant going against the wishes of his fam-ily, who were ready to involve his boss in setting consequences, which made it easier to comply. The behavioral expectations led to a change in his behavior, which in turn changed his attitude.

The third myth claims that we know what motivates us to make change in our own lives. Much to our collective astonishment, social scientists have repeatedly shown that this is not true. For instance, while most people claim they are not motivated by what other people do or say, social scientists tell us that this is our greatest motivator. Social norms, which indicate the established and approved way of doing things, are powerful forces for change. Whether we know it or not, we have a high tendency to do what we see other people do.

Research has shown that reporting prosocial behaviors—such as "nearly all people recycle" or "most people reuse their towels in hotel rooms"—has the effect of changing behaviors in favorable ways. Consistently stressing high expectations through social norms produces desired results. Reporting negative social behaviors, however, changes people's conduct in an unfavorable way. For instance, when it was announced that people were pilfering petrified wood from national forests, the number of people taking petrified wood increased. Research repeatedly shows that emphasizing a social norm, either in the positive or negative, increases behaviors that conform to the norm.[31]

There is a growing trend in the treatment world to reframe relapse as a normal part of the process. Addiction is called a *chronic relapsing brain disease,* which is fine for researchers, but is this what we want to tell addicts? The impetus behind this movement is the idea that when we reduce feelings of shame associated with relapse, the addicted are more likely to return to treatment once they've started drinking and drugging again.

Perhaps there is truth in this hypothesis, but we really don't know if a lack of shame is a primary motivator for returning to treatment. It would be as easy to argue the opposite. It is even reasonable to assume that shame (which is quite different from the toxic experience of being shamed by others) is a normal response to failing to maintain one's sobriety.

Shame has fallen out of favor in therapeutic circles, but it seems that some behaviors appropriately elicit shame whereas others trigger shame's first cousin, guilt. For example, if I steal money from my beloved grandmother's purse, feeling shame is probably an appropriate emotional response. Such a behavior should give rise to questions such as, "Is this who *I* am? Is this who *I* want to be?" Whereas, if I borrow my sister's sweater when she asked me not to wear it, guilt would trigger a different kind of self-examination. "Should I have done *that?*" When the transgression is attributed to the general value we place on ourselves, we feel shame. When it's attributed to a short-lived behavior, we feel guilt.

Webster's Revised Unabridged Dictionary helps highlight the differences between the moral emotions of shame and guilt. *Guilt,* it says, "is a feeling of regret or remorse for having committed some improper act." But *shame* is a different emotion, described as a "painful sensation excited by having done something that injures reputation." The *Century*

Dictionary further clarifies the emotion of shame as a feeling caused by an awareness of "having done something unworthy of one's own previous idea of one's excellence."

Interestingly, cultural differences determine how people respond to shame and guilt. When one values *feeling good,* as is common in many North American contexts, the idea of being evaluated by others is presumed to be bad or something to be avoided. In this context, shame is viewed more negatively than guilt. But in cultures that value interdependent concepts of self, such as in European and Asian American cultures, other people's thoughts and feelings are as important as one's own feelings and thoughts. They view shame in more positive terms: an instructive emotion that triggers a need for self-improvement.

Relapse is almost always an indication of a particular set of behaviors that are in conflict with our personal standards and represent a failure to meet our responsibility to ourselves and others. Not everyone survives a relapse, and many who do, do so at great cost to themselves and their families. This most certainly triggers negative moral emotions, whether we name them guilt or shame. With Structured Family Recovery, people closest to the addict can respond to these emotions with care and loving concern, modeling the road back to recovery and setting up behavioral expectations.

Based on what sociologists know about social norms, we can also hypothesize that normalizing relapse might have the opposite effect of what we're after and actually trigger a relapse. By creating an expectation that relapse is a normal part of the recovery process, we might be signaling that it is the normal and approved way if we aren't careful.

As a long-recovering alcoholic told me, "It's a good thing this wasn't the thinking when I was getting help. My addict brain would have grabbed onto that idea immediately. The first time I wanted to go out with my old drinking friends, I would have reminded myself that relapse is a normal part of being an alcoholic."

These trends give us greater cause to become more involved in creating positive social norms within our families. When an entire family is participating in the recovery experience, we raise the bar and create our own normal. Relapse is most often a symptom of the lack of adequate support over time. As we've seen, doctors participating in Physician Health Programs experience extraordinarily low relapse rates. Their social norm is successful recovery, and the results tell the story.

So, what do social scientists ultimately teach us about motivating alcoholics and addicts to stay sober? *Never depend on motivation to carry the addict into long-term recovery.* Motivation plays an important role, but put into proper perspective, it's only good for a sprint in a long-distance race. Families are much more effective when they model the recovery behaviors they want to see in their addicted loved ones. We need to repeatedly ask ourselves, "What social norms am I demonstrating today?"

We've also learned that we waste a lot of time trying to change attitudes, when it is behavioral expectations that get results. If we want to change an attitude, we must first change the corresponding behavior. When we, as family members, model recovery behaviors, we set up behavioral expectations in the form of social norms. But the opposite can also be true. When we model a lack of commitment and involvement in recovery, we create a social norm that supports the opposite of what we want the addict to achieve, and we create a behavioral expectation that works against recovery.

The paradox is that if we are resistant to recovery, which, as we've learned, most addicts are, it takes getting involved in recovery to change our attitudes about it. Lasting recovery is the result of what we do, not what we think. Our actions will change our thinking. These words are found in the Big Book:

> "There is a principle which is a bar against all information, which is proof against all arguments and which cannot fail to keep a man in everlasting ignorance—that principle is contempt prior to investigation." —Herbert Spencer[32]

Contempt prior to investigation keeps us in our heads, dependent solely on our own thinking and opinions, which, when generated by the addict brain, are likely to resist new experiences and ideas. This applies to families, too. To change our thinking, we first need to change our behaviors. The end result is that we create a new world for ourselves.

In each alcoholic's history, it isn't difficult to identify the limits of motivation in the journey from drinking to sobriety. Motivation alone, as we will see in the following story, is not effective when it's up against the closed mind and distorted thinking of the addict. Involvement of a family team gives motivation muscle. But, even then, motivation is of short duration and cannot be relied on as the foundation for lasting sobriety.

Greg is a thirty-six-year-old husband and father. He's been drinking heavily since high school and started smoking pot in college. For the last four or five years, he's been doing cocaine, first with his buddies and now in the mornings to get a start on the day. His primary care physician prescribed Adderall, an amphetamine, for what Greg describes as an inability to concentrate. He made plans to go to a psychiatrist for a second prescription for the drug.

Greg began to experience negative consequences. He was spending too much money on cocaine, squandering funds from the family's monthly budget. His wife became furious about the shortfalls and interrogated him about where the money was going. He borrowed from his parents to secretly cover drug costs and didn't pay them back. Using Adderall and cocaine, he felt like a powerhouse on the job, but his boss brought him into her office one day to ask him if he was all right. She said he didn't seem quite like himself. He could tell she thought something was up.

Greg's wife found a tiny bag with residual white powder in his jeans pocket. She called him at work demanding to know what was going on. She threatened to call his parents. Greg told her a friend had left it in his car and he put it in his pocket, planning to throw it in the trash. She accused him of lying. The pressure was building, and Greg was getting nervous. He made a pledge to himself that he would quit the cocaine and cut down on the booze. He'd allow himself an Adderall in the morning and two or three beers to get to sleep at night, nothing more. He was highly motivated to get things under control and get everyone off his back. Greg's resolve lasted a week and a half before he called his coke dealer.

A few months later, he was spending more money than usual for cocaine. When his wife was paying bills and balancing the checkbook, she discovered they didn't have enough money to write the mortgage check. It was the last straw. After a blowout fight with Greg, she called his brother. "We have to meet right away," she said.

Greg's brother called a clinical interventionist, and together, they formed an intervention team of family and friends. Intervention, they learned, creates a moment of clarity, and in that moment, most alcoholics and addicts agree to treatment. But the resulting motivation to accept help is short-lived. For that reason, they prepared to take Greg to treatment immediately after the intervention, when his motivation was at its highest.

Once admitted into treatment, Greg was actually relieved. He was tired of the secrets and lies. He burned with shame when he thought of the loan from his parents and the financial troubles he had caused his family. He thought about cocaine all the time—how to buy it and how to hide it—and it was exhausting. Getting caught filling double prescriptions for Adderall at two different pharmacies was something he couldn't even think about.

But ten days into treatment, Greg began feeling agitated. He wanted out. Everything was irritating him. His counselor told him he was experiencing cravings, but Greg insisted he was never going to drink or drug again. He complained to his wife that his roommate was a heroin addict on probation for theft. "I'm not as bad as the rest of these people," he said. "I'm ready to come home. I've learned everything they have to teach me. I know better than to use another drug."

His wife might have been convinced by his arguments, but by then, the entire family was engaged in Structured Family Recovery. They were prepared for Greg's motivation to fail and had learned that education and "knowing better" weren't cures. The family team quickly consulted with the professionals. They scheduled a family conference call with Greg and his counselor. The conversation was carefully planned so each person knew what to say. They were loving and supportive of Greg but firm in standing behind the recommendations of the treatment team. The family was prepared to introduce negative consequences but never needed to use them. The negotiations went well and Greg agreed to stay. By the next day, he was feeling positive and, once again, engaged in treatment.

When Greg returned home after completing treatment, he was highly motivated to stay sober. He said his desire to drink and drug was gone. He began going to AA meetings. But the family knew that motivation in early recovery can eventually dwindle down to nothing—just like it did while Greg was in treatment—so his optimistic mood didn't give them false hopes. The urge to drink or drug could hit at any time. For that reason, they invited Greg to join their Structured Family Recovery team. Everyone on the team was already engaged in family recovery and the Twelve Steps of Al-Anon. The team met weekly by conference call. As a family team, they created positive social norms. As a result, Greg agreed to random drug testing and remained involved in AA. He enjoyed being part of a family in recovery.

His family's involvement created a strong desire in Greg to be successful in his own recovery. Participation in Structured Family Recovery set up behavioral expectations for the entire family, which led to a common empathy and a growing recovery intelligence. Working as a team, the family returned to their values determined not to let addiction win.

Following the wisdom of AA—*"One day at a time"*—Greg took his recovery in extremely small bites. He made a commitment to set aside one hour a day for an AA meeting. At each meeting, he'd introduce himself to one person, saying, "Hi, my name is Greg. I'm new in AA." He'd ask for the person's phone number, knowing it was one more person he could call for support. Greg took five minutes every morning and every night to read his recovery meditation book.

Initially, Greg was mostly going through the motions. He followed directions and did what he was supposed to do, but his heart wasn't completely into it. But with time, he experienced a growing sense of belonging. In the long tradition of Twelve Step programs, he began to laugh. As a result, he started looking forward to the camaraderie he experienced in meetings.

He often arrived at a meeting feeling weighed down by frustrations and discontent, but by the time he left, his load was lightened and his mood elevated. He began to follow the AA slogan, "Easy does it." He learned he didn't need to solve all of his problems at once. The most important thing he could do was not make things worse by picking up a drink.

By going to a meeting every day, Greg was practicing new social norms. He was modeling a group of sober people, learning to relax and have fun. He gradually gained confidence in his ability to make it one more day. Reading the literature at night quieted his mind before sleep. These simple steps took much less time than drinking and drugging had taken.

Greg made many new friends at the meetings. Some had long-term sobriety, measured in years or decades; some had only weeks or months. He chose a home group and agreed to help organize the snacks. He started coming earlier and staying later. He'd become acquainted with an older and wiser member of AA and finally worked up the courage to ask him to be his sponsor. They began working the Steps together.

For Greg, staying sober was now part of sticking with the group. These weren't choirboys, and Greg appreciated their sharp humor and willingness to help. They were an unusual group, people who otherwise had little in common, coming from all walks of life, but he valued their experience. It was like finding his way from a sinking ship into a lifeboat with other castaways, where everyone worked together for a common survival.

Rather than looking forward to evenings as a time to drink, he looked forward to his AA meetings and the easy camaraderie he enjoyed with his new friends. When he arrived home to his wife, he was a man who could be part of a family.

● ● ●

A Closer Look at Relapse

When an alcoholic or addict relapses, everything is up for grabs. Even one drink or hit of a drug creates a change of mind and spirit. Of course, one is never enough when you're addicted. It's as if a demon is unleashed, launching an insatiable lust for more alcohol, more cocaine, more pills. It becomes a singular focus where work, home, friends, children, and spouse are again shut out by the obsessive need to use the drug and hide the truth. As one relapsed crack addict described it: "My mind was constantly saying, 'I need it, I need it, I need it, I need it.'"

A friend of mine, Grayson, a former heroin addict with twenty years of abstinence-based Twelve Step recovery, tells a story that perfectly illustrates what happens when a drug is reintroduced into an addict's system. It began when he was hospitalized for surgery. After the operation and back in his room, the nurse hooked him up to an IV with a morphine drip to manage the pain, which was quite severe. Grayson describes what happened next. "The very second the morphine hit my blood, the reaction was instant and vicious. I wanted to get my wife, pregnant with our first child, out of the room, and get the nurse back in. All I could think was, I need more of this *now*."

Grayson's morphine experience, however, was up against his solid recovery program. "I keep myself right in the middle of AA," he said. "That way I always have thirty eyeballs on me." Both before and after surgery, he called his sponsor to openly discuss the fact that he would be given an opiate for pain. He talked about it at meetings. He and his wife had discussed it. Grayson knew he couldn't depend on himself once the drug coursed through his bloodstream. He needed other recovering people and family to create a safety net. By being forthcoming and applying rigorous honesty, Grayson placed himself in the hands of people he could trust. The disease of addiction couldn't stand up to the power of that kind of recovery. Grayson never acted on his desire to get more morphine. His wife stayed by his side, and he immediately got honest with her about what he was thinking. "It's just the difference between life and death," he said.

Relapse isn't random, like a cancer reoccurring. A medical team can do everything possible to eradicate cancer, only to have it come back with a vengeance. When a relapse in addiction occurs, however, it isn't a mystery. It's usually a sign that a recovery program is lacking something. Most people who relapse can point to exactly what was missing and describe quite incisively how they slipped back into drinking or drugging. The signs and symptoms of relapse are well established.

With Structured Family Recovery, we decide on an action plan in advance of a relapse. The alcoholic or addict is central to making decisions about how the team can best help if she were to fall back into her addiction. By communicating and planning together, relapse doesn't have to mean failure or a full return to active addiction. Regardless of how bad the addict might feel about herself, when the family team comes together *with love,* guided by the predetermined relapse plan, most alcoholics and addicts respond positively and accept an appropriate level of care. Family members also need extra Al-Anon meetings for added support while coping with the stress of a relapse.

Kerry was sober twenty-six years. He owned a fly fishing shop in a small northwestern town and was a mainstay in the AA community. Everyone knew Kerry; he was funny, outgoing, and an open book about his recovery. He loved AA and the legion of sober friends he had made over the years. When the economy crashed, his thriving shop began to suffer. There were times when he looked at his checking account and wondered if he'd have to shutter the business he'd spent much of his adult life building.

As the economic downturn lingered, Kerry managed to keep his fly fishing store open, but had to cut down on employees and do more of the work himself. Although days were long and stress was high, he always had his AA meetings and his recovering friends. "But then," he said, "I started slacking off. It seemed harmless. I'd been sober a very long time and hadn't experienced a craving for a drink in twenty-five years."

Eventually, he stopped going to meetings altogether. Looking back, Kerry says he could see the shift that took place in his thinking. Once recovery wasn't central to his life anymore, it slowly lost its importance until he had all but abandoned it. "I did what you are warned about over and over again in AA," he said. "I became indifferent. Other things in creasingly got in the way of my meetings, and I stopped going." Kerry explained that once he became disconnected from the recovery behaviors that kept him sober, he was already in trouble. "I wasn't drinking, but it was a full-blown relapse nonetheless. The drink was simply a matter of time, but I couldn't see it happening to me."

Kerry began visiting a casino and entertaining himself with small-time gambling. He thought he could sit at the bar if he just ordered a diet soda. "One night, I went to play video poker and this guy I'd met a few times bought me a beer. The bartender set it down in front of me. I looked at it, and even though I knew it was wrong, I picked it up and took a sip," he said.

"When I tasted that beer, all the flags went up in my head telling me this was absolutely the worst thing I could ever do but, inexplicably, I downed the entire glass." He said, "What I'd always heard is true, 'AA ruins your drinking.'" Sober all those years, Kerry had a well-developed conscience, and it led him to feel miserable about himself. Yet he couldn't stop.

"That first beer awakened my disease, even after all my sobriety. I totally lost control over alcohol," he said. "Throughout that week, I'd return to the casino to drink, worrying someone might see me. Then I'd think, 'I don't care! I hope you see me!' It was that crazy alcoholic mindset, 'I'll show you, I'll hurt me!'"

It was pride that kept Kerry from telling his friends in AA. "I almost didn't make it back into the program because of pride," he said. "But the terrible shame and guilt, and the relentless pain it caused me, trumped my pride."

An old AA saying that kept replaying in Kerry's head—"You can't save your face and your butt at the same time"—finally pushed him to pick up the phone. "I called my longtime friend, Sam, who told me exactly what I needed to hear. 'Get yourself to a meeting. You have to admit to it.'"

"Once I did that," said Kerry, "my shame and guilt were cut in half. I began to feel hope again. I knew I could make it." People in AA didn't shame Kerry for his relapse, they embraced him. An old friend with thirty-two years of sobriety said to him, "Come on, let's go to lunch so you can save my life." He took Kerry's admission of relapse as a gift. It was a powerful reminder, "But for the grace of God, there go I."

"Pain," said Kerry, "is an addict's best friend." He then recited his favorite quotation from Proust, "To goodness and wisdom we make only promises. Pain we obey."[33]

Attending to the chronic nature of the disease is a prerequisite to avoiding relapse. Whether it's early in recovery or after years of sobriety, when a person stops working a thorough Twelve Step program as part of a recovery plan that includes building a support system of family and friends, the risk of eventually drinking again is almost certain. Knowing better doesn't keep people sober. Alcoholics and addicts can go on a dry drunk—abstaining from mood-altering substances but still behaving like an addict—for varying lengths of time. But eventually the pain of living with emotional unmanageability leads to relapse.

A person who abuses alcohol or other drugs, but is *not* suffering from the disease of addiction, can stop on his or her own. But, among true alcoholics and addicts, quitting on their own is risky business. It's estimated that 96 to 98 percent eventually relapse or switch addictions.[34] The alcoholic switches to pot, the cocaine addict gets a prescription for Adderall, the opiate addict starts drinking. The new drug eventually becomes a problem or sets off cravings for the former drug, or both. The brain, once addicted, reacts to all mood-altering substances. This change in the brain doesn't go away with time or by switching drugs.

I was walking with a recovering friend through Greenwich Village, a neighborhood in New York City, where she had lived while attending college. She was telling me about the severity of her cocaine addiction in those days and that this was the place where she had bought her drugs. Suddenly she stopped and turned toward me, "You won't believe this," she said. "I can taste cocaine in the back of my throat." After eighteen years of sobriety, her addiction was triggered by strolling through the streets of her past cocaine use, and she could taste the drug as if she'd just used it. This illustrates how powerful the imprint of drug addiction is on the brain.

The addict may know what actions are required for lasting sobriety, but if there isn't a rigorous recovery plan and consistent family support that ensures he'll follow through, an addict will be vulnerable to triggers, and relapse can happen in many different ways. Here are some of the most common rationalizations that can lay the groundwork for relapse as well as what Structured Family Recovery can do to intervene.

I've been through treatment. I can do the rest on my own. This is a combination of false pride and underestimating the power of the disease and what it takes to stay sober. The addict, fresh out of treatment, often has an inflated opinion of himself, called *grandiosity.* He puffs up his self-importance to disguise feelings of inferiority and may resist going to AA or other Twelve Step groups because of stigma. Structured Family Recovery can reassure him by setting an example. "We are with you all the way. We understand the insidious nature of this disease. We are teaming together for success." When the addict finds himself in the middle of a recovery family, he no longer feels like the odd man out. When the entire family is working at recovery, attending family Twelve Step groups, discussing what they've learned and how they're struggling, recovery becomes the social norm. The addict feels the warmth of belonging, something he may not have felt in a very long time, disarming his sense of inferiority.

I attend meetings but don't have a sponsor. The addict may be showing some effort and a modicum of commitment, but not enough. Perhaps the addict has learned how to get along in life by giving less than full effort. He translates these past experiences to his recovery program. The addict thinks, "I'm doing enough. This works for me." Again, this is the mark of underestimating what it takes to stay sober. By engaging in Structured Family Recovery, the family sets up behavioral expectations for everyone. By modeling a program of recovery and maintaining unity and accountability with weekly family meetings, the alcoholic follows suit, not to please the family and comply with their wishes, but because he knows they willingly do it for themselves out of love.

I have a sponsor, but our relationship is superficial. When the addict remains emotionally removed from his sponsor, he is usually reluctant to reveal the true nature of his problem, especially the resentments he has against others. He presents an idealized image of himself rather than getting to the truth. This is his protective shield of pride, driven by fear. When family embraces their alcoholic through the lens of their own recovery, accepting the fact that no one can change the past and knowing it is what we do today that defines our tomorrow, the need to blame is lifted. With acceptance from family, demonstrated through the action steps of Structured Family Recovery, the alcoholic may realize enough self-acceptance to stop fearing the truth. Bill Wilson, in *Twelve Steps and Twelve Traditions,* wrote, ". . . we began to get the feeling that we could be forgiven, no matter what we had thought or done."[35]

I get to meetings late and leave early. The addict is isolating even while attending meetings. By coming to a meeting late and leaving early, he avoids personal interaction with others. He's fulfilling a cursory responsibility to attend meetings but without engaging others and building supportive relationships or making friendships. Addiction is an isolating disease; recovery requires connecting with others in recovery. With no emotional connection to people in AA, the addict feels like a perpetual outsider. He'll soon fall away from his meetings, telling himself he has nothing in common with *those* people. But how different the expectation when a family engages in Structured Family Recovery. Right away, the addict is no longer in isolation. When a family defines a new norm through their actions, it helps the addict to see recovery through a more positive lens. As the family connects with Al-Anon, the enthusiasm is contagious.

I don't bother with service work. It's easy for the newcomer to see service work as unimportant or to think he has nothing to offer. Making the coffee, putting out the snacks, arranging the literature—it all seems small and insignificant. But it is insignificant only on the surface, in the *thinking* about it. In the *doing,* it has the deep, resonating significance of giving back. AA is not so much about getting help as it is about giving help. Ultimately, it's through helping other alcoholics that people stay sober. People tend to think those new to AA aren't ready to help others, but they can set up chairs, greet people at the door, or make sure the lights are turned off as they leave. Even more importantly, any time the addict tells his story or shares in a meeting, he may be giving others exactly what they need to hear to help them stay sober. It's a critical first step in learning to give rather than receive. It creates a sense of belonging to the group. Families do the same in Al-Anon. In Structured Family Recovery, as we share about our service commitments, we create a spiritual expectation of giving back.

I've been sober a long time. I really don't need meetings anymore. This is the reemergence of the inflated ego, and it gets alcoholics and addicts in trouble. The fewer positive and constructive recovery experiences addicts have in the early days of recovery, the less capital addicts build up against relapse. This relapse process often happens when life seems to be good. The addict assumes she now no longer needs to do the work that recovery requires, instead of understanding that her life is good *because of her efforts in recovery.* For families who are not participating in recovery, this rationalization can sound sensible. Someone might say, "I don't see why you need to go to AA anymore. You're doing great." But families in Structured Family Recovery know better. Moreover, when an entire family is involved in Twelve Step recovery, an addict sees recovery as a normal way of life.

I don't make time for spiritual practice. Alcoholics Anonymous is a spiritual program, but newcomers frequently misunderstand this to mean religious or as having no real significance. Keith Humphreys, a professor of psychiatry and social sciences at Stanford University, explains that in AA, "Someone will say something profound that everyone can connect to beyond themselves, and it can be very moving. That is a spiritual process." He goes on to say that "the basic frame is about minimizing selfishness, minimizing grandiosity, giving to others, accepting character flaws, and apologizing when you're wrong."[36]

Spiritual practices also include reading recovery literature (such as meditation books), taking time to reflect, and connecting to other people in the program. These practices help prevent the disease from once again gaining strength. Positive spirituality spreads to the emotional brain, which sends positive messages to the thinking brain. Spiritual practices are action steps that create positive attitudes and fortitude. This process is as important for the family as it is for the addict. Anger, resentment, and blame, which keep families tied to the pattern of addiction, are put into perspective when they experience a power greater than themselves at work. Structured Family Recovery helps each member of the team set up spiritual practices that are simple, consistent, and effective.

I have thoughts of drinking, that I don't talk about with others. This is a combination of pride and perfectionism. Even in AA, the addict wants to look as if he has no problem. In recovery, a sign of growth is to be honest, even when it is embarrassing. Lack of honesty is a lack of humility and a retreat back into the self. Recovery flourishes in the light; addiction grows in the dark. For this reason, rigorous honesty is one of the main tenets of the program. When alcoholics and addicts aren't honest, they eventually relapse. In Structured Family Recovery, the entire family begins to let go of blame and each individual begins to focus on him- or herself, and what he or she needs to do to foster recovery. The entire family team learns to model humility and honesty. The family discovers a newfound acceptance of one another. In this atmosphere, the addict learns that it is safe to be honest with himself and others.

Monica is a forty-year-old executive for a multinational corporation who travels the globe for business. A glamorous life from the outside, but, for years, alcoholism was destroying her from the inside. No longer able to hide her drinking problem, she agreed to attend a world renown treatment center. Once home, she joined AA and then relapsed in early recovery. What follows is her narrative of a journey into relapse and back into recovery.

"Once I entered recovery, my life began to turn around quickly. My health came back, my liver healed, relationships were restored, and I made several new friendships. I was no longer the target of office gossip, and even my golf game was improving. Shame was starting to lift, and I was experiencing a freedom I had long forgotten. It was due to my recovery, and I was working what I believed to be a strong program: I attended daily AA meetings, committed to service work, read, prayed, and worked the Steps with my sponsor.

"After my health improved and my confidence returned, life was on an upswing. I quickly forgot the pain, fear, and shame that alcohol ultimately produced, despite hearing about it nightly at my meetings. I forgot how grateful I was to have been given another chance in this world. I began to get bored with my routine and started missing the glamour associated with alcohol. I began fantasizing about the conviviality of drinking with others in swanky bars. I desperately wanted the feeling of 'ahhh' again, as alcohol washed away my cares.

"It was the type of dangerous thinking that I should have been discussing in meetings and with my sponsor. Instead I let my ego run away with concerns such as *what will they think of me?* Even while dreaming about drinking, I wanted to look like the AA poster child. It wasn't clear to me at the time, but I hadn't grasped the concepts of acceptance, surrender, and honesty. My obsession with alcohol was still very present.

"Before long, it became a daily fight to stay sober. Despite the forewarnings from people in AA who said, 'It just takes the first drink,' or 'The disease progresses even when you're not drinking,' or 'Relapse is planned,' my disease was telling me that I was smarter than those people, and besides, no one ever needed to know. I began to believe drinking would be different this time. Without taking that first sip of alcohol, I had already relapsed.

"My secret thoughts finally drove me to drink. There was no 'ahhh' feeling with that first drink, nor with the ones that followed. Instead, each drink brought stronger feelings of guilt, shame, and self-loathing. There was no conviviality or companionship or swanky bars. I drank alone in fear of being found out, having to hide from anyone who knew I was in AA, which included my husband and my entire family.

"Not only had I been unable to recreate my fantasy about drinking, there were so many precious things I lost: clarity, self-respect, confidence, serenity, and, most of all, freedom. While no one suspected yet, I was consumed by planning my next drinking escapade—where I could go, how I could hide it, how much I could have before it was noticeable, how much I could drink and still drive, what to say and how to say it, what excuses to make, how to minimize the aftereffects, how to push what I'd done out of my mind. It was an all-consuming, horrible feeling.

"The next day always brought some version of a hangover and a sick feeling of doom. I needed to get back on track, which of course required a few stabilizing drinks. Even though the slip went unnoticed to the outside world, the cycle had started. The cravings and obsession were back in full force. It was all I could do to maintain any semblance of control. I was determined to portray myself as successful to everyone around me, fearful that unless I conducted myself perfectly they would catch on. It was exhausting. I felt like a complete fraud.

"I had achieved freedom with recovery, but with that first drink, I relinquished it. Again, I felt captive to alcohol and the paralyzing fear that went along with it. In the end, it was fear that led me to prayer, which led me to only one answer—the one I was desperately trying to avoid—*honesty*. My relapse started with self-deception, which manifested itself to outward deception, which then turned into shame, guilt, and fear. I was now drinking to drown out the terrible negativity and emotional pain.

"There was only one way to break the cycle: I had to get honest with myself, others, and the God of my understanding. It is humbling and terrifying to make an admission of relapse. But I really wanted to get better, and I knew there was only one way out. There was something in me that had changed in those early months in AA, and I simply could not continue to act one way and live another. Of course I was afraid of judgment, looks of disgust, and dismissal, but that fear originated with the way I was judging myself. In my ego-driven head, I was afraid people would think less of me. It was far from the truth. What I found instead was support, care, concern, and, yes, some colorfully worded candor. I found love, acceptance, and the strength to move forward. Today, by working an honest program of recovery, I have more than two years clean and sober."

Recovery in AA, NA, and other Twelve Step programs replaces a drinking and drugging life with something of value. In the Twelve Steps, addicts embrace a higher set of principles that supports a higher standard of behavior. Working a program gives addicts and their family members a framework for realizing major changes in character and personality. Maintaining these changes requires staying active in recovery. For those who don't, even after years of sobriety, tales of relapse abound. The storyline almost always begins with the same admissions: "I stopped going to meetings" and "I wasn't being honest."

Families can relapse, too. Behaviors and attitudes well practiced while addiction raged don't work in recovery. Resentments and anger often burn long after alcoholics get into recovery. In many cases, families believe it's the addict's job to make everything right again. But it's not possible for a recovering person to do what family members need to do for itself.

Recovering alcoholics who receive criticism from their spouses, as compared to alcoholics who have their support, have a higher relapse rate, according to research from the State University of New York. Researchers found that families who work together in recovery, however, have greater success.[37]

• • •

Tiny Tasks

In the words of Irish author Derek Landy, "Every solution to every problem is simple. It's the distance between the two where the mystery lies." Finding better ways to motivate alcoholics and addicts to stay sober is an ongoing pursuit. We educate, we attempt to change attitudes, and we ask alcoholics to tell us how they can best motivate themselves. None of these alone has proven to have the power to sustain lasting change. It isn't as though effective strategies for sustaining change don't exist; it's that we're not using them in a consistent way.

B. J. Fogg, PhD, professor of social sciences at Stanford University and behavior-change expert, has created a model that helps us think clearly about behavior change. Designing for behavior change is systematic, he says. It's not guesswork. There are just a few things that drive behavior.[38]

But first he lists five approaches that do not work well for sustained changes in behavior:

1. Present information, hoping it will change attitudes, and new attitudes will change behavior.

2. Give people a big goal and then focus on amping up motivation and sustaining willpower.

3. Move people through psychological stages until they are ready to change.

4. Assume all behaviors are a result of choice.

5. Make persuasion techniques, such as scarcity and reciprocity, the starting point for a solution.

What's startling is how often these five approaches are used as motivators for lasting sobriety. They might have varying degrees of value for short-term change by advancing alcoholics and addicts forward from one stage of care to the next: from intervention to treatment to aftercare planning to Twelve Step groups. Each move forward represents a short-term goal. When a family wants to motivate a loved one to accept treatment, they use a short-term motivator called *intervention*. It's what's needed to get the job done, and then treatment takes over for the next phase. But when we mistakenly believe short-term motivators magically produce long-term sobriety, we set up unrealistic expectations that can lead to relapse.

As families, we have been expecting a kind of success from people suffering from the disease of addiction that not even dieters have achieved. Our myths can lock us into false solutions, which invariably lead to disappointment, resignation, and even estrangement. People in general are resistant to change, alcoholics and addicts only more so. Our loved ones who are suffering from a disease that discourages its victims from reaching out for help can't be expected to self-motivate for recovery. This is an important fact to keep in the forefront of our minds.

As we've learned, decades of research have found that traditional motivational approaches alone usually only produce temporary change. Dr. Fogg concurs, "Relying primarily on motivation to change your behavior long-term is a losing strategy, and similarly for will power."[39] He is speaking for all people. But addiction creates the added burden of dismantling the will and defeating motivation. So knowing that these two forces—motivation and willpower—aren't central to lasting change is good news.

Change doesn't happen by placing our focus on the outcome; it happens by focusing on the behaviors that produce the outcome. Still, it is the expected outcome of treatment that we typically fixate on—staying sober—rather than centering our attention on the behaviors that need to happen *after* treatment that lead to ongoing sobriety. This harkens back to our misreading of treatment's role in the recovery process, which leads us to the false belief that the required behavior changes all took place during treatment—a *fait accompli*—and now we can just sit back and witness the results.

As we've seen, it is more accurate to say that when treatment ends, recovery begins. This is when the make-or-break work of managing a chronic disease gets under way. It calls for the acquisition of new behaviors and skills. If simply announcing, "I will never drink again!" is an addict's recovery plan, he's probably heading for relapse. Why? Because he is skipping over the necessary behaviors required for sobriety, such as going to AA meetings, getting a sponsor, and working the Steps. Instead, he's aiming directly for the outcome. It's a sign of overconfidence.

Alcoholics and addicts who utter these proclamations usually can't explain how they will make "never drinking again" possible, other than through sheer willpower. If you ask them, you're likely to learn there is no reasonable plan; you're lucky if you'll hear something as fundamental as "I am following my aftercare plan and going to my AA meetings!"

Alcoholics Anonymous and other Twelve Step programs are based on the premise that behavior drives attitude change; their logo could be "Action before motivation." Still, we commonly hear people theorize, after an alcoholic has relapsed, "I guess she wasn't ready." This presumes *readiness* as the key ingredient for success. In other words, the right attitude will lead to the right behavior. It also sends a message that our feelings of readiness are unwavering or that we can somehow measure them. Nothing could be further from the truth. Every day, approximately 350 alcoholics and addicts die before they feel ready to get sober.[40]

Where does all of this leave us? If motivation, willpower, education, changing attitudes, psychological stages of change, personal choices, and persuasion techniques aren't sufficient approaches on their own for initiating sustained change, what do we have left? The answer lies with social scientists, the experts on creating change.

Dr. Fogg and his Stanford team break the process of change into three steps.

1. Define what you want and the behaviors required to get there.

2. Make it easy, because simplicity changes behavior.

3. Trigger the behavior, because no behavior happens without a call to action.

When all three steps happen at the same time, the desired behaviors materialize.

Let's take a look at each of these three steps and how we can use them to create reliable programs of recovery that lead to lasting sobriety. Both Structured Family Recovery and Twelve Step programs complement this three-step model of change. Combined, they present a serious challenge to relapse behaviors.

1. Define what you want and the behaviors required to get there.

Alcoholics, addicts, and families don't need to guess at what behaviors keep people sober. The program has it well figured out. Over the last three-quarters of a century, alcoholics and addicts in AA and other Twelve Step groups have demonstrated precisely how to stay sober—and how not to stay sober—by taking a few simple actions.

- Go to meetings
- Choose a home group
- Get a sponsor
- Work the Steps
- Read the literature (especially the basic texts, *Alcoholics Anonymous,* known as the Big Book, or *Narcotics Anonymous*)
- Volunteer for a service position (make the coffee, greet people, put out the snacks, or help clean up)

Attending meetings is the glue that holds it all together. Taking these simple steps "One day at a time" changes the lives of alcoholics, addicts, and their families in immeasurable ways.

The spiritual principles that underlie these actions, recommended by Twelve Step programs, are equally simple. They are represented in the acronym HOW, which stands for honesty, open-mindedness, and willingness. This is what members refer to as the "HOW of the program." This may seem like a tall order for an addict, but these spiritual principles can be broken into tiny tasks. An addict can start by being honest with his sponsor. He can practice open-mindedness as he learns about the principles of the program. He can become willing to do the small things every day that lead to big changes over time. The Big Book provides the following clarification.

> Many of us exclaimed, "What an order! I can't go through with it." Do not be discouraged. No one among us has been able to maintain anything like perfect adherence to these principles. We are not saints. The point is, that we are willing to grow along spiritual lines. The principles we have set down are guides to progress. We claim spiritual progress rather than spiritual perfection.[41]

2. Make it easy, because simplicity changes behaviors.

Social scientists at Stanford and members of Alcoholics Anonymous understand that keeping it simple is a function of lasting change. It doesn't take much motivation to do something simple. Simplicity removes blocks and difficulties that get in the way of a behavior, and requires less motivation. But this doesn't mean the task of recovery is easy, which implies something quite different. In practice, it's said that recovery is simple but not easy. Easy suggests it requires minimal effort to get results. AA corrects this notion with a few words: "Half measures availed us nothing." We're up against a disease that regularly drives people to risk everything, even their lives, for the next high. But recovery doesn't ask alcoholics to tackle the whole problem all at once, instead they're asked to take small, manageable steps forward.

AA co-founder, Dr. Bob, on his deathbed, famously told Bill Wilson, "Remember Bill, let's not louse this thing up. Let's keep it simple." "Keep it simple" is a favorite slogan among people in recovery, both addicts and their families. We are only expected to do what we can do *today*, which is captured by another popular slogan, "One day at a time." Alcoholics and other addicts quickly learn that they stay sober twenty-four hours at a time. In Al-Anon's meditation book *Courage to Change,* it says,

> Al-Anon reminds me to "Keep it simple." Instead of approaching the task as a whole, I can simplify it by taking it only one step at a time. . . . That takes the pressure off having to know all the answers and solve every problem that may arise before I've even begun. . . . By focusing on one thing at a time the impossible can become likely, if I keep it simple.[42]

Dr. Bob, speaking at AA's first international convention in Cleveland, Ohio, during the last days of his life, said:

> There are two or three things that flashed into my mind on which it would be fitting to lay a little emphasis. One is the simplicity of our program. Let's not louse it up with Freudian complexes and things that are interesting to the scientific mind, but that have very little to do with our actual AA work. Our Twelve Steps, when simmered down to the last, resolve themselves into the words "love" and "service." We understand what love is, and we understand what service is. So let's bear those two things in mind.[43]

3. Trigger the behavior, because no behavior happens without a call to action.

Certainly we've long understood triggers that lead to relapse, but "triggers for recovery" isn't a common concept in AA or Al-Anon. If we want to make a behavior a lasting part of our lives, the Stanford social scientists say we must pair it with a trigger: another behavior we already perform every day.

Let's look at an example that's easy to understand. About a year ago, I set out to do twelve push-ups a day. I was only meeting my goal every two or three days, and soon, I quit entirely. In the back of my mind, I had a lingering regret over my lack of fortitude. I decided to try again, following Dr. Fogg's model of behavior change. First I created a tiny task. I would only do two push-ups at a time. Then I paired my push-ups with something I already did several times a day—wash my hands. Since I wash my hands about ten times a day, I was immediately doing twenty push-ups without needing to motivate myself. I've successfully maintained this new behavior day after day, week after week, month after month without losing my resolve, because I didn't need any resolve.

I think it's possible that many alcoholics and addicts have relapsed precisely because they didn't have access to this simple strategy of matching recovery behaviors with triggers in daily life. Addicts who've completed treatment know what to do for their recovery but, inexplicably, don't always do it. Who among us isn't guilty of the same? The heart patient who doesn't take the daily walk, the diabetic who forgets to check blood sugar, the student who doesn't keep up on daily reading assignments. These omissions all come with varying degrees of consequences, some quite serious.

There are a number of behaviors that are associated with lasting sobriety, but let's look at meeting attendance and triggers. To discover the right trigger, an alcoholic can ask herself, "At what times did I drink or drug?" If it was after work, leaving work is the trigger to drive directly to a meeting. If drinking started after dinner, then finishing dinner triggers going to an evening meeting. A morning drinker gets out of bed and heads directly to an early-bird meeting. For a midday drinker, it's a lunchtime meeting. If getting to a meeting still proves difficult, an addict can start with an even smaller task. He can set up a telephone appointment with another member of AA or a member of the family recovery team at the times he typically would drink or use.

Alcoholics no longer have to think about what meeting and what time. "I always started drinking by lunch, so I go to the Lunch Bunch meeting," says a stay-at-home mom, who brings a bag lunch, and looks forward to the camaraderie in her otherwise uneventful day. "I don't have to wonder when I'll fit a meeting into my schedule. At the same time I normally reached for the wine bottle, I'm on my way to my group."

But here is where we need to revisit motivation. Remember, the Stanford team's first step to behavior change requires defining what one wants and the behaviors required to get there. Alcoholics and addicts typically do not want to change their behavior, at least not for long. Social scientists' clarity about motivations informs us of its usefulness: motivation is necessary for initiating change. Not everyone has the same drive to change, and some have none. This is when families and professionals can play a crucial role, creating just enough willingness to light a spark. Motivation is a powerful stimulus that points alcoholics and addicts in the right direction and gives them a little push.

Motivation generally comes in the form of a family intervention where family members express their needs and concerns, or when upheaval and suffering are so sufficient that treatment and recovery look like a good option. However, as soon as pain recedes so will motivation. That's why families play such a major role in an addict's desire to change. They can either create motivation by expressing their needs and concerns, thereby modeling honesty and willingness, or extinguish motivation by trying to fix the addict's problems.

We know that people who fully adhere to the principles of Twelve Step programs stay sober in dramatically higher numbers than those who don't. The problem comes when alcoholics and addicts fall away from their recovery programs or, freshly out of treatment, refuse to work a recovery program, convinced they can make it on their own. And they may prove themselves right for a period of time. But relapse in the days, weeks, or months ahead is almost always the end result in these cases. Once the disease is fully active, there is no reasoning with an addict. His brain is fully hijacked once again.

Treatment centers do considerable work to create motivation. They do it primarily by dismantling the denial system—which actively sends messages telling the addict that change isn't necessary. The treatment professionals are continually stoking motivation. They strive to keep patients from leaving treatment early and work to persuade them to adhere to their aftercare plans. A family that is engaged in Structured Family Recovery, working as a team, is in the best position to support the efforts of the treatment team.

An addict leaving treatment may initially be eager for AA and all things recovery, and dive right into the meetings, but if he doesn't make connections with other recovering people, including finding a sponsor, he can feel like a fish out of water. So, not knowing anyone, he sits in the back quietly and leaves meetings as soon as possible, too uncomfortable to speak to people. He was close to his peers in treatment, but AA doesn't feel the same. Everything is new and unfamiliar. Recovery is proving to be more difficult than he imagined. He's not sure what to do next and feels awkward. So, he drops away from AA, reassuring his family that he has no plans to drink again, but he simply can't find time to get to the meetings and they're not doing much for him anyway.

We often hear that alcoholics and addicts must want to stay sober *for themselves.* The unspoken message is, "If you don't want it for yourself, it won't work." This assumes that having a reason to change is the motivating factor for a person's success. But, since social scientists say research repeatedly shows that we don't do well at identifying the single factor that truly motivates us to change, this is unlikely.[44] And since these scientists have proven repeatedly that social norms are the most powerful drivers of behavior, being motivated by the people you love is expected and even desirable. Motivation simply starts the process. New behaviors fostered by new social norms are responsible for changed attitudes, so why worry about what fuels a call to action? Our only concern should be that we and our addict keep working our recovery programs.

Anne went to treatment after a family intervention. She initially refused to accept help, so her family established bottom lines as a method to motivate her to say yes. It was her husband's bottom line that persuaded Anne to change her mind.

> You know I love you and want our marriage to work. But first I have to say, I haven't been a trustworthy husband or father. I've done nothing to help you these last years, letting this disease overtake you and our home life, ultimately affecting our children. I was blaming you for something you could never have done on your own: just quit. But now I know better, and I apologize with all my heart. Today, we must join forces to eradicate addiction from our home and our lives. If you can't join our recovery team, it

is important that you leave our home until you can choose treatment and recovery. You and I must protect the children from this insidious disease. Only with recovery can we rebuild our lives together.

The entire time Anne was in treatment her motivation for staying sober was to save her home. Counselors and peers said she needed to stay sober for herself or she would relapse. When she joined AA, she heard the same. But she couldn't quite muster the impetus to be motivated just for herself. It was keeping her children and her husband that mattered. Some might say her attitude wasn't optimal, but as we know, changing attitudes doesn't change behaviors. Her early motivations were perfectly workable for driving change. We don't really care what fuels motivation as long as it sparks new behavior. Anne did everything that was asked of her: she went to meetings, got a sponsor, worked the Steps. With a daily program of recovery, Anne was eventually able to say, "I'm doing this for my family, but I'm also doing it for me."

Once an addicted person has completed treatment, a family recovery team keeps the ball rolling by modeling new behaviors that support recovery. Creating a strong social norm within a family inhibits relapse behaviors. Regardless of all the talk of individuality, it is in our nature as human beings to want to conform and belong. We are social animals. When addiction separates and isolates us, we experience pain. When we reunite through recovery, it is easier to be happy, joyous, and free.

The sixth chapter of the Big Book, titled "Into Action," describes the result of working the Twelve Steps. These are the promises that recovering alcoholics and addicts around the world have learned to be true. And so have their families.

We are going to know a new freedom and a new happiness. We will not regret the past nor wish to shut the door on it. We will comprehend the word serenity, and we will know peace. No matter how far down the scale we have gone, we will see how our experience can benefit others. That feeling of uselessness and self-pity will disappear. We will lose interest in selfish things and gain interest in our fellows. Self-seeking will slip away. Our whole attitude and outlook upon life will change. Fear of people and of economic insecurity will leave us. We will intuitively know how to handle situations which used to baffle us.[45]

Fr. Joseph Martin, a Roman Catholic priest, recovering alcoholic, and renown educator, speaking on these very promises, said, "You are learning lessons of life from those who lived it and lost it and regained it. It's a beautiful way. . . . We are the thrice blessed of the world."[46]

* * *

9

A New Look at Enabling Addiction

Enabling is a word that has found its way into our everyday vocabulary, popular media, and armchair psychology. It's a word thrown out blithely to draw attention to dysfunctional behaviors in every corner of life. It's commonly acknowledged that families of alcoholics and addicts are most culpable as enablers, much to the detriment of their addicted loved ones. If you are being called an enabler, it's not likely a compliment. But why then is it so hard for families to stop enabling their drug addict? Is there more to the story than we think?

The commonly accepted definition of enabling is when we take responsibility for another person's harmful conduct and prevent the negative consequences that motivate addicts to accept help. What this definition isn't telling us is why families, once they learn that enabling exacerbates addiction, continue to do it anyway. We tell people to stop, but we don't ask them why they don't. Most don't even know themselves.

Oftentimes, our beliefs become well-worn paths that are too easily traveled again and again without asking if they are still relevant or accurate. Beliefs about enabling are so universally accepted without question that exclaiming, "Mother, you're such an enabler!" requires no further explanation. But this comfortableness with words and beliefs can easily put our critical thinking skills to sleep.

A shallow understanding of enabling serves to pit family member against family member. A sister is furious with her parents for enabling her brother. Husband and wife are on the brink of divorce over disagreements about enabling their son. Family members argue, stop talking, blame, and fume over the notion of enabling. Everyone can get bogged down in the problem with no visible way out. The resulting chaos makes it easier for addiction to thrive, because families have little chance of making meaningful change until they unite. But uniting is impossible when we define each other as the problem.

Taking a closer look at what is happening within a family, we see that saving the alcoholic from negative consequences is not the end of the story but rather a means to an end. When we enable an addict, we're really doing so to save *ourselves*. If our loved one dies or gets arrested or fired from the job or any of the other bad things that tend to cascade downward in the addict's life, we suffer in a multitude of ways. When we're told to simply detach, the risk feels too great.

A young mother of small children needs her husband's paycheck to keep a roof over their heads and food on the table. An aging couple can't bear to watch their son die before they do. Parents' hearts are shattered by the thought of the sweet little girl they raised turning to prostitution to feed a drug habit. A dad doesn't know how to cope without a mom tending to the children. People closest to alcoholics and addicts intrinsically understand they hit bottom along with the alcoholic, so it is in their interest to make every effort to keep that from happening. We conventionally called it enabling, but calling it survival might be closer to the truth.

Saving the addict is about saving our families. Addiction crashes into lives, altering families in a manner that threatens all we hold dear. When we rescue the addict, it feels as if we're saving the family, but we aren't. We're protecting the addiction. The result is the progression of the disease, mounting problems, and ongoing damage to the entire family system. Yet, we believe, in our heart of hearts, that we are doing the right thing. In the words of the American writer Robert Brault, "An old belief is like an old shoe. We so value its comfort that we fail to notice the hole in it."[47]

We all hold dear our own version of our family's story, and no two stories are exactly alike. Each member of a family has a perspective and a history unique to that person. Stories have parallel plot lines, defining who we were before addiction took hold, who we are now, and who we could be if things were different. The actions we take to maintain and defend our families against addiction are usually forms of enabling. How we enable is usually determined by our version of the family story.

A father and son, both attorneys, shared the same suite of offices in a small Southern town. Since the first day the son expressed an interest in law, the father had dreamed of passing his thriving law practice down to him. Working with his son for the first five or six years after he graduated from law school was a joy. Then this bright, engaging young man began to change. His moods were erratic. He missed important appointments and court dates. He showed up to work late, always with a reasonable excuse. Dad began working overtime checking up on his son's clients and cases. He instructed his assistant to monitor his son's calendar closely, making sure he showed up for appointments. When a fellow attorney asked him if his son was having problems, he vehemently denied it. When his daughter told him it was drugs, he blew up. "Nonsense, he's just going through a rough patch. He'll pull himself through." Dad was determined to preserve the dream he held so dear.

Enabling is a promise for something better or avoidance of something worse. No one wants to believe that their actions are going to contribute to more unmanageability. Each enabler assigns him- or herself a role in the family story. The closer a person's fate is tied to the alcoholic, the more furious the enabling. A cousin who isn't close to an alcoholic or involved in his daily life, for instance, is probably not engaged in major enabling behaviors because the alcoholism isn't central to his or her survival. But it's different for a wife, a parent, or a child who lives with the alcoholic and experiences the ravages of his drinking directly.

The wife of a senior executive of a large company puts up with his glass after glass of scotch every evening. She tries to stay out of his way until he stumbles off to bed to avoid triggering his wrath. She's lonely with all the children grown, but leaving him feels worse than staying. He is central to her family story. Her home, car, clothing, travel, and social status are tied to him. She likes having the children and grandchildren in the big house for holidays and at the lakeside cottage for summer weekends. Divorce means giving it all up at this late stage in her life. She fears if she rocks the boat, he'll find a younger woman and she'll be turned out to live alone in an apartment. Being a sixty-something divorcée is not in her story.

People want solutions for addiction that preserve family rather than break it apart. If solutions force them into positions they're madly trying to avoid, they're not likely to move forward. If a wife who doesn't want a divorce is told she needs to leave her husband if he keeps drinking, it's likely she will dismiss professional help or sabotage the process. Divorcing her husband is asking her to give up the story she spent forty years creating. She doesn't really care that she is enabling if it results in preserving her home life.

However, if a solution offers her a way to strengthen her family and help her husband, she'll probably listen. Creating a recovery team with her grown children, their spouses, and other close family members can change the dynamic. It feels good to work together as a team. Group decisions can be made about intervention, treatment, practicing Structured Family Recovery, and the best ways to support one another. These actions preserve what is best about us and rebuild what addiction has torn asunder.

Even when family members say they want to end their relationship with the addict, there is usually a wide gulf between the saying and the doing. Family members often announce decisions that feel good to say but not to put into action. If they back away from these decisions, it appears they are returning to old enabling ways, frustrating other family members and professionals. But it's more likely that it wasn't the end result they truly wanted. Most people want to come together, not fall apart. And we know, in our heart of hearts, that when we're family, we're never really free of one another.

Certainly, there are cases when a relationship with an addicted person needs to end. Sometimes so much bad has happened it's impossible to look toward the future with that person. Even so, the web of relationships for the addict can include other family members and mutual friendships. The story doesn't generally allow for a clean severing of ties. A mother must send her child off for shared custody. A woman's brother is still invited to holiday and birthday celebrations by their parents. An ex-husband tries to juggle friendships he shares with his former wife.

Separation doesn't guarantee an end to unmanageability. A physical change rarely leads to emotional emancipation. Simply getting away from a person doesn't automatically change everything for the better. Anger and resentment can persist and grow with problems that were never anticipated. It isn't that we don't have a relationship anymore; we now have a different relationship. We're still tied together through emotions, memories, regrets, family, friends, children, and geography. We struggle to create a new story that makes sense of how this plays out in our lives and the lives of others, and we're not necessarily happier right away when we leave the family story behind.

Our brains want to believe in the best even while we are fighting against the worst. But when we need to enable, it signals we're in trouble. It takes a great deal of faith to let go of enabling, because we fear what might happen. For this reason, we need a good solution to grab onto and then it isn't as difficult. And, when we do this as a family team, together letting go of the anger that paralyzes us, we find a power we didn't know we had.

The Power of Enabling Recovery

Enabling is a family's attempt to be part of the solution, but left to their own devices, families unwittingly contribute to prolonging the addiction. When families are provided with good direction and learn to work together for both the addict's and their own health, they are transfigured into a remarkable source of energy and strength for enabling recovery.

It doesn't matter if family relationships are rocky. Addiction always damages relationships to one degree or another. The process of working together rebuilds families. Structured Family Recovery creates a framework that helps families succeed at recovery and avoid the pitfalls that lead to relapse. We make it together, not by fixing each other, but by mending ourselves. We enable recovery.

One dictionary definition of enabling is "rendering capable or able for some task." Simply put, it means we can support each other in developing the qualities or skills necessary for the work ahead. This functional definition empowers us to do something about the problem. We can begin enabling recovery at any point on the road to sobriety. Family participation is a game changer before, during, and after treatment. It's never too late to begin. When we connect in a meaningful way, we strengthen our family.

Alcoholics and addicts don't respond well to empty words, but actions attract their attention. When the entire family is on the same page—not telling the addict what to do but doing it themselves—it is clear that something has changed. When families model recovery, not one or two people but everyone, it has a tremendous force no words can match. It is so radical a shift that the addict can be momentarily stunned. As a recovering alcoholic said to me, "I thought, could this really be my family? I was so moved by what they were doing that, of course, I pursued my own recovery."

Working together is the key to enabling recovery, but we don't have to do it perfectly. Each member of a family must have a degree of willingness to put aside grievances for the greater good. It's through our recovery behaviors that we begin to let go of anger, resentments, and other unhelpful emotions in a more dependable way. We cannot enable recovery when we are full of venom. In a television interview, author Toni Morrison said of anger, "It's helpless . . . it's absence of control—and I need all of my skills, all of my control, all of my power . . . and anger doesn't provide me any of that. I have no use for it whatsoever."[48] We can get stuck in our anger, just as the alcoholic is stuck in his addiction, and then no one is going anywhere.

Enabling recovery returns us to our integrity, because we can't enable recovery if we aren't participating in the solution, just as we can't enable addiction without participating in the problem. Rather than staying stuck in the quagmire, we move toward a sense of purpose, productive behavior, and clear goals. We'll never get worthwhile results with anything less.

The Eight Essential Elements used for physicians in recovery, described in chapter two, create a proven path to follow for enabling recovery. Structured Family Recovery modifies each element to suit the needs of a family recovery team.

1. *Positive Rewards and Negative Consequences.* A clear understanding of rewards for recovery behaviors and consequences for relapse behaviors is key to recovery. For the newly recovering addict, positive rewards come in the form of family cohesiveness and restoration of privileges. Reconnecting with family and engaging in sober fun is one of the greatest gifts of recovery. Negative consequences are identified in advance and recorded, so the addict understands that relapse comes with repercussions. This is not done in the spirit of punishment. It's a promise a family makes to an addict, vowing not to support addiction. For instance, paying for college tuition is linked to improved performance at school made possible by ongoing recovery. Living at home and creating a safe, stable environment for children requires sobriety. With relapse, these privileges are no longer appropriate and are withdrawn. Families also receive rewards and consequences. In Structured Family Recovery, family members are aware that their actions impact the entire family system and can help facilitate relapse. If a family member returns to old behaviors that support addiction, the recovery team calls a meeting to discuss how that member can return to recovery.

2. *Frequent Random Drug Testing and Monitoring.* A monitoring program for addicts in recovery is set up. Random drug testing creates accountability. Families relax knowing a relapse will be detected early. The relapse-related consequences are written in a document and signed by the alcoholic and the family team.

3. *Twelve Step Programs and the Abstinence Standard.* When an entire team engages in family Twelve Step recovery, they create an active expectation that the addict will engage in his own Twelve Step recovery and that they will do the same. Understanding that Twelve Step involvement is central to long-term recovery, this is not left to chance. Family teams understand that alcoholics and addicts must abstain from all mood-altering substances. Aftercare recommendations are shared with the entire family team, and the addict agrees to follow directions. When addicts

are transparent about what they are doing for recovery, they feel accountable to the team.

4. *Viable Role Models and Recovery Mentors.* Doctors have built-in role models: other recovering doctors. This works well, because doctors relate to other doctors. Following the lead of the Physician Health Program, the newly recovering addict, in the early days of recovery, makes a recovering friend he can easily identify with and follows his example in working a recovery program. Once engaged in a Twelve Step program, the addict will begin to identify with a wider circle of people, coming to understand that they are similar in more ways than they are different. Being in an environment where recovery behaviors are the norm and having a mentor or recovery coach until he finds a sponsor, the addict has a guide who supports him in the early days of finding his way into recovery. As family members also look for sponsors in Al-Anon, they will readily relate to the struggles and concerns that come with being new in recovery.

5. *Modified Lifestyles.* There are two questions every newly recovering person needs to ask. How am I going to fill the time I used to spend using alcohol or other drugs in a way conducive to recovery? What do I need to do differently to stay sober? In AA, newcomers are cautioned to avoid "wet faces and wet places." Therefore, spending time at bars or with old drinking or drugging buddies is a relapse warning sign. Driving by the spot where the addict frequently bought his drugs or liquor is another relapse sign. Making lifestyle changes requires forethought and planning. A twenty-four-year-old college student living in a sober house changed the message on his cell phone to help avoid contact with his old drug-using friends. "Hi, you've reached Mike. I'm making some changes in my life. If you don't hear back from me, you're one of them." Newly recovering people need to pinpoint what needs to be extracted and what needs to be added to their lives. Making good lifestyle choices reduces relapse triggers and increases triggers for recovery.

6. *Active and Sustained Monitoring.* The success of doctors is largely attributed to five years of monitoring. When an entire family is in recovery, family dynamics change in a way that naturally supports long-term recovery. It becomes exceedingly difficult to relapse when a family system supports the principles of recovery through its actions. Structured Family Recovery (SFR) meetings are a form of monitoring and can continue indefinitely. Family meetings are known to benefit all families, not just alcoholic families. So taking an hour to invest in the most important people in our lives is a small act that provides big payoffs. Doctors in the Physician Health Program are also randomly drug tested for five years, with the number of tests decreasing over time as long as sobriety is sustained. Our addicted loved ones can easily incorporate a similar program into their SFR plan. There are monitoring plans that families can access that include drug testing, tracking AA attendance, and more.

7. *Active Management of Relapse.* In Structured Family Recovery, families and addicts work together to identify relapse signs and symptoms, sharing them with the team. Everyone discusses ways they can help each other if they notice signs and symptoms of relapse. Family members write commitment letters, and addicts write relapse agreements. Everyone agrees to a plan of action. By being prepared, relapse is never ignored. This component also serves as a relapse prevention tool.

8. *Continuing Care Approach.* The continuing care plan is designed to address the chronic nature of addiction. The components include Structured Family Recovery, a Twelve Step recovery program, and an aftercare plan created by a treatment team. This ongoing support, similar to the programs designed for doctors, promotes a high rate of success for all alcoholics and addicts.

Sometimes families engage in Structured Family Recovery on their own, before their addicted loved one gets into recovery. Most addicts don't accept help until something happens that has enough power to break through the barriers of denial. It's often the cumulative effect of years of mounting consequences or a single earth-shaking event, such as an arrest, threat of divorce and loss of children, or a serious medical problem. But getting into recovery through catastrophe is risky. Countless addicts lose their families, homes, careers, and even their lives. Our prisons and jails are overfilled with the addicted. Others slowly waste away, all their promise in life traded for a drink, a pill, a powder. Being in an environment where recovery behaviors are the norm, and where having a mentor, sponsor, or recovery coach available to guide and support the addict in working a rigorous Twelve Step program, can provide the necessary power to break through the denial and avoid catastrophe.

Hitting bottom can lead to many things besides treatment and recovery, things families are urgently trying to avoid. For this reason, enabling recovery often begins with a well-planned, structured family intervention. When properly done, approximately 85 percent of alcoholics and addicts agree to accept help. Of the remaining 15 percent, most eventually change their minds and get some type of treatment or go directly into a Twelve Step program.

Following are two different scenarios of families reacting to a crisis caused by a loved one's addiction that illustrate the difference between enabling the disease and enabling recovery.

1. A thirty-two-year-old alcoholic loses his job and begins burning through his savings. He spends most days on the couch drinking and watching television, telling his family he's out looking for work. Running out of money, he can no longer pay his mortgage and is soon receiving notices. He calls his mother for help. Filled with panic, she pulls out her checkbook. The alcoholic's sense of emergency spreads throughout the family, whose immediate reaction is to fix the problem. Once the mortgage is paid, the mother is relieved and the alcoholic makes some half-hearted attempts to find work. But mostly he drinks, setting up the groundwork for the next crisis and the need for more enabling.

In this example, the mother reacts to her son's crisis by paying his mortgage bills, unwittingly supporting his addiction. Alleviating his panic over losing his house, she misses a perfect opportunity to launch him into recovery. Writing a check was an easier, quicker solution. It didn't require thinking, communicating, or planning. But for this mother and son, things got progressively worse. Negative consequences continued to pile up, costing more money and causing ongoing stress.

2. A mother receives a call from her alcoholic daughter asking for help. The daughter's house is going into foreclosure. Mom listens carefully and then tells her daughter she will call back after talking with her father. Mom and Dad decide to retain the services of a clinical interventionist. They bring together a family team and execute a well-planned intervention. Their daughter is admitted into a treatment facility. Crisis created a sense of emergency in this family, too, but they chose to enable recovery.

Here the mother doesn't react to the crisis. She buys herself some time by telling her daughter she needs to talk with her father. Together, the parents decide to seek professional advice and, working with other family members and friends, leverage the crisis by implementing a family intervention. For this family, the up-front work required more effort and some stressful moments. But in a relatively short period of time, their life became easier. With an entire family joining together, they began enabling successful recovery.

During the planning and implementing of a family intervention, families have a well-defined and powerful role to play in initiating treatment. It's after the alcoholic is discharged from treatment that families once again may not know what to do or what to expect. Their beloved addict, who was wildly out of control just a few weeks earlier, is now making major life changes essentially on his own. Is he really going to AA meetings? Is he resisting the urge to drink and drug? Is he hanging out with old friends who do drugs and frequent the bars?

The family isn't sure what's right or what's wrong. The alcoholic tells them what his counselor recommended, but they don't know if it's true. Is it okay to drink nonalcoholic beer? Is going out bar hopping okay as long as he sticks to drinking cola? Should family get-togethers still revolve around lots of drinking? Is a little pot okay if he doesn't drink? Is it true he only needs one or two AA meetings a week?

With so many concerns, the fear of relapse looms large. There is no system in place that allows for meaningful family communication and mutual support. The family is left on the sidelines with limited information and no role to play. This is why Structured Family Recovery is crucial. Without a systematic plan designed for enabling recovery, too many factors work against recovery. When everyone in the family begins participating in recovery, the family dynamic changes and the addict begins following directions, too.

The biggest problem in recovery from addiction—as is true across the spectrum of health care—is a lack of compliance. The World Health Organization reports that effective interventions that lead to patient compliance are more valuable than the creation of new treatments. Noncompliance is a primary cause of relapse. Structured Family Recovery is designed to create compliance. As a team, we all do what we need to do to make recovery work.

Let's look at two more families and compare how they responded to their newly recovering addict's return home after treatment.

1. Sam returned home after treatment for alcoholism and marijuana addiction. His wife is elated at the changes in him. He's on what is commonly referred to as a *pink cloud*. Treatment was great, he feels like a new man, and he knows he'll never drink or drug again. Sam goes to some Alcoholics Anonymous meetings, but is not really connecting with anyone and begins to think the meetings aren't for him. His wife, unaware of his private struggles, proudly tells her in-laws that he's going to meetings and doing great. She's sure everything will be better now that Sam is sober.

Sam joined a gym to get into shape and worked harder at his job to catch up for lost time. Soon, he's only hitting a recovery meeting now and again. His wife begins suspecting that he's going less often than he claims. She asks him about it, and he snaps back, "It's my program. Quit looking over my shoulder." She and Sam have no system that allows for recovery communication, and she's never seen his aftercare plan developed by his treatment team. One evening, when Sam returns home from work she swears she smells a whiff of marijuana.

2. Paula is admitted into treatment after a family intervention. The clinical interventionist recommended to her husband and extended family that they participate in Structured Family Recovery. In their in-

tervention letters, they wrote, "Addiction is a family disease, so we are all committed to Structured Family Recovery. You are not alone on this journey. We're in this together."

While Paula was in treatment, her family scheduled their first Structured Family Recovery meeting and continued meeting weekly by conference call. Before Paula was discharged from treatment, her family invited her to join their team. Paula's counselor participated in a call to discuss the treatment team's aftercare recommendations. Family members had an opportunity to ask the counselor questions so they clearly understood the plan. Each team member was working his or her own recovery program—the family was in Al-Anon and Paula in Alcoholics Anonymous. Random drug testing eliminated the need for guesswork. Everyone talked openly about their progress, and if someone was struggling, they had the support of the entire family. Everyone knew the language of recovery.

Let's examine the different experiences of each family with early recovery.

Sam's wife felt isolated and alone. She couldn't bring herself to tell her in-laws that Sam was smoking pot again. Without a family recovery team or her own Twelve Step program, she didn't know where to turn or who to talk to. Sam's anger frightened her, so she kept her mouth shut. All she could do was hope for the best, but she was filled with dread. All the no-talk rules were back in place, offering no safe place for communication, openness, or problem solving.

Paula, on the other hand, moved from treatment into a family recovery team. Everyone was living a transparent life, talking about their recovery programs and what they were learning. It was a smooth transition from treatment, and Paula felt that she fit right in with the rest of her family. She knew, working together, they were rebuilding trust. She and her husband planned recovery date nights. He attended Al-Anon, and across the hall, she attended her AA meeting. Afterward, they would have a nice dinner and take time to enjoy each other's company.

The quality of our future is determined by the actions we take today. It is not where we begin that counts, but where we end up. Living in recovery, we can begin to forgive. As Leo Buscaglia so beautifully wrote, "Too often we underestimate the power of a touch, a smile, a kind word, a listening ear, an honest compliment, or the smallest act of caring, all of which have the potential to turn a life around."[49]

. . .

10

Families Pay a High Price

Chronic stress changes our brains. It also causes disease. There is a great deal of the truth in the statement, "I'm worried sick."

Short-lived stress doesn't hurt us. But stress reaches a point when it can become toxic. Since emotions impact every cell in the body, when stress persists over time we are set on a course for declining health and even premature aging. Since this doesn't happen instantly (in the way a heart attack or a broken bone does), it doesn't always set off our alert systems. We don't worry about how much we worry; instead, we learn to live with it.

Families of alcoholics suffer from *psychosomatic illnesses,* caused by emotions (psyche) changing the body (soma). Often described as psychological factors affecting medical conditions, these diseases aren't imaginary. They are very real, caused by direct changes within organ systems due to the ongoing stress that can be caused by another person's addiction and its consequences. Stress can ultimately lead to conditions like hypertension, stroke, and irregular heartbeat. It also decreases our ability to defend ourselves from bacteria, viruses, and, at the extreme, cancerous cells by damaging our immune system.

According to Robert M. Sapolsky, PhD, professor of neuroscience at Stanford University in his book *Why Zebras Don't Get Ulcers,* "Stress can wreak havoc with your metabolism, raise your blood pressure, burst your white blood cells, make you flatulent, ruin your sex life, and if that's not enough, possibly damage your brain."[50] He goes on to say that if we experience each day as an emergency, we will pay the price.

When we feel we are in danger, which is what stress is telling us, our body undergoes rapid change. It releases two hormones, cortisol and adrenaline. Adrenaline creates an instant state of readiness by increasing our pulse rate, our blood pressure, and creating a sudden burst of energy. It's deceiving because it can also temporarily increase our strength, make us more agile, and allow us to take in information more quickly. Cortisol is released after adrenaline to calm us down. We begin breathing normally, our heartbeat slows, and muscles relax. Our defense reaction is designed to keep us alive by protecting us from dangers that are brief, such as escaping from a fire or evading a suspicious person or, in earlier times, running from a bear. But, in modern life, many less obvious stressors can persist for months or years.

When we are under constant stress, we produce too much adrenaline and cortisol. When they circulate in our bodies long enough, they hurt us. Overdoses of adrenaline scar blood vessels, which can cause heart attacks and strokes. Cortisol damages cells in an area of the brain called the *hippocampus,* affecting our capacity to learn and remember. When we experience prolonged episodes of stress, our bodies enter a stage of exhaustion, preventing us from functioning well in everyday life. In adulthood and as we age, the areas of our brains that decline most rapidly are vulnerable to the destructive forces of stress hormones.

According to John J. Medina, MD, developmental molecular biologist and brain development expert, the worst kind of stress we can experience is feeling we have no control over a problem—a sense of helplessness. The more we feel out of control, the greater the stress. This is how most families of alcoholics and addicts experience stress.

Dr. Medina writes in his bestselling book *Brain Rules*:

> Stress hormones can do some truly nasty things to your brain. . . . Stress hormones seem to have a particular liking for cells in the hippocampus, and that's a problem, because the hippocampus is deeply involved in many aspects of learning. . . . Stress hormones can disconnect neural net-

works, the webbing of brain cells that act like a safety de-
posit vault for storing your most precious memories. They
can stop the hippocampus from giving birth to brand-new
baby neurons. . . . Clearly, stress hurts learning. Most important, however, stress hurts people.[51]

Every structure in our brains is influenced by what is happening
in our surroundings. If our family environment isn't healthy, it's likely
our brain isn't either. According to Elizabeth Gould, PhD, of Princeton
University, chronic stress causes the brain to starve. Her groundbreaking
research in neurobiology shows that, when under stress, brains stop creating new cells. Our existing cells retreat inward, and the brain becomes
disfigured. Stress is changing our neural anatomy. Dr. Gould explains,
"When a brain is worried, it's just thinking about survival. It isn't interested in investing in new cells for the future."[52]

What stress does to the brains of family members is similar to what
drugs do to the brains of alcoholics and addicts. The thinking and the
emotional brain systems are impacted. Researchers at Yale have found
that the prefrontal cortex—the thinking brain—is most affected by
stress.[53] As nerve tissue in this area of the brain begins to diminish, we
lose gray matter, which affects our emotions, self-control, and ability to
adapt to life's challenges.

The mood center of the brain also shrinks, resulting in increases
in depression and anxiety. These reductions in brain function make it
more difficult for families to deal with stressful events. This is particularly detrimental, since addiction is a progressive disease; over time, we
can expect more problems. With less capacity to handle stress, problems appear unsolvable. Families resort to temporary solutions, which
do not eliminate the impact of addiction or the resulting stress. Similar
to the alcoholic's and addict's relationship to alcohol and other drugs,
families now experience enabling as a need not a choice—as a matter
of survival.

Stress can also lead to insomnia. Alcoholics don't sleep well due to
the toxic effect of alcohol, which disrupts sleep patterns. Family members
also experience a lack of sleep caused by worry, anxiety, and depression.

Stress can make it difficult for many to fall asleep and stay asleep, and it affects the quality of sleep. According to the National Sleep Foundation, stress causes hyper-arousal, which upsets the balance between sleep and wakefulness.[54] Poor sleep creates more stress.

Chronic insomnia disrupts the brain's ability to pay attention, analyze information, and concentrate. Scientists are now learning that it also leads to a reduction in the brain's ability to clear out a buildup of waste, specifically a type of protein associated with Alzheimer's and other forms of dementia. A number of research studies have shown that one of the crucial jobs of sleep is cleaning out the debris that builds up every day. Chronic insomnia slows the brain's ability to do its maintenance work. Scientists are hypothesizing that this may age the brain, damaging it in ways that could lead to a greater vulnerability to brain diseases such as dementia and Parkinson's.[55] These diseases may occur far sooner than they otherwise would. Chronic loss of sleep, as it turns out, isn't easy to make up; brains don't fully recover. More research is needed, but studies thus far offer evidence that sleep is more important than we thought. Sleep aided by pills isn't the same as natural sleep. Reducing stress and using nonmedication sleep techniques boost brain health.

Learned helplessness, caused by unmanageable stress, is another phenomenon that affects people in addicted families. It was discovered in 1965 by two scientists, Martin Seligman and Steven Maier, who exposed animals to prolonged and unpredictable stressors over which they had no control. When the animals were then given a way to avoid the stressors, they didn't do it. For example, when rats were given a series of shocks they could not avoid, they quickly developed learned helplessness. When they were put into cages with safety zones and lights warning of upcoming shocks, the rats continued taking the shocks rather than escaping. The control rats, who hadn't been previously shocked, easily avoided the shocks. When the light flashed, they quickly fled to the safety zone.

Rats who develop learned helplessness demonstrated motivational problems. They had difficulty handling ordinary tasks and rarely engaged in activities that were life-improving. They no longer paid much attention to the world around them. When they would attempt to cope, they showed confusion, not knowing if their efforts were working. They didn't interact with the world in the same way that normal rats did.[56]

Another scientist, Donald Hiroto, has conducted experiments showing how little it takes to create learned helplessness in humans. First, he exposed a group of subjects to piercing noises they couldn't escape. The second group of subjects had access to a mechanism that turned off the noise. Later, when both groups were presented with a simple task that would end the noise, the first group did considerably worse, demonstrating learned helplessness. They also showed diminished abilities in performing other tasks such as solving word puzzles and functioning in social coping situations. The deficits led to feelings of hopelessness, lowered self-confidence, poor problem solving, and a limited attention span.[57]

Learned helplessness is common in alcoholic families. A close relationship with an alcoholic or addict causes prolonged and unpredictable stress, and a sense of having no control. Families never know what the alcoholic or addict might do next, and nothing they do stops it from happening. This creates laboratory-perfect conditions for learned helplessness.

It's easy to recognize family members who are impaired by learned helplessness. When offered help, they usually refuse to take it. Much like the animals being shocked, they don't see a way out. They famously use the phrase "yes, but . . ." to dismiss solutions. They can't believe anything could possibly work. Efforts to help an addicted loved one are hampered by a family member who suffers from learned helplessness.

Michael, a forty-five-year-old husband and father, is addicted to alcohol and sedatives. His older sister, Betsy, decides something must be done after he's lost yet another job. Their parents are retired and can't keep bailing him out financially. She approaches Kathleen, her brother's wife, who agrees to help intervene. But as Betsy moves forward, consulting with a clinical interventionist and building a family team, Kathleen begins subtly sabotaging the process. She's too busy with the children to attend a meeting. She isn't sure anymore that intervention is the best idea. She talks to Michael's parents without Betsy knowing, telling them about promising job interviews. "Treatment is going to interfere with Michael getting a job," she says. Betsy finally confronts Kathleen out of frustration, asking, "Don't you even care about your kids?" But Kathleen can't see solutions. Instead she talks in circles about why Michael will never accept treatment. Lacking the ability to evaluate her situation properly, Kathleen isn't able to protect her children or help her husband. In anger, Betsy lashes out, "You are keeping my brother sick! You are crazier than he is!"

Not understanding learned helplessness, the entire family defines Kathleen as "a little nutty." Intervention plans fall apart, Michael gets another job, and the addiction goes unaddressed. Betsy never forgives Kathleen, and family relationships sour. The entire debacle has made it much easier for Michael's addiction to progress unchallenged.

This same situation is approached very differently when the family quickly understands that Kathleen is experiencing learned helplessness. Rather than thinking she is "sick," they realize she is responding to the ongoing crisis in an expected manner that is beyond her control. Kathleen can't see how she's been changed by her husband's addiction.

Betsy and her parents temporarily postpone the intervention and call a meeting with other relatives who are close to Michael and Kathleen—a favorite uncle and aunt, a cousin, and a younger brother. They create a recovery team and initiate Structured Family Recovery. By doing so, they demonstrate something very important to Kathleen: *You are not alone. As a family, we are standing together. We are here for you, Michael, and the children, not for a few days or weeks, but for the long haul.* The family creates a growing sense of safety for Kathleen, presenting her with an entire team of trusted people to lean on.

By participating in Structured Family Recovery—before, during, and after treatment—Kathleen wasn't the only one who benefited. Stress throughout the entire family began to dissipate. Michael achieved more than lasting sobriety. He found a closeness with his family he hadn't felt in a very long time.

When it comes to the disease of addiction, the cost is too great to ignore. Some people give addiction a pass, saying, "He's not hurting anyone but himself, so if that's what he wants to do, let him." This simply isn't true. Addiction hurts everyone closest to the alcoholic in very real ways. Addiction is everybody's business, and so is recovery.

We Begin and End with Family

A woman recently said to me, "My sister and I disagree on many things, but I know if life hands me a lemon, she's the one who'll be there holding my hand." After all, the highest goal of any family is to sustain its members. How often do we hear someone say, in the face of loss or tragedy, "As long as I have my family, I can overcome anything."

There is so much talk about dysfunctional families, but I think this catch phrase does us a disservice. What exactly does it mean to be dysfunctional, and who decides? Where do we draw the line between functional and dysfunctional? Does this word unfairly imply something is inherently wrong with the many families responding to crisis?

I find it interesting that families facing the crisis of addiction are commonly called dysfunctional, yet the same word isn't prevalent when describing families responding to Alzheimer's, another brain disease. Both groups often cope with years of crisis and similar correlating emotions and consequences: denial, depression, anxiety, guilt, anger, uncertainty, grief, isolation, embarrassment, secret-keeping, multiple losses over time, difficulty explaining the illness to others, concerns about safety, not knowing where to turn for help, and financial stress.

To call a family dysfunctional is stigmatizing. It is far more accurate and supportive to call a family coping with addiction a *family in crisis*. By doing so, we remove the implication that something is wrong with the people who make up the family and, instead, signal that they are in a state of emergency and in need of help. Most of us, when called dysfunctional, adopt a defensive position. But when other people acknowledge we're suffering from a crisis, there is a sense of being cared about and understood. Others are more willing to reach out to a family in crisis than to a family labeled as dysfunctional. One solicits compassion, the other condescension.

Families living with addiction know only too well how this disease breaks down relationships, and many books are written that recount the devastation. But rarely do we talk about the many noble ways families demonstrate resiliency. Working with families of alcoholics and addicts for more than twenty years, I've stood in awe of families again and again. Determined to help the one they love get into treatment, fortitude and goodness of spirit is the norm, not the exception. They sacrifice so much and work so hard to ignite a spark of willingness in their addict. After receiving solid, reliable direction, they follow instructions willingly, show amazing vulnerability, and drop their resentments and anger in favor of love. They walk through fear and trepidation to do what needs to be done. They put aside differences and hurts in favor of what is important for the well-being of the addict and the family.

So often when I meet with a family preparing to do an intervention, the first thing they do is show me photos of their beloved addicted son, brother, mother, daughter, father, or sister. They want me to see the real person—the person they cherish—so I know there is more to them than addiction. It's the humanity of the person they want to share—the kind heart, sense of humor, generosity. "He's a good son and a good friend," they might say, and then tell me all the wonderful things about him. And these things I want to hear, because then I know what this family is fighting for. It is the magnificence of the loved one, not the addiction, that inspires everything we do. Standing up to addiction requires the fuel of love.

The alcoholic may seem undeserving in a thousand ways and the family may be seething with anger, but under it all lies the smoldering power of love. That's what drives families. Love. Not wimpy sentimentalism but courageous, never-giving-up love. I've worked with other families who struggled to think of nice things to say about their alcoholic or addict, but they, too, were there to intervene on the disease because of love. It's illogical, some might say, but in spite of the many difficulties that they may have had with the addict, they shared a rich and complex history that isn't always easy to capture in words. The depth of a relationship is rarely understood if we don't factor in the power of belonging to one another.

Several years ago I began working with a mother concerned about an adult daughter. The professional who referred her to me warned that she was impossible to work with and exhibited signs of emotional instability, so I was expecting the worst. During our first meeting, however, it became clear to me that she was simply a mother who wasn't going to let anyone tell her she couldn't do anything more to help her daughter. She was dogged and intense, but her resoluteness was understandable, and she made sense. Her only child was a bright, beautiful, young woman terribly addicted to alcohol and other drugs. She had watched over the years as addiction robbed her daughter of all her accomplishments and left her dependent on any man who would have her. Now, she believed, her daughter was at risk of dying. She was going to do whatever it took to turn things around and make sure her daughter had a chance at life, and she didn't care what anyone else thought. So, together we devised a well-thought-out plan, designed not only for her daughter's needs, but possibly more importantly, built to her strengths. It was by invoking a higher calling that we reached her daughter's heart, creating enough spiritual clarity to give her the capability of saying yes to receiving the help she needed.

But when families are not given a central role to play after their loved ones enter treatment and recovery, and don't have a clear direction in the recovery process, they often start falling apart. Teams created for intervention splinter, and the momentum dies. Feeling out of the loop, family members retreat into old survival skills they used for dealing with addiction's crises and are now trying to apply them to addiction's recovery. Using the old ways in this new world of recovery won't work. Just as addicts cannot bring the old ways of an addiction lifestyle into recovery, families cannot keep using their old ways of coping.

Our strengths—the bedrock of who we are—are often buried under the many disturbed emotions that come with coping with addiction. We can't always feel love because anger, recrimination, and hurt seem more urgent and true. But they are simply clouds, family symptoms of the disease of addiction that prevent healing for the addict and his loved ones. It's not unusual for families to hang on to disturbed emotions in the same way alcoholics hang on to drugs. Oftentimes, an alcoholic is in recovery, yet his family refuses to move forward, still tending to their anger.

Have we been trained to always look for the negative in our families? We can just as easily, and with better results, view each other with understanding and compassion. Just as medicine is changing to be more health-oriented rather than disease-oriented, we need to be more strength-oriented when talking and thinking about our families. This requires a clear-eyed inventory of ourselves that will allow us to make a decision to let go of what isn't congruent with our values.

Structured Family Recovery is about strengths—the ones we have and the ones we need. The crisis of addiction, over time, creates unhealthy patterns in families. Engaging in recovery, as a team, changes these patterns in much the same way a solid recovery program changes the alcoholic or addict. We learn to loosen our grip on disturbed emotions as the addict loosens his grip on drugs and the emotional and spiritual damage they've caused.

Structured Family Recovery based on the Twelve Steps promises a spiritual change that can reveal who we really are as family, as the haze of fear and mistrust lifts to reveal the real person behind the addiction. We witness the powerful spiritual shift that comes with recovery, not just in behavior, but in the countenance of addicts *and* their loved ones: the look in their eyes, the sound of their voices, the glow of their skin. Healing truly becomes a family affair.

Don't Forget the Children

Parents, as they gaze at their newborns, wonder, "Will she be a happy child? Will she make friends? Who will she be when she grows up?" They develop streaming videos in their minds of the perfect life for this little bundle of joy. But a healthy, productive life doesn't happen by chance. Who a child becomes is decided by many things: genetics, nutrition, even luck. But, possibly more than anything else in life, it is family and home that shapes and molds a child, providing the springboard into life.

Babies tucked safely in their mother's womb are already interacting with the outside world. The unborn child isn't shielded from the goings on of life. Mothers pass their emotions on to them. If a mother is happy and secure, her baby is bathed in warm emotions. But when there is marital strife, the baby feels a mother's anger or fear. These babies hear how their parents talk to one another, if they are loving or arguing. Some neurologists suggest that babies' brain development, even before birth, is influenced and changed by the emotional states of their parents.

When a father is drug addicted, for instance, the relationship between mother and father is already filled with tension before this new life arrives. The mother is releasing stress hormones that travel through the placenta into her baby's bloodstream, affecting the neurochemistry of the baby's brain. Once born, the baby is living in an unpredictable world, marked by toxic stress. When the mother is actively using, the toxic effects of the drugs are passed on to the fetus, resulting in severe cognitive impairment, stunted growth, and, in some cases, permanent brain damage.

Since developing babies cannot process alcohol through their livers, they have the same blood alcohol content as their mothers. In babies with fetal alcohol syndrome (FAS), the size of the overall brain is smaller and brain systems are underdeveloped. Alcohol affects all developing organs, but the brain is especially vulnerable. Areas of the brain most affected cause problems in executive functions, impulse control, judgment, learning, memory, motor control, and emotions.

Sometimes an alcoholic mother, in an attempt to control her drinking, binges on alcohol sporadically throughout her pregnancy rather than drinking continually. This, too, harms the developing brain of the fetus. Whatever part of the brain is developing during the binge is damaged. This can cause tangles in neurons that mix up connections between brain cells, migration of brain cells into the wrong areas, and the death of brain cells.

Receiving a call from a woman whose pregnant sister was alcoholic, I recommended immediate action in the form of an intervention and treatment. She said, "Our family is quite confident my sister isn't drinking. She promised us that she wouldn't touch a drop." Making it clear that the disease of alcoholism can make it difficult to keep such a promise, I could not persuade her to reconsider and get her sister help. She was steadfast in her conviction that her sister would never hurt a developing baby. She just wanted to know what she should do if her sister started drinking once the child was born. Three months later, I heard back from her. She'd just learned that her sister had been sneaking drinks all along. We had no way of knowing how much damage was done. Even the love for an unborn child cannot change the fact that a mother suffers from addiction.

Baby's Brain Development and Stress

As babies develop, they create a half million neurons a minute and generate links between billions of brain cells. How an individual brain develops depends largely on what it is experiencing in its environment. Babies who are stressed in utero show a lowered threshold for stress after birth. They can often experience higher anxiety for years, sometimes throughout life.

Nature Reviews Neuroscience reports that exposure to prenatal stress has three major effects on adult behavior: learning impairments, enhanced sensitivity to drugs of abuse, and increases in anxiety.[58] Research shows that toxic stress during key points in development isn't always fully realized until later in life.[59] For instance, childhood stress can lead to health problems in adulthood such as heart disease, diabetes, and depression. Because it is often presumed that unborn babies, infants, and toddlers aren't aware of problems in the home, many people believe these children aren't affected. So the children are left unprotected from the ongoing harm caused by addiction.

Growing children navigate the world with brains ill-equipped to handle intense and prolonged stress. When raised in the toxic environment of addicted homes, they are more likely to have underdeveloped "thinking" brains and overdeveloped "feeling" brains. This imbalance leads to a variety of abnormal behaviors: hyperactivity, poor problem solving, antisocial behavior, difficulty regulating emotions, and trouble soothing themselves.

Toxic stress, according to the Center on the Developing Child at Harvard University, occurs when a child experiences strong, frequent, or prolonged adversity such as a caregiver's addiction to alcohol or other drugs, neglect, emotional abuse, violence, or accumulated hardships in the family.[60] The more stress a child experiences, the greater the probability of delays in development.

Research at Children's Hospital and Baylor College of Medicine has found that among neglected children, the cortex—the thinking part of the brain—is 20 percent smaller on average than in a control group.[61] When we understand that most children who live in homes where there is active addiction experience some form of neglect or abuse, this finding is startling.

When children look to an impaired parent to give them guidance on how to negotiate in the world, they are depending on a parent who isn't fully able to attend to his or her own needs, much less the child's. An opiate-addicted mother sleeps away much of the day and leaves her children to their own devices; an alcoholic father has a personality change, and his kids know it's risky to cross his path.

A seventy-year-old attorney confided in me that as a little boy, he'd cry into his pillow at night, afraid his dad wouldn't come home—and afraid that he would; over sixty years later, he's still carrying grief for that little boy.

A report from Partnership for Learning, a nonprofit organization dedicated to improving K–12 education, says, "When young children are stressed by too much noise, abuse, or violence, they use all their brain power for survival instead of for learning." The child's brain is doing exactly what stressed brain cells do: work to stay safe in the present rather than investing in the future. The price paid shows up later with a deficit in logical thought and creative problem solving.

Lost Childhood

The non-addicted parent is often unwilling to acknowledge that the other parent's addiction affects their children. "They never actually see their dad smoke crack," a mother might say. "They really don't know anything is wrong." By not witnessing the drug use, it's assumed they are protected from the negative consequences of having an addicted parent.

People often say their children don't even notice when a parent is inebriated. "It's normal to them," says a dad about his wife's drinking. "It's just how their mom is." One mother felt assured that her children weren't affected by their dad's alcoholism, saying, "My parents both drank every night until they were drunk, and I turned out just fine." When I asked her to describe how it felt when she was a little girl as her parents were getting more and more intoxicated, she couldn't get the words out without crying.

Perhaps the saddest of all are the stories of the children who take on the "hero" role in their alcoholic homes, unknowingly accepting the role of the perfect child who brings respectability to the family by being the best at everything. These children are often excellent students, have lots of friends, and are good at sports, music, or any variety of extracurricular activities. A parent will say, "Our little Janie hasn't been affected by her dad's drinking. She's the perfect child. She does everything right. She's just like a little adult."

The truth is, Janie is giving up her childhood to play the role of adult and isn't likely to get professional help. Instead she's likely to grow up to be a perfectionist, never allowing herself to make mistakes. She'll probably obsess over details often to the point of paralysis. Due to fear and shame, she will sidestep challenges she cannot do expertly. She'll have friends, but will always carry a secret: "If you really knew me, you wouldn't like me." Her life is clouded with dread as she constantly tries to show the world that she is in control. She often dates men who are irresponsible or emotionally unavailable, because she is most comfortable as the caretaker. It's not surprising that hero children often grow up to marry alcoholics or addicts.

Diana, a thirty-nine-year-old pediatric nurse, was raised with a father who was called a *functional alcoholic.* "People call alcoholics functional because they go to work," she told me. "But do they ever take a peek inside the home? Maybe they'd see things aren't so functional after all." She went on to say, "When I was older, my father said to me, 'You were never a child.' I took this as one of the few compliments he ever gave me, but now I know his alcoholism stole my childhood." It also affected Diana's adulthood. She twice married and divorced alcoholics.

Jerry Moe, one of the foremost experts on children in addicted and recovering families and founder of the Betty Ford Children's Program, describes the burden carried by the hero child. "Despite all their accomplishments, as they grow into adulthood, they never feel satisfied. Every achievement leaves the hero child feeling hollow. The sad irony is that they never succeed at the one thing most important to them: stopping the alcoholic from drinking. No one ever told them that they didn't have the power to do that."[62]

Joseph Califano Jr., former United States Secretary of Health, Education, and Welfare and chairman of The National Center on Addiction and Substance Abuse at Columbia University, says:

> Bluntly put, the time parents need to conquer their substance abuse and addiction can pose a serious threat to their children who may suffer permanent damage during this phase of rapid development. Little children cannot wait; they need a safe and stable home and nurturing adults now in order to set the stage for a healthy and productive life.[63]

Recovery and the Child

By age three, a child's brain is twice as active as an adult's. During the teenage years, the brain is going through the last phase of rapid development. If toxic stress interrupts any of these prime periods of brain growth, a child's development is compromised.

While toxic stress is occurring, whichever brain system is developing at that time is affected. The hippocampus, which is important for learning and memory, is most vulnerable to stress before the age of twelve. The prefrontal cortex, which is responsible for cognition, personality, decision making, and social behavior, is most susceptible between ages twelve and eighteen. By introducing recovery into addicted homes at the earliest possible time, we reduce stress and allow children's brains to begin evolving normally.

Since young brains still have a high degree of neuroplasticity, they can begin to reorganize if given the opportunity. There is no better reason for an entire family to pursue recovery together. An alcoholic going through treatment isn't enough. We all need to participate in the recovery process if we hope to heal as a family. We may fool or trick ourselves into believing otherwise, but brains of children won't be deceived. When we join together as a family recovery team, however, we accomplish amazing things, even things we cannot see, that have profound effects on children that last a lifetime.

There are many people who could break the silence and potentially change the trajectory of a child's life. But most people do nothing, not because they are uncaring, but because they see no workable solution. But solutions exist. When families work together as a team, including grandmothers and grandfathers, aunts, uncles, godparents, friends—whoever is close enough to care—there is a power we harness for the good of the child.

When an addicted woman is pregnant, swift action is required. By learning the best way to help, change becomes possible. Intervention has become a household word and, done properly with good guidance, is very successful. If you are concerned about a pregnant mother, use the resource section of this book to locate a clinical interventionist to help you get her into treatment immediately.

Sis Wenger, president emeritus of the National Association for Children of Alcoholics and advocate for children who suffer from adversity due to addiction in the family, says, "In face of clear evidence that children with alcohol- or drug-addicted parents are harmed emotionally and sometimes physically, we are stunned that so many children are allowed to suffer in silence without any meaningful intervention or support from adults they encounter in their everyday life."[64]

Getting the addicted parent into treatment is just a beginning. Too many go to treatment, stay sober for weeks or months, and then relapse, plunging the entire family back into turmoil. Structured Family Recovery is important for keeping recovery on track and building a family recovery team that protects the children. The youngest in our families need trusted loved ones who are capable of helping them, even when their parents cannot.

With consistency, children live in a predictable world. They need to know what to expect in their daily lives. Beyond sobriety, children need harmony and love. They need regular schedules so they know what time to go to bed, what time to wake up, and when they're going to eat. They need to know the rules and the consequences of breaking the rules. They need play and laughter. They need to trust. With consistency, they don't need to worry so much. Their brains can open up to all the good things the world has to offer them.

In Structured Family Recovery, we build great families. We want the kids to grow up saying, "I am the luckiest person ever! I grew up in the greatest family!" Recovery, after all, is about finally finding happiness. Children thrive when home life is happy. It creates wonderful futures and marvelous memories. We grow together rather than apart. As children get older, marry, and have families of their own, they come back to us with love. They want to spend time together. Siblings like each other and are good friends. We change the future of our family by what we do today.

Sister Molly Monahan says it best in her book *Seeds of Grace,* when she speaks of families in recovery.

> Imagine the lives of those babies if their alcoholic parent or parents were still drinking. The erratic behavior, the emotional turmoil, the fights, the terror, the shame they would experience. Instead, even given the genetic factor in the disease of alcoholism, there is a good chance that the awful chain linking one alcoholic generation to another will be broken.[65]

But recovery often happens later, when children live with the addiction for years or their whole lives. Children are in kindergarten or third grade or middle school or older before a parent gets help. Just because a child's mom or dad or brother or granddad is sober, that doesn't mean all of the child's troubles are solved. The child needs a place to begin healing, time to reframe the experiences of a parent's addiction, and the chance to learn about the gifts of recovery. Children impacted by a parent's addiction need to understand *both in their heads and their hearts* that they didn't cause the addiction. They need to know it isn't something Mom or Dad purposely did to them, but instead is a sickness that hurt everybody and is no one's fault. And they need to understand that there are things people do to get well from this disease all the time.

If at all possible, parents need to find a facility that has a children's program. If one isn't available, get help from a therapist who specializes in working with children of alcoholics. This can provide a strong foundation for children as they participate in Structured Family Recovery at whatever level their age allows and discover their own roles in the mutual healing that takes place. Too often families don't make this choice because they are still mired in secrets and shame, both terribly toxic for these little souls. Our secrets and shame are often the reasons we are afraid to get help for our children. But children's programs, family therapy, and Structured Family Recovery can liberate a child from the grip of this disease and, as a result, the entire family can experience a new freedom.

When little children go through programs designed just for them, learning about addiction and recovery in a manner they can readily absorb, they demonstrate acceptance and love in amazing ways. Children can inspire the whole family. They stand up and say, "This is my dad," pushing out their little chests with pride. "He has a disease. It's not my fault, and it's not his fault. But he's getting better, and he loves me."

Children today get help at much younger ages than at any other time in history, experiencing the joys of recovery as they grow and develop. Whereas children once entered adulthood still carrying all of the pain brought on by growing up in an addicted home, parents now have resources to help their children grow up with skills and tools that prepare them for dealing with the daily challenges of life. The Betty Ford Center has pioneered a marvelous program for children, ages seven to twelve. Besides their own program, they have listings of other programs available around the country. Call them and ask.

Jerry Moe, director of the Betty Ford Children's Program, says,

> It takes much courage and strength for parents or grandparents to bring kids to the children's program. With the silence and secrecy so pervasive in addicted families, many children make up a story to make sense of all the stress and chaos. These stories are usually way off base and add to the guilt and shame children carry. Without help, these stories can become life scripts which severely limit one's potential and actualization. Providing accurate age-appropriate information about this insidious disease helps children to realize that it's not their fault, they are not to

blame, and they are not alone. This liberates kids in enormous ways.

Then equipping youth with a feelings vocabulary, a safe place with structure and consistency, and counselors who listen with their hearts encourages kids to get real by pouring out their feelings, worries, and concerns. Slowly their true self emerges. Empowering them with coping skills, self-care strategies, and ways to stay safe gives them hope. Children build a strong spiritual connection to the group and one another as they truly believe they belong. The beginning of a new future blooms as the possibility of changing the family legacy takes root.[66]

● ● ●

PART II

What We Need to Do

THIS SECTION OF THE BOOK launches Structured Family Recovery (SFR), a cooperative approach to lasting sobriety. While many families may choose to work with an SFR counselor, this section is written as if your family will be working without a professional. It is written to cover major eventualities, but each family is unique and will face specific challenges. Follow the guidelines closely, and your family should do well. However, if you come up against problems or roadblocks that require extra help, consult with an SFR counselor at least until you've overcome the difficulty. Consult the resource section to find referral sources. Additionally, if one of the family team members has a seasoned sponsor, you might arrange a group discussion with that person to seek his or her guidance.

As with doing anything new, it takes time before it feels comfortable and natural. It's my hope that you and your family give yourself the time. The rewards for the entire family are well worth it.

It Takes a Family

From the beginning, we've had family, sometimes with great joy and other times, sorrow. It is our most cherished institution, and the health of the family is a reflection of each member within it. Our definition of family may vary—the one we were born into or the one we created—but the value of family is uncontested. Our very nature depends on sharing a common life with other people. As David Mace, author and family specialist, said, "Nothing in the world could make human life happier that to greatly increase the number of strong families."[67] If we've lost family to death, divorce, abandonment, or other crises, we can create new families with people in our lives who we trust and love.

All families face crisis at one time or another; it's how we handle crisis that determines our welfare. While some crises can be irreversible, addiction is not one of them. It is the most treatable chronic illness. When we compare addiction to other brain diseases—Alzheimer's and Parkinson's—we understand why we have hope. Recovery is not only possible, but those who achieve recovery can live full and productive lives. Yet, most alcoholics and addicts never get help or don't get the kind of ongoing help they need. Their families' suffering continues. As we discussed in Part I, we've never before created a central role for the entire family in the recovery process.

Structured Family Recovery brings family into the middle of recovery to meet this critical need. We've seen the uncommon success that comes from a team approach with addicted doctors who participate in long-term monitoring programs. We will now explore how families can replicate the structure of these programs and add the greatest ingredient of all: *love.*

Before putting Structured Family Recovery into action, we need to review some key points from the previous chapters. Much of this information is counterintuitive, and without reinforcing these ideas, our common sense can lead us astray. The power of addiction requires that we are greatly prepared.

1. *Treatment only addresses the acute stage of addiction.* Treatment plays a very important role for many addicted people who might not succeed without it. It addresses the most severe symptoms of addiction—physical, mental, and spiritual. Treatment centers cannot cure addiction, but they can prepare alcoholics and addicts for their release by giving them an aftercare plan, including working a Twelve Step recovery program. Although they provide aftercare plans, treatment programs do not attend to the chronic nature of addiction. This process begins when treatment ends and happens primarily in Twelve Step groups and by rebuilding addicts' relationships at home, at work, in their place of worship if they are religious, and in the community. Since addicts often don't comply with their aftercare plans, or do so inconsistently, the relapse rate during the chronic phase of the disease is high.

2. *Relapse isn't random.* Relapse is a sign that something is missing in a recovery program, usually as a result of underestimating the disease and what it takes to stay sober. Many alcoholics and addicts don't get adequate support in early recovery, and without it, relapse is all too common. We know how addicted people succeed and how they fail—it isn't a guessing game. Addicts who respect the chronic nature of their disease and work a consistent and honest Twelve Step recovery program and restore key relationships for support at home and in the community have high success rates; those who don't usually drink again.

3. *A high percentage of addicted doctors succeed but not because they are doctors.* Doctors are the recovery winners, not because they are easy to treat or compliant, but because they engage in a five-year plan of action, called a Physician Health Program (PHP). The expectation of Physician Health Programs is that everyone will succeed and work a Twelve Step recovery program. In the first five years of recovery, 78 percent of doctors never have a single relapse.[68] With SFR, we can create a similar plan of action, greatly reducing the probability of relapse.

4. *Motivation alone doesn't drive success.* According to social scientists, our beliefs about the role of motivation in creating lasting change are wrong. Motivation works for us in the short term, much like a sprint in the long-distance race of recovery. Education is beneficial for breaking through denial, but it isn't a reliable way to change behavior. When we attempt to change attitudes to change behaviors, we have it backward; we change behaviors in order to change attitudes. Social norms—what other people are doing or saying in modeling behavior—are a leading force for change as is keeping things simple and doable with immediate rewards and using concrete calls to action to trigger new behaviors.

5. *Enabling addiction.* When families enable alcoholics or addicts, they do so to save themselves. When an alcoholic hits bottom, the family usually does, too. Enabling is a method family members use to prevent this from happening. It is seen as a promise for something better or prevention of something worse. Most people want solutions that heal the family, and enabling is often their well-meaning, although self-defeating, attempt to help themselves survive the crisis of addiction.

6. *Enabling recovery.* With good direction, efforts that go into enabling addiction can be redirected to become a driving force for enabling recovery. When families transform themselves into recovery teams, they create new social norms based on recovery

values. Everyone in the family begins speaking the language of recovery.

7. *Structured Family Recovery.* Structured Family Recovery transforms recovery into a shared journey the family takes together with the newly recovering alcoholic or addict. It creates positive social norms, behavioral expectations, tiny tasks, triggers for enabling recovery, accountability, structure, family cohesiveness and fun, and serves as a relapse prevention program. It does all this while keeping it simple.

Recovery from addiction is a process of changing behaviors to change thinking, which in the end changes us spiritually. There are no magic solutions or pills that can do what we have to do for ourselves. I am thankful for that, because if there were, we'd miss out on one of the greatest journeys a family can take together.

Begin with a Team

As long as we live and breathe, we have the choice to do something different, to move forward, to embrace solutions. We can't see results from where we stand at any given time—especially in the beginning. We must live results one day at a time, and we do this best with the support of a team.

The person who is initiating the selection of the team can be anyone who is willing to take the responsibility to begin the process by identifying a core of team members who will work together to fill out the list. By reading this book, you have shown a willingness to take on at least part of that responsibility yourself and to engage others to help you go to the next stage.

In the words of Henry Ford, "Coming together is a beginning. Keeping together is progress. Working together is success." All we need to do to get started is to *come together.* This simple act creates a powerful change of direction. Family becomes a force for recovery. By creating a team, we can do things we couldn't do before. As Henry Ford went on to say, "If everyone is moving forward together, then success takes care of itself."

Once we unite as a recovery team, we begin creating a strong family culture that does more than stand up to addiction. It cultivates love and support in the larger picture of our lives. Team meetings, simple in concept, are a powerful source of transformation in practice. We greatly improve the quality of family life, while we address issues associated with addiction in team meetings, by developing healthier ways of communicating, greater respect of one another, and tolerance of our differences. None of us is perfect, but in healthy families we know we are loved. When we begin undoing the damage of addiction, we clear out the emotional debris that gets in the way of our happiness.

Selecting a team for Structured Family Recovery begins with defining what we mean by *family* as we list the people who are closest to the alcoholic or addict. As I indicated at the beginning of this book, these are people who have a vested interest in the addict's and their own well-being. These are usually close family members (including older children), serious romantic partners, close friends, clergy or spiritual advisors. If the addict has become isolated in his addiction, recovery leads to positive spirituality (defined as a willingness to open up to other people). So we don't worry about the current state of relationships since addiction by definition creates differences and fallouts. All that's required is that team members are willing to mend the relationships through cooperation in family recovery.

Everyone on the team can't help but be affected by the addict's disease, if for no other reason than they are closely related or intimately connected. The alcoholic or addict is cherished by them even if he isn't particularly liked at the moment. Addiction makes most of its victims unlikable, at least some of the time. In recovery, however, alcoholics and addicts are among the best people you'll ever meet.

Occasionally, someone denies having been affected by addiction at all. An addict's sister recently told me she was completely untouched by her brother's alcoholism. "We live in different states and almost never see each other," she said. I asked her to describe what her relationship with her brother was like growing up and what it's like now. She told me they were close as kids. "He was funny and made me laugh," she said, "and he always looked out for me." But over the years, he pulled away in his addiction and she began a family of her own. Their two lives weren't a good fit anymore, she said. When I asked her if she could choose to make it different, what would the relationship with her brother look like today. She paused a long while. "He'd know my children, he'd love them," she said. "He'd be the world's best uncle."

Addiction takes from us not only the things we had but the things we might have had. *What never happened because of this disease?* It's not just the consequences we can tally up—smashed cars, lost jobs, money problems, arguments, broken promises, disappointments, estrangement, divorce, jail. It's also all the really wonderful stuff of life that didn't happen, all the memories we didn't make. Talking to a family the other day, the mom said, "This was the first Christmas we've spent together in five years." Recovery is about reclaiming the person we love—the *real* person—and making our family whole. It's about changing the memories we create in the future. No one of us can manage to do this alone; it requires all of the family members who have come together as a recovery team.

Make a list of everyone who comes to mind when you think of a recovery team. Don't edit the list by thinking someone won't be interested or is too mad to care. People can live near or far; they may have demanding schedules with kids and work. But people who understand family and the power of its legacy will be willing to make the necessary sacrifices and do it not just for the alcoholic and not just for themselves, but also for the generations to come. When a family is wounded by addiction and it goes unaddressed, the pain is handed down, unknowingly, to future generations. A family team can stop the pain in the here and now. Ask people to join together, give them the information they need, and then let them decide if they want to make this commitment.

Be prepared for questions and doubt. You'll likely get mixed reactions among the candidates you've identified as potential team members. The best way to build a team is to start with a small coalition of the willing by approaching those who are most likely to say, "Absolutely! When can we get started?" With the enthusiastic people onboard, approach those who may be somewhat reluctant and then, finally, even the ones you suspect may be fiercely opposed. Meet everyone at their starting point. Usually people's reactions to participating on a family recovery team are tied to their reactions to the addiction. The angrier they are, the more resistant they may be to participating in solutions. They might say, "I'm done! I'm not wasting any more time on him."

Don't try to talk people out of how they feel. Listen to them. Their feelings come from real experiences. Put your proposal aside for the moment, and hear what they have to say. It'll give you valuable information about the ways their relationship with the addict has affected them. Their anger, after all, is usually the result of hurt and a sense of injustice.

Refusing to participate is usually a result of strong emotions flooding the brain. As a result, decision making is based on a deep sense of pessimism caused by repeated failures and past hurts. Therefore, the potential good that can come from family recovery is overshadowed by the ravages of addiction. It's a common reaction among family members: *I refuse to be victimized by the addiction, so I can't participate in a solution that may only result in further hurt and disappointment.* They really may be saying, "It's hard for me to trust. I need more information and time to think about it," or they may be truly unwilling to take the risk.

Before you talk to each person on your list, set your goals. Ask yourself, "What do I want to get out of this call?" The most successful people in business know that the goal of the first meeting is to get the second meeting. You might know, for example, that Aunt Mary will agree without a moment's hesitation. But your dad is so mad, he'll react negatively at first. Building a team requires a certain kind of choreography, selecting each step carefully. Bring Aunt Mary and other supporters onto the team first. Then, as a group, approach the others. Perhaps if your dad has a good relationship with Aunt Mary, she should be the one to approach him. Since he respects her, there's a better chance he will listen. Decide who will talk to whom. Take it in small steps. Begin with something nonthreatening and positive such as, "Would you be willing to learn something new?" or "Perhaps we can avoid future relapses and treatment."

In the end, if a family member or friend doesn't want to participate, respect that person's wishes. It is better to stay on good terms than to force the issue. You might invite those who are reluctant to attend a couple meetings as observers, so at least they understand what everyone else is doing. While the door always remains open to them, it's for them to choose.

Team size varies from family to family. Include people who should definitely be part of the team and no more—the inner circle that might feel comfortable sitting casually around the kitchen table. While an employer might be part of an intervention team, for instance, it might not work for him or her to join a family recovery team, unless he or she is truly like family.

If you don't have the makings of a team from your immediate family, you and your recovering loved one can still engage in Structured Family Recovery by involving your Twelve Step sponsors from AA, NA, and Al-Anon, friends you've met in your recovery programs, members of your extended family, good friends from other areas of your life, or a therapist certified in Structured Family Recovery. Since meetings take place on conference calls, these people can be located anywhere in the country.

Children can be invited to participate with consideration for their ages, maturity, and emotional readiness. It's wise to select specific meetings that will be helpful to children, because not all will be. Children need to learn about the disease of addiction, know that it is genetic, and that the addicted person didn't choose to get sick. Celebrate milestones with children, such as sobriety dates. When a mother is six months or a year sober, make it a time for everyone to get together and have some fun. Whether six or sixteen, children who witness members of their family coming together to take responsibility feel safe. And they learn how to be responsible by watching adults do what is right, even when it's tough.

When possible, it's best to begin holding weekly meetings *before* inviting the addicted loved one to join the team. It's crucial that the recovery team be confident about group cohesiveness and steadiness of purpose before going to the next stage of bringing the addict aboard. Team members need time to work through questions of their own and develop a degree of self-assuredness in how Twelve Step recovery works—especially if the addict has been through a full treatment program and will know more about recovery than the family.

When asking the addict to join the team, he may immediately assume Structured Family Recovery is all about him and instantly feel suspicious. You can reassure him by saying something like, "We understand that addiction is a family disease. So we are taking responsibility by doing our part in the recovery process. We have begun Structured Family Recovery for *ourselves,* but we'd like to invite you to join us, so we can all recover together."

Although Structured Family Recovery can start at any time, it's helpful to begin while the addict is in treatment, whenever possible. This gives the team time to become established. If you begin when your newly recovering loved one is home, you can explain that you're involved in family recovery, but invite him once your weekly team meetings are underway, basic questions are answered, everyone has gone to at least one Al-Anon meeting, and the team feels prepared. When the addict comes on board and sees that the family is already engaged in recovery, he will take you seriously, even if he's not entirely committed.

When an addict is still in treatment, the recovery team can arrange a conference call during the last week to review aftercare planning with him and his counselor. This will require signed permission from the addict, saying the counselor has his permission to participate. Everyone can then learn what kinds of support are being recommended for the addict when he leaves treatment. Aftercare plans are designed to encourage ongoing recovery. They should always include Twelve Step meetings. As John Schwarzlose, the former president of the Betty Ford Center, said, "I can give you a guarantee. When you leave here, if you don't go to AA, you won't make it." This meeting with the addict and counselor is a good time to explain Structured Family Recovery, what the family team has been doing, and invite the addict to join.

If the addict isn't in treatment yet, and the family is planning an intervention, this is a perfect time for family members to discuss Structured Family Recovery. It creates a seamless recovery process before, during, and after treatment. Once the intervention is completed, appropriate members from the intervention team (using the guidelines above) convert into a recovery team. This should happen even if a loved one refuses treatment during the intervention. A family engaging in Structured Family Recovery is a powerful example of *doing the right thing,* which will turn many refusals into agreements. Addicts will generally notice when family members are "walking the walk."

The team invites the addict to participate *only if he is abstinent.* Structured Family Recovery is designed to support recovery, so alcoholics and addicts must be in treatment or a program of recovery. If an addict is still drinking or drugging, the family team must place intervention at the top of the agenda: *How do we best motivate him to accept help?* Start by consulting with a clinical interventionist—an addictions therapist trained in intervention—or read a comprehensive guidebook on intervention. (Refer to the Resources section in part IV.)

When we are ready to invite the addict into the group, every participant must have already made a firm commitment to the recovery process. We are creating a social norm for recovery, which requires modeling integrity. The word *integrity* comes from the Latin word *integritas,* which is "untouched, whole, entire." Wholeness, a shared commitment to recovery values, speaks to the strength of our team. Webster's Dictionary defines it as "moral soundness; honesty; freedom from corrupting influence; and the fulfillment of contracts." With Structured Family Recovery, we are making a contract with the addict, our family, *and* ourselves. We promise to take a firm stand for recovery. We can only ask the addict as a member of the team to do what we are willing to do ourselves.

When we waver or a team doesn't honor its contract, we create a very different social norm for the alcoholic to follow. We open the door for him to waver or stop honoring his commitments. Structured Family Recovery is a sacred promise we make to each other. We may not know exactly where we're headed, but once we launch, we keep going.

As Hank Aaron, one of baseball's greatest players, once said, "My motto was always to keep swinging. Whether I was in a slump or feeling badly or having trouble off the field, the only thing to do was keep swinging."

How Do I Talk to My Addict?

The alcoholic or addict freshly out of treatment is often tired of being the center of attention. Although the family commotion has really been about the *disease,* usually members haven't understood this in a meaningful way and have made it about the *addict*—with their anger and frustration directed at him instead of the disease. The differentiation may appear subtle, but it doesn't feel that way to the addict. It gets mixed up in his brain and can be translated as, "I'm sick of everyone jumping all over me and talking about me behind my back!" This is surprising to families, who recoil at the very idea that the addict accuses them after all they've been through. To addicts, the family's mad attempts at surviving the onslaught of addiction felt like a war of words and actions directed at them.

So when an addict returns from treatment, all those feelings of anger and resentment still linger. He's been the problem in the family for a long time. Then he becomes "the patient." Home again, now he's the point of contention for the train wreck he left behind and a person of suspect because around every corner lurks the possibility of relapse. All eyes are on him *always* (and for good reason, from the family's perspective). It's emotionally exhausting and can easily call up his already festering resentment. He may lash out at the suspicion and real and implied accusations, causing more reason for family apprehension. Everyone can get fed up pretty quickly with both addict and family focusing on the other yet again, and with everyone harboring unrealistic expectations. The cycle of mistrust and recrimination can build on itself and eventually undermine everyone's recovery efforts.

There are ways for family members to communicate with the addict to break the cycle and establish terms for their relationship that are different than what they've had. We do it through our actions, *true-to-ourselves actions.* In other words, we work a Twelve Step family recovery program. We demonstrate support of our alcoholic while simultaneously participating in the recovery process for ourselves. The effect on addicts can be profound. Initially they may be suspicious of our motives or assume we won't follow through for long, but if we demonstrate commitment and perseverance, they're likely to experience a quiet, growing respect for us and begin to internalize the recovery norms that we are modeling.

We need to demonstrate that Structured Family Recovery is about the family, not the alcoholic. Because we have all shared in the disease, and we all need to recover. The message is, "This is something we are doing for ourselves. We would really like you to join us, but this is for each of us individually. Recovery is about making our family great by all of us healing together."

This doesn't mean we're ignoring the messes needing attention and the problems that need solving. Addiction can play havoc on every area of our lives. But we have a choice to sort things out as adversaries or partners. Alcoholics and addicts are overwhelmed at what they need to do to straighten out their lives. Working the Twelve Steps with a sponsor helps guide them in doing the right things and in being painstakingly thorough in beginning to repair the damages to their body, mind, and spirit. Structured Family Recovery keeps us all focused on recovery. By trusting the process, we can feel a little calmer. Life will come back together, but it doesn't happen overnight.

Recovery becomes a two-way street when we share with the addict what we've learned in Al-Anon or little light bulb moments during our daily meditation or self-insights when working a particular Step. When these moments are truly for and about our recovery and *not a thinly veiled attempt to influence the addict,* they create warmth and belonging. When we share our recovery, we can experience feelings that unite us.

Invite the addict back into the normal activities of family life: *Do you want to go shopping with me? Would you like to catch a movie? I'm going to run over to Grandma's, would you like to come?* These are the small things that make up our existence. Don't underestimate how difficult this might be for the newly recovering person, so don't make a big deal out of it. Strike a balance between lightly encouraging the addict's involvement in activities and being respectful of the addict's need for his own space, both of which are important for the brain to adjust to life without chemicals. Remember the Twelve Step slogan, "Easy does it."

We need to take a look at our family life, too. Does it give the impression of a happy place? Or have we become frenzied, short-tempered, disorganized, or just plain no fun? Do we all sit around with our faces in screens, television blaring, everyone hunkered down in a private spot? Does everyone grab a bite to eat willy-nilly or by racing to a drive-thru? Do we have lots of excuses at the ready for why we live this way, each person left to his or her own devices? Let's take a good hard look at what the addict is returning home to, at what the family "real estate" looks like.

Ask: How would I define a healthy family life? How would others in the family answer this question? Are there tiny changes that we can begin making now? What do we need to give up? Let's clean out our cache of family life habits like a long-neglected closet. What are we going to keep, throw away, and add? Where can we find guidance to help us do this democratically and effectively? How can we use what we've learned in this book to make lasting changes? As Bruce Feiler, author of *The Secrets of Happy Families,* wrote, "Want to have a happier family? Tinker with it all the time."[69]

Bring fun back into the family. Not just going out to restaurants or shopping, but by trying the novel and new. Have some days that end with, "Wasn't that great? Who knew that could be so much fun (interesting, challenging, intriguing, exciting, inspiring)?" Fun doesn't require big and grand and expensive. There's so much out there in the world. Let's open up the windows and doors of our family life. Let the sunshine in and breathe in the fresh air. Let's make it a place where everyone wants to belong.

How Do I Talk to My Family? Advice from a Longtime Recovering Drug and Alcohol Addict

When I came home from treatment, it was difficult to talk to my family. I knew what my behavior as an active alcoholic had been. I was sometimes kind, sometimes entertaining, sometimes angry, sometimes manipulative, and always dishonest. But what was my role now? How was I supposed to act? Strange as it may seem, in the early days of my recovery I almost didn't know how to communicate. I wasn't comfortable in my own skin and was dimly aware that I'd been letting everyone down for a long time, to put it mildly.

The first thing I realized—and probably the most important thing—was that I needed to win back my family's trust. As an alcoholic and drug addict, I'd shredded their trust again and again until there was nothing left of that precious fabric that binds people together. There's an old saying, "Talk is cheap." That was more true of me than of most people. There's another old saying that provides the remedy, "Actions speak louder than words." If I was going to win back the trust of family and friends, I was going to have to show them I was trustworthy. My actions would prove what my words never could.

I went to a Twelve Step meeting every day and followed through with the rest of my aftercare recommendations from the treatment center. I did what I was supposed to do, whether I felt like it or not. The immediate effect of doing these things was that I never picked up the first drink or drug. I stayed sober, and although my family didn't believe their eyes for many months, my sobriety was something that I could only achieve one day at a time.

The second thing I did was talk a little bit about what I was learning at the meetings, maybe something funny, maybe something insightful. I wasn't trying to prove anything about my meeting, but if something really struck me, I related it to someone in the family.

For example, after the close of one of the meetings, when I was helping clean up the coffee and putting the chairs away, I happened to pass Alan in the hallway. I asked him how it was going. Alan was a short guy with curly hair and thick glasses. I admired the quiet and thoughtful way he talked. He stopped dead in his tracks, as though I'd asked him the most important thing in the world. I stopped too, just waiting for his reply. After some reflection, he said, "It's going just the way it should. Not that I like it!"

We both had a good laugh over that and then continued on our separate ways. I was so struck by his remark that I repeated it when I went home. My family wasn't sure whether to laugh or scratch their heads, but it made a big impression. And I remember Alan's comment still, these many years later.

The third thing I did was to rejoin the life of the family, which I did by asking questions: "How's Aunt Audrey doing?" or "When is that little nephew's birthday?" or "What are we doing for the Fourth of July?" These questions always brought answers and opened the door to conversations that weren't about me. *Thank God.* And they allowed me a chance to offer a little help. *"Do you want me to pick up something for the birthday party?"*

When I was drinking and drugging, my interest in family was scanty at best. But in the early days of my recovery, I learned that interacting with others and trying to be part of the family gave me less time to be worried about myself and my many self-centered fears.

Twelve Step programs put a great emphasis on service work and for good reason. When we help others, we help ourselves. We find relief from our countless anxieties. We can extend that to our families, too. Actions not only speak louder than words, they open the door to real conversation. We find a shared sense of quiet gratitude. We're together again.

Keeping It Simple

"Life is really simple, but we insist on making it complicated," said Confucius, the Chinese teacher and philosopher, more than two thousand years ago. When we overcomplicate recovery, we can overwhelm ourselves, and when we get overwhelmed, we're risking relapse for the whole family. When it all becomes too much, we're tempted to quit, and the addict is tempted to drink. To succeed in recovery, we do simple things that *work*. Simplicity changes behavior.

Structured Family Recovery is simple. But simple doesn't mean simplistic. When we oversimplify complex issues, we don't get the results we want. A simplistic approach is a sign that we underestimate what's required of recovery. Simple, on the other hand, is finding the most uncomplicated solution to a problem.

Structured Family Recovery consists of two activities for the SFR team. First, we attend a weekly Al-Anon or other Twelve Step meeting. This is our connection to the recovery community.

Al-Anon is the most common Twelve Step group for families. However, there are other excellent options such as Families Anonymous, Adult Children of Alcoholics, and Nar-Anon. Families Anonymous is popular with parents of addicted children of all ages. Adult Children of Alcoholics consists primarily of grown children of addicted parents. Nar-Anon is specifically for family members of addicts who use other drugs besides alcohol and who attend Narcotics Anonymous. Find meetings by searching online or using your telephone directory. In choosing a meeting, make it easy for yourself. Select the best day and time to go. Pick a convenient location. Identify your recovery triggers. What already happens in your day that will trigger you to go to a meeting? Can you create recovery triggers?

Second, we participate in an SFR meeting by conference call. This is our connection to our family recovery team. Each meeting lasts only one hour, more if needed on occasion.

After Jillian's husband came home from treatment, she knew she needed to go to Al-Anon but initially dreaded it. "I'm not unique, I suppose, but I saw it as a burden," she said. "I resented going to these meetings when drinking was *his* problem." But after her first few meetings, she began to see a benefit. "I felt calmer, more hopeful, somehow."

Jillian decided to make Al-Anon a special outing for herself midweek, when she most needed a break from the kids. "Since Wednesday night was my meeting night, I thought it could also be Dad's night with the kids," she said. Jillian and her husband, Richard, decided to make it special for the kids, complete with pizza and board games. "It's good for everyone to be without Mom once a week," she said, "and Richard gets some fun time with the kids." On her way to Al-Anon, Jillian always stops for a caramel macchiato and savors it throughout the meeting. "We make the evening a treat for everyone, including me."

Jillian created a recovery trigger, making attending Al-Anon easy, not only for herself, but for her entire family. She modeled self-care to her children and avoided meltdowns by making it special for them. Rather than creating dread and contention, Wednesday nights became a favorite for everyone. Jillian met her sponsor at her Al-Anon home group, and the kids had great fun being with their dad. Richard felt he was making up for his drinking days by spending quality time with his kids every week.

"Lucinda and I've been married twenty-eight years," said Peter, "and drinking was always part of our lives. But in the last five years, alcohol became a problem for Lucinda." Peter and their adult daughters intervened, and Lucinda agreed to attend an outpatient program.

"The idea that I should go to Al-Anon came as a surprise to me," Peter said. "I agreed to do it, but my meetings were erratic." The family finally challenged Peter and, together, worked out a simple plan. "The way I had been approaching Al-Anon made it feel unmanageable," he explained. "But we came up with a recovery trigger that worked for me."

Peter and Lucinda loved their Saturdays together, so they decided to build recovery time into the day. "There's a church that has both AA and Al-Anon scheduled at the same time on Saturday mornings," said Peter. "Lucinda and I go to our meetings and then have lunch together at our favorite cafe."

Alcoholics and other addicts identify their recovery triggers, too. Using triggers makes attending meetings a no-brainer. Josephine is a morning person. She loves her early bird meetings before work. Coffee and donuts are in good supply, but she always brings a breakfast yogurt. "It's a great way to begin my day," she says. "I leave the meeting in a sober state of mind, and it carries me throughout the day."

Tyler eats dinner with his parents every night and then is off to an evening meeting. "I'm young, and I need to get out of the house at night," he says. "So going to an eight o'clock meeting is perfect. Plus, I hang out with my sober buddies at Starbucks afterward."

Ben is unemployed, so he attends two meetings a day to give himself structure. "I'd be smoking pot in no time if I just hung around the house," he said. "Instead, I start out with a morning meeting, do some job hunting, and then catch a meeting at the Alano Club." Ben calls his sponsor every night to report on his day. "If I think about skipping my meetings, I think about that call with my sponsor," he said.

Families working Twelve Step programs of recovery share a common experience with their addicted loved ones. When struggling to schedule one hour of Al-Anon into their week, they have a new appreciation for their alcoholic who is jump-starting recovery often with a meeting every day for the first critical three months. One mother said, "I didn't have much trouble going to meetings, but when it came to asking someone to be my sponsor, I really struggled." She and her daughter, who was new in AA, commiserated about how difficult it was to walk up to someone and ask the sponsorship question. "My daughter finally found a great sponsor," she said. "She bolstered my courage, so the next week I got a sponsor, too." It is a profound experience for family and addict to take this journey together. It creates empathy, compassion, accountability, and sometimes a bit of healthy competition!

Using conference calls simplifies Structured Family Recovery. No one has to drive anywhere, no need for childcare, no worries about clothes, makeup, or hair, and family members can participate from anywhere. If you're on vacation in Florida and your family is in New York or if you are at your daughter's soccer game or if you are in bed with a head cold—no problem. With a conference call, the meeting comes to you.

Setting up conference calls is easy. You can choose from several services. We use freeconference.com and schedule all our calls online. By email, each family member automatically receives a telephone number to dial, connecting them to the conference call. These services are free. Callers only pay the rate they're charged by their own phone company.

Attempting to plan weekly meetings that work for everyone's schedule can be time consuming, requiring multiple calls or emails. It's far easier to hold meetings at the same time every week or use a free website, like doodle.com, to coordinate. Everyone is polled by email to determine the best time to meet. It simplifies group scheduling and will even sync appointments to calendars. Accessing technology makes managing meetings a breeze.

Structured Family Recovery Counselors

There are a growing number of counselors who families can work with. These specialists are experienced addiction therapists who have been certified in SFR counseling and who work their own Twelve Step recovery programs. Some are also trained as clinical interventionists. SFR counselors are skilled in working with the whole family.

By participating on the weekly conference calls, SFR counselors facilitate communication, guide interaction, and navigate the family team through the unexpected. They also answer questions or assist in a crisis between SFR meetings. They have expertise working through complex family issues associated with addiction and are proficient in conflict resolution. SFR counselors help families implement the Eight Essential

Elements (described in chapter 2) and develop relapse plans that become agreements that addicts and family members commit to. These specialized counselors also offer an abundance of practical wisdom that comes from having traveled the road of recovery themselves.

Most families decide to work with an SFR counselor once a week for the first few months or longer. Once a family is comfortable with recovery, their SFR counselor meets with them less frequently, such as every other week or once a month. As the needs of a family team change, they work with their SFR counselor more or less intensely as circumstances require. Eventually, family teams who have been working solid Twelve Step programs only need to involve their SFR counselor periodically for checkups. The ultimate goal is to reach a place of self-sufficiency that no longer requires professional help.

Some families have greater needs than others. Trust is dramatically diminished, not only with the alcoholic, but between other family members. These circumstances initially require additional meetings with an SFR counselor to stabilize the family system. Once these families are able to work together in recovery, however, they experience dramatic changes. The impact on the alcoholic is profound. When a splintered family begins to coalesce around recovery, it is more difficult to return to drinking and drugging.

Structured Family Recovery without a Counselor

For varying reasons, such as financial limitations, some families will need to participate in Structured Family Recovery without working with a professional. However, since families do not have a recovery knowledge base, the key to success is finding good Al-Anon sponsors just as the addict or alcoholic makes finding an AA or NA sponsor a priority. Team members need to choose sponsors as quickly as possible, preferably within two weeks after forming the recovery team. Attending additional meetings will help accelerate the process. Sponsors provide everyone on the team with their own recovery guide. Team members get the help they need but in a different way than from an SFR counselor.

Talk with your sponsor before each weekly SFR meeting, exploring the topics you'll be discussing with your family. Also bring up the topics during Al-Anon meetings. Gain as many insights as you can, so you are prepared to share thoughts and ideas in your SFR meetings that are firmly grounded in recovery. Keep in mind that without an SFR counselor to guide you, it is critical that everyone follow the SFR format closely. When everyone participates fully, family recovery can flourish.

"My husband is working part-time, and our parents are on fixed incomes. We all struggle financially," said Mattie. "We couldn't afford working with a counselor, but we made a family pact to go to meetings and find sponsors." The entire family was true to this promise. "My dad had a knee replacement a few months ago, but he didn't let that stop him," she said. "And even my mom got an Al-Anon sponsor. I could hardly believe it."

Mattie's health insurance only covered detox. "I was given five days at the treatment center and then sent home," she said. "I went directly to Alcoholics Anonymous. It was tough, but with my whole family joining together, I'm doing really well."

Every Sunday, Mattie and her family hold a meeting after church and review their recovery progress. They share wisdom gained from sponsors and other people attending Twelve Step meetings. "We make scrambled eggs and bacon and sit around my mom's kitchen table to talk," said Mattie. "We've never felt closer."

In some cases, problems are beyond what families can handle on their own. The following is a list of challenges that call for professional guidance. If your family is facing any of these, it is highly advisable to set up an initial consultation with an SFR counselor or other professional counselor with expertise in addiction, family issues, and the Twelve Steps to review needs and determine the best course of action for your family. (Use the resource section of this book to locate a certified SFR counselor.)

These challenges require professional guidance:

- Addicted person has a history of multiple treatments followed by relapse
- Evidence of serious mental health problems or past suicide threats or attempts

- History of family violence

- Evidence of cross addictions, such as gambling or sex addiction

- Addicted person consistently refuses to follow aftercare recommendations

- Key family members are resistant to Twelve Step recovery

- Untreated addiction among other close family members

- Family relationships deteriorated to the extent that cooperation isn't possible

- Too few people to form a family team (only one or two people are available)

- Family members feel more comfortable working with a professional

If you are facing any of the above circumstances but don't have the financial means to work with an SFR counselor, consider a one-time consultation. An SFR counselor will help create a plan, determining the best direction for the family to proceed. Get additional support by identifying free or low-cost counseling services in your community or at your place of worship. Ask about professionals with experience in addiction and recovery issues.

Regardless of the unique problems families may face, when the entire family engages, we create a positive force for recovery. But when serious challenges threaten to block recovery, accessing professional help is the appropriate choice.

● ● ●

Twelve Step Meetings

Family members can feel as nervous going to their first Al-Anon meeting as alcoholics feel about their first AA meeting. Nobody knows what to expect when they walk into the room. There's such a buildup of emotions, it can feel overwhelming, even downright frightening.

Here are brief introductions to Al-Anon for the family members and to Alcoholics Anonymous for the alcoholic or addict. Many people whose drug of choice isn't alcohol also go to Narcotics Anonymous or other drug-specific Twelve Step meetings, such as Cocaine Anonymous or Pills Anonymous. However, these more specialized meetings aren't as plentiful and not available everywhere. There are also groups for people with co-occurring addictions and mental health disorders such as Double Trouble In Recovery and Dual Recovery Anonymous. For the most part, the information for AA applies to these other groups except for the specific drug involved.

Your First Al-Anon Meeting

Listening is always a good first step, and there's never pressure to speak in Al-Anon. You'll notice that people who've long been in Al-Anon rarely talk about their alcoholics. They attend Al-Anon for their own personal benefit, because a loved one's addiction had an effect on their mental, emotional, and spiritual wellbeing. If we stop to think about it, when alcoholics attend AA, they focus on themselves. Family members do the same in Al-Anon. This can be confusing for newcomers who initially need to talk about their addict. It seems the natural starting point for them, but remember, Al-Anon is for *you.*

Although this section is about Al-Anon, most of it will apply to other Twelve Step programs for families, such as Nar-Anon, Families Anonymous, and Adult Children of Alcoholics. Since there are fewer of these meetings, most family members will often attend Al-Anon, recognizing that what's said about alcohol can apply to all other drugs as well.

During meetings, members share their experiences, strengths, and hopes. When listening to others, take what you like and leave the rest. You may not relate to everything being said, but somebody is likely to say something you needed to hear. It's the passage of wisdom from one Al-Anon member to another, in the same way Alcoholics Anonymous works, with one alcoholic talking to another, that makes the experience valuable. In time, you'll begin to identify ways you've been changed as a result of your relationship with your addicted loved one.

Janice grew up in a home with an alcoholic father. In her twenties, she always came to realize that her boyfriends, no matter how promising, were alcoholic. She didn't see the pattern at first, but over time, it became apparent. "I had a serious relationship with a successful financial manager," she said. "I thought I had finally met the one." On a lovely Saturday morning, they arranged to meet at a favorite Chicago restaurant. "I found him chugging Manhattans-on-the-rocks at eleven o'clock in the morning," she said. "He ordered me one, and when I refused it, he started belittling me. That's when I knew I needed counseling." Janice found a therapist who worked with adult children of alcoholics.

"My counselor told me I needed Al-Anon," she said. "But I was terrified at the thought of it. After six weeks of counseling—and always admitting I hadn't yet gone to a meeting—I forced myself to attend Al-Anon." Janice described entering the church basement where the Al-Anon meeting was being held. "The meeting had already started and the clip-clop of my high heels seemed to echo throughout the room. I wanted to turn and run, but I knew they all saw me. I thought it'd be rude to leave," she said laughing. Janice sat down at a table with eight other women. As she looked around, she realized none of the women could possibly have anything in common with her. "At this particular meeting," Janice said, "everybody was much older than me, and I could tell these women had lived hard lives.

"Once I began listening to these women speak, I was spellbound," she said. "The wisdom and spirituality in that room was like nothing I'd ever heard before." Janice went on to explain that with all the hardships these women had experienced, they found a serenity she deeply longed for. "Without knowing it, I was given a lesson in principles before personalities," she said. "I prejudged these women, who had so much to offer me."

In Al-Anon, it's said, "Though you may not like all of us, you'll love us in a very special way, the same way we already love you." This addresses the idea of "principles before personality." In Al-Anon, we focus on the *principles* of the program that help us change our defects of character. If we habitually try to control other people, for example, the principles teach us to put our focus back on the only person we can change: ourselves. *Personality* speaks to our individual differences. From time to time, a member of Al-Anon may rub us the wrong way. Some members may even seem to be insufferable at times. But we look beyond personality, past the outside shell of a person. We don't know their individual circumstances or pain. We accept each person as a gift: an opportunity for us to practice patience, tolerance, and forgiveness. The principles of the program stand steady, while personalities, ever changing, come and go.

Al-Anon describes the practicalities of the program in a few short paragraphs.

> The Al-Anon Family Groups are a fellowship of relatives and friends of alcoholics who share their experience, strength, and hope, in order to solve their common problems. We believe alcoholism is a family illness and that changed attitudes can aid recovery.
>
> Al-Anon is not allied with any sect, denomination, political entity, organization, or institution; does not engage in any controversy, neither endorses or opposes any

cause. There are no dues for membership. Al-Anon is self-supporting through its own voluntary contributions.

Al-Anon has but one purpose; to help families of alcoholics. We do this by practicing the Twelve Steps, by welcoming and giving comfort to families of alcoholics, and by giving understanding and encouragement to the alcoholic.[70]

Most Al-Anon meetings are held in churches, not because of religious affiliation, but because churches are numerous throughout neighborhoods and have good, inexpensive meeting spaces. You'll also find Al-Anon meetings in hospitals, office buildings, schools, community centers, and government offices. Some offer childcare. Meetings are available most days of the week depending on where you live. Smaller towns may have fewer meetings per week, but in larger cities you're likely to find that Al-Anon meets morning, noon, and night in a number of locations.

There are women's meetings, men's meetings, and mixed meetings. There are meetings for beginners, discussion groups, Twelve Step study groups, and speaker meetings. At a speaker meeting, an Al-Anon member will share his or her story: how it was in the past, what happened to initiate change, and how it is today. It's fairly easy to find an Al-Anon meeting scheduled at the same time as Alcoholics Anonymous, but held in separate rooms. The alcoholic and family member can go to their respective meetings and then go out for something to eat or a coffee.

"My wife is in AA and our family is doing Structured Family Recovery," says George. "Every Saturday morning, my daughter and I go to our Al-Anon home group together. It used to be that I hardly ever saw her, as busy as she was with her career and social life. Now, every week, we have our morning meeting. Then we go out for coffee and a bagel. It's our quality time. We talk about everything."

In Al-Anon, people don't give counsel. There is no cross talk in meetings, which means you do not have to endure any unwanted advice. Members learn how to solve their common problems by listening to others share and working the Steps with their sponsors. The ways we've changed as a result of coping with a loved one's addiction will often bring out the worst in us, and Al-Anon helps us transform shortcomings into assets and, as a result, gives us the tools to mend broken relationships.

There are no leaders or professionals in charge of Al-Anon. Members volunteer to chair meetings. They read the opening and closing statements. Nobody acts as a group facilitator, and it's not group therapy. Nobody takes attendance, and there's never an obligation to attend. Al-Anon asks members not to discuss therapy techniques, psychology, religious affiliations, intervention, non-Al-Anon literature, and treatment programs during meetings. These boundaries keep Al-Anon pure.

Al-Anon is anonymous. Members use first names only. Discussions are confidential, which affords safety and trust. Newcomers sometimes worry they'll see someone they know at an Al-Anon meeting. A woman told me she saw a married couple she knew from church at her first Al-Anon meeting. Horrified that they might see her, she scurried to the back of the room. "After the meeting, they came up to me and gave me a hug," she said. "They told me their son was addicted to heroin. I started to cry and told them my daughter was a heroin addict, too."

When we walk into Al-Anon, we'll notice that members look like people we see in the grocery store, at work, in school, at church or synagogue, and around our neighborhoods. They come from every walk of life. We find a mix of retired people, young people, middle-aged people, rich, poor, and middle class, often of diverse cultural backgrounds and religious beliefs. Some have been attending meetings for years, and others are first-timers. Regardless of backgrounds, everyone comes because they have been affected by someone else's addiction. While Al-Anon is specifically for loved ones of alcoholics, the recovery principles apply to all addictions. *We all share a common problem.*

Family members, faced with the prospect of going to Al-Anon, often react in ways much like the alcoholic when he's told he needs to attend Alcoholics Anonymous. One of the most frequently heard objections is, "I don't have time!" It's not always just a dodge; people have busy lives. When we sit down and look at our schedules, however, I've never known anyone who couldn't fit an Al-Anon meeting into the week. If anything, it gives us time to pause and reflect, something we're in short supply of in modern life. Every struggle we have with attending Al-Anon is an opportunity to understand our alcoholic's struggles. It's easy to be judgmental until we have to do it ourselves.

Elaine worked for a nonprofit organization in Washington, DC. "My job was all consuming and then I went home to my kids," she said. "When my husband Marc was in treatment for his drinking, I was told to go to Al-Anon." Elaine was so overwhelmed with work, the kids, and taking care of responsibilities while her husband was away, she couldn't find a free minute. "When he came home, he was going to AA every night. I didn't know when people thought I'd go to Al-Anon," she said. Elaine learned about an Al-Anon meeting within walking distance of her office after a chance encounter with a friend. "I ran into an old friend and told her about Marc's treatment," she said. "My friend told me about a noontime Al-Anon meeting right on DuPont Circle, a few blocks from my work. I now brown bag it there several days a week."

When looking for Al-Anon meetings, try and find those near your home or workplace to make it as simple as possible to attend. Is it easiest right after work, in the morning, or on the weekends? What will trigger you to go? Try several Al-Anon meetings and choose the one that fits the best. Ask people for recommendations to other meetings. Look for people who are working an enthusiastic Al-Anon program. If you can say, "I want what they have," you are in the right place. Attend a meeting several times before you decide, but when you finally choose, *make it your home group*. This is the meeting you never miss. You'll most likely find your sponsor here, and it's the place where everyone knows your name. Get involved if only to volunteer to make the coffee or put out the literature. As one Al-Anon member said, "I've made a commitment to always show up at my home group. I greet newcomers and make myself available to them. My sponsor is there, so we always have this meeting together. It's a place where I know I'll find support and friendship."

Meetings generally last an hour. During each meeting, a basket is passed around to collect donations to cover group expenses. Most members put a dollar or two in the basket, but contributions are strictly voluntary. To find local meetings, search online, use your telephone book, or visit the Al-Anon website at www.al-anon.alateen.org. The website also provides helpful information and video of members anonymously speaking about their experiences with the program. It also offers information on Alateen, the Twelve Step groups for teenagers who have a parent, stepparent, grandparent, sibling, or friend with an addiction problem.

Let's imagine for a moment what it is like to walk into an Al-Anon meeting for the first time. We might feel any number of ways, from terrified to mildly uncomfortable to annoyed that we're expected to go at all. In this moment, we can imagine how our alcoholic or addict feels going to his first AA or NA meeting. Rather than sitting in judgment of our addict, we're suddenly standing in his shoes. Everything looks different from this perspective, and we have empathy. *Wow, this is harder than I imagined.*

When we want to turn around and go home, we think of what we'd say to our addict. *Stick with it; it'll get easier.* So we stay. We've practiced ahead of time what we're going to say when we arrive. We walk up to someone who looks like they know what they're doing, stick out our hand, and say, "Hi, my name is (you give your first name only). This is my first Al-Anon meeting and, to tell you the truth, I'm really nervous." Just getting that out makes us feel better.

An Al-Anon member might greet you and say, "Welcome! My name is _____. Let me get you a newcomer's packet of information. The meeting is going to start in a few minutes. Would you like to sit next to me?"

When the meeting begins, the volunteer chairperson or another member reads the opening welcome, which offers an overview of the purpose of the program.

> We welcome you to this Al-Anon Family Group Meeting, and hope you will find in this fellowship the help and friendship we have been privileged to enjoy.
>
> We who live, or have lived, with the problem of alcoholism understand as perhaps few others can. We, too, were lonely and frustrated, but in Al-Anon we discover that no situation is really hopeless and that it is possible

for us to find contentment and even happiness, whether the alcoholic is still drinking or not.

We urge you to try our program. It has helped many of us find solutions that lead to serenity. So much depends on our own attitudes, and as we learn to place our problem in its true perspective, we find it loses its power to dominate our thoughts and our lives.

The family situation is bound to improve as we apply the Al-Anon ideas. Without such spiritual help living with an alcoholic is too much for most of us. Our thinking becomes distorted by trying to force solutions, and we become irritable and unreasonable without knowing it.

The Al-Anon program is based on the suggested Twelve Steps of Alcoholics Anonymous, which we try, little by little, one day at a time, to apply to our lives along with our slogans and the Serenity Prayer. The loving interchange of help among members and daily reading of Al-Anon literature thus make us ready to receive the priceless gift of serenity.

Al-Anon is an anonymous fellowship. Everything that is said here, in the group meeting and member to member, must be held in confidence. Only in this way can we feel free to say what is on our minds and in our hearts, for this is how we help one another in Al-Anon.[71]

Introductions are made, beginning with the chairperson. "Hi, my name is Jenna and this is my home group," followed by others saying things like, "Hi, I'm Bill, and this is my first time at this meeting," or "My name is Anne, and this is the first time I've attended Al-Anon." The group responds, "Hi Anne! Welcome." It may sound corny in theory, but in practice it creates a sense of warmth and belonging. When we share our names and welcome each other, we begin to connect.

Someone will send around a basket, and members throw in a dollar *if they so choose*. If addiction has damaged family finances, and every dollar is needed to buy milk or put gas in the car, no one expects a dollar in the basket. But, if you have it, it helps pay for the free literature, the coffee in the pot, and rent for the meeting space.

The type of meeting you are attending determines what happens next. If it's a speaker meeting, a member of Al-Anon gets up and tells his or her story. Everyone listens and, at the end, there may be time for questions or discussion. If it's a Step meeting, the group discusses one of the Twelve Steps. In discussion meetings, the chairperson or the group chooses one or two topics. "Today, we're going to discuss fear and the slogan, 'One day at a time,'" the chairperson might say.

Meetings end with the chairperson or another member reading the closing.

> In closing I would like to say that the opinions expressed here were strictly those of the person who gave them. Take what you liked and leave the rest.
>
> The things you heard were spoken in confidence and should be treated as confidential. Keep them within the walls of this room and the confines of your mind.
>
> A few special words to those of you who haven't been with us long. Whatever your problems there are those among us who have had them, too. If you try to keep an open mind you will find help. You will come to realize that there is no situation too difficult to be bettered and no un-happiness too great to be lessened.
>
> We aren't perfect. The welcome we give you may not show the warmth we have in our hearts for you. After a while, you'll discover that though you may not like all of us you'll love us in a very special way, the same way we al-ready love you.
>
> Talk to each other, reason things out with someone else but let there be no gossip or criticism of one another. Instead, let the understanding love and peace of the pro-gram grow in you one day at a time.[72]

Al-Anon sets a tone for congeniality and kindness, acceptance and warmth. We learn that when we change ourselves, magically it seems, the world around us changes. Helen Keller could have been speaking of the benefits of Al-Anon when she wrote, "Your success and happiness lies in you. Resolve to keep happy, and your joy and you shall form an invincible host against difficulties."

Alcoholics Anonymous and Other Twelve Step Meetings

From a little spot on the map in Ohio, Alcoholics Anonymous has spread around the globe, reaching more than 170 countries—each meeting autonomous, self-supporting, nonprofessional, and without anyone who leads or commands the activities of the group. It's supported by the dollar-in-a-basket contributions, thrown in by alcoholics who have it to spare.

AA spread throughout the world for one reason: it worked. No commercial interest built a chain of AA meetings, one on every street corner like Starbucks or McDonald's. Every meeting was started by one alcoholic talking to another and sustained through attracting others who want what they have. There are no promotions, fundraising campaigns, or sales pitches. But in any minute of any day, there are alcoholics and addicts in AA, NA, and other Twelve Step recovery groups in every imaginable place, drinking coffee, laughing, and working the Twelve Steps to stay sober another day.

Twelve Step recovery is at the heart of Structured Family Recovery's success and the success of addicted doctors in Physician Health Programs, but it is also true of the majority of alcohol and other drug treatment programs throughout the country. The application of the Twelve Steps in treatment began when Hazelden opened its doors in 1949. Ever since, treatment programs that do the best job of preparing alcoholics for Twelve Step recovery are the most desirable places to seek help. There are even Twelve Step immersion programs, such as The Retreat in Minnesota, that primarily establish a solid foundation in recovery based on the principles of Alcoholics Anonymous.

The structure of AA, NA, and Al-Anon meetings are just about identical. Opening and closing statements are a little bit different, but the Twelve Steps are the same. AA has speaker meetings, discussion groups, Big Book meetings, and Step meetings. There is a special designation for

AA and other Twelve Step meetings: *open* and *closed*. Anyone can attend open meetings. You don't have to be an alcoholic or addict. Closed meetings are only for people who identify as alcoholic or drug addicted. This provides a greater level of confidentiality for those suffering from a disease that is still stigmatized in our society. Anonymity also helps alcoholics and addicts put principles ahead of personalities.

For newly recovering alcoholics and addicts coming into AA, following a few guidelines can help build an effective program of recovery.

1. *Attend meetings regularly.* As mentioned earlier, it's often suggested that newcomers go to ninety meetings in ninety days. The obvious reason, of course, is the high relapse rate in the first three months. But frequency also creates familiarity and habit. Attending every day, the addict goes to a variety of meetings and chooses his favorite for a home group. He gets to know a variety of recovering people, which helps him find a sponsor. He begins feeling familiar and comfortable with the program. When walking through the doors of a meeting, there's nothing better than hearing, "Hey, Joe, good seeing you! How's it going?" As for habits, psychologists have found that regular folks need up to eighty-three days to develop a new habit. Addiction creates its own challenges, so ninety-in-ninety sounds more than reasonable.

2. *Choose a home group.* As in Al-Anon, this is the meeting the addict never misses. He sees his sponsor here, knows all the regular members, and volunteers for a service position. When he's sober long enough, he even chairs the meeting. This is just what the name implies: *home.* Walking into this room is so comfortable and friendly that the addict looks forward to it and relies on the people in this meeting more than anyone else. He laughs and jokes with them, but can also be dead serious about his recovery and his life. These are people who often become lifelong friends.

3. *Get a sponsor.* Sometimes alcoholics tell me they only need their families to help them stay sober. If a family alone couldn't keep the alcoholic sober before treatment, it isn't likely they can do it

after treatment. Nobody understands an alcoholic like another alcoholic. They can see through the baloney faster than anyone and speak knowledgeably from personal experience about drinking and recovery. As one fellow's sponsor told him, "I drank for twenty-five years, and I've been sober for twenty-five years. There's nothing I don't know about either one."

4. *Follow the directions.* As one old-timer put it, "Something amazing happens to alcoholics and addicts after they've had about one minute sober: they think they are recovery experts. Well, they're not. They are drinking experts." Twelve Step programs offer *suggestions* on how to stay sober. Alcoholics who follow these suggestions stay sober; those who don't are likely to start drinking or drugging again. There's nothing like a former relapser to tell a newcomer what doesn't work.

5. *You're not different.* Alcoholics and addicts suffer from "terminal uniqueness." A million sober alcoholics could line up to tell an alcoholic what works, and he'd probably think, "Well, maybe it works for all of you, but I'm different." Even some professionals buy into this notion, saying, "AA isn't right for everyone. Some people have personality and cultural differences." Alcoholics Anonymous meetings are in Zimbabwe, Laos, Mongolia, and Uganda, to name just a few. When we focus on the recovery principles that are at the heart of Twelve Step meetings, personality and cultural differences don't matter. We're all more alike than we are different. As alcoholics and addicts continue attending meetings, they begin to understand this.

6. *It works if you work it.* Talking to chronic relapsers over the years, I always hear the same thing. "AA didn't work for me." AA or NA won't work if the alcoholic or addict won't work the program. This is comparable to the student who flunks out of school, saying, "College just didn't work for me." Ask him, *Did you go to class? Read your textbooks? Study for exams?* You'll probably learn he didn't work for his college education. The same applies to recovery.

AA Comes to Kazakhstan

Jim Balmer, president of Dawn Farm, a residential treatment program in Michigan, told me a story that illustrates what life would be like without Alcoholics Anonymous. One day, he received a call from a Catholic mission organization working in Kazakhstan. "Would you be willing to come here and help us?" they asked. "Because the most frequent question we get is if we have anyone who knows anything about alcoholism."

Kazakhstan is a country in Central Asia that was once part of the Soviet Union. Jim described it as having a post-Soviet pall that made everything dreary and depressing. "People drank a lot of vodka," he said, "and it was cheaper than bottled water." As it turns out, the people of Kazakhstan drink more alcohol than any other country in Central Asia, and they're seventh in the world in vodka consumption. When Jim got that call, there were no AA meetings in Kazakhstan.

"Americans don't visit Kazakhstan very often, and my arrival created a flurry of invitations from universities and sanitariums," said Jim. "But I was most interested in a German priest who had a parish in Karaganda, Kazakhstan."

As it turned out, the priest had discovered a Russian translation of the Big Book of Alcoholics Anonymous and gathered about a half dozen drunks from his congregation. "I began meeting with these alcoholics, reading to them from the Big Book," he told Jim, "and they all got sober. So we kept reading." His group had grown to more than twenty sober men. He asked Jim if he would like to meet some of them.

Jim had an appointment with the staff of a hospital known for treating alcoholics. He decided to take one of the priest's success stories with him. Boris was two months sober and had been a patient at the hospital several times. When they arrived there, Jim said it reminded him of the "snake pit asylums" of nineteenth-century America.

"We walked into a room, and they had put out a big spread of food for us," he said, "and all the white coats were lined up to meet me." He was first introduced to the medical director, who began talking to him about treating alcoholics and addicts. At a certain point, Jim

continued

introduced him to Boris. "Boris is sober sixty days," he said. A commotion ensued as the medical director turned to Boris and began speaking with great animation. Puzzled, Jim asked the interpreter what was happening. As it turned out, the medical director, in his entire career of treating alcoholics, had never known anyone to stay sober that long. "I realized at that moment," said Jim, "what it was like to live in America before 1935."

In our own country, it is incumbent on us to use the best method of achieving and maintaining sobriety available, which are Twelve Step groups based on Alcoholics Anonymous. Addicts who want to access other programs that promote abstinence, through churches or other organizations, certainly can do so. But they are wise to always pair these other programs with meeting and sponsorship in Alcoholics Anonymous or other Twelve Step groups to ensure lasting sobriety. Structured Family Recovery is designed to help addicts and their families engage in Twelve Step recovery, because it changes lives. Nothing would have spread around the globe, as AA has done, if the program didn't work. It would have been swept into the dustbin of history long ago, like so many other failed endeavors.

Alex

Alex was twenty-six years old when he went to treatment for alcoholism. He didn't know anything about AA or recovery, but he went to a couple of meetings while in treatment. Arriving home, he learned his parents were attending Al-Anon. "Seeing my parents go to Al-Anon rocked my world. My dad was a very busy attorney, and for him to make time for those meetings *for me*, well, what could I do but go to AA?" Now many years sober, Alex thinks back on his first meeting out in the world.

"Although my first AA meeting was many years ago, I remember it quite clearly. I wasn't sure I was ready for sobriety, and I wasn't at all sure what my life would be like without alcohol. Fortunately, I had my family's support and decided to follow the recommendations of the treatment professionals.

"I had asked my counselor how many AA meetings he thought I should go to every week, hoping he'd go easy on me and perhaps recommend two or three. The counselor looked at me, and without answering my question, asked, 'How many days did you drink every week?'

"I was a daily drinker, and I took his point. The treatment team recommended I start out with ninety meetings in ninety days. It seemed a bit much, but then everyone thought my drinking was a bit much. So I decided to give it a try.

"I was discharged from treatment on a Monday morning and was home by lunchtime. The world already seemed like a different place without alcohol. I was nervous about going to AA that night. But truthfully, I was glad to get out of the house after dinner, if only to get a break from my family. Everyone was walking on eggshells with me back home.

"Since I'd been to AA in treatment, it wasn't totally foreign to me. But this meeting would be in my home neighborhood, and I'd be walking in alone. Would I see someone I knew? What would the people be like? Was I really going to sit around for an hour with a group of hometown rummies? The whole thing seemed surreal.

"The meeting was at a church a few miles from my home. It was early evening and already dark. But there were cars in the parking lot in the vicinity of the parish hall. So I figured I was in the right place. Two minutes before the appointed hour, I got out of my car and walked in the door.

"About a dozen people were meeting in one of the rooms that opened off a long hallway. It was a small meeting, an intimate group of friends who appeared to have nothing in common. That is, they were men and women of all ages and walks of life. I couldn't imagine them getting together under any other circumstance.

"When I walked into the room, I was greeted warmly. Needless to say, with such a small group, the newcomer stood out. They offered me a cup of coffee and pointed me toward an assortment of cookies on a side table. They were an affable bunch, and I could tell they were genuinely pleased to have me join them.

"I don't remember what was said during that meeting, but I remember the feelings their words imparted. First, there was kindness. They weren't roughnecks or holier-than-thou types. They were thoughtful in what they said and seemed to understand my discomfort. They immediately made me feel at ease, accepting me as one of the group.

"Second, I could feel their sympathy, and their precise knowledge of my situation. They understood me, because we suffered the same illness. Their knowledge didn't come from books or classes. They had lived through the madness, and now were living in the solution. Their personal experience, combined with compassion, made them ideal teachers, even though they didn't try to teach. Rather, they shared their experience, strength, and hope. It was a great comfort.

"Third, they had something I wanted or perhaps needed. They were content and good-humored. They seemed comfortable in their own skin. They believed in themselves and something greater, too, and whatever it was, it was working for them. They made me feel that I could have it, too—that it would be freely shared with me, along with the next cup of coffee. I was part of the club, and, as one of the older guys said, 'This club has the highest initiation fee in the world.'

"I understood their jokes, and they understood my fragility. They handled me with care. The hour went by quickly, and I was sorry our time together was done. I got a couple of names and phone numbers, along with tips for good meetings around town. But the most important thing I got out of my first meeting was a commitment in my own heart to show up again tomorrow."

The Sponsorship Relationship

Each of us needs someone in our Twelve Step program who can help us figure out how to navigate these new waters, someone who comes without emotional baggage and isn't related to us. We need someone who can impart wisdom, who understands our struggles because they've been there, too. That someone has worked all of the Twelve Steps and has a sponsor of his or her own.

An Al-Anon member wrote in *Forum Magazine* about her experience working with a sponsor.

> I was sitting there . . . with someone who knew who I was
> and accepted me for who I was. I felt connected to the

world in a completely new way. I no longer had to go it alone as I had done for so many years. To have the unconditional love from another human being without being judged, without feeling ashamed, was a great turning point for me in my recovery. I had been working long and hard, but always alone. Now I was connected. . . . The fear I lived with (because of my secrets) had changed to hope, because someone took the time to care. It gave me the courage to move forward in my recovery with confidence.[73]

The value of this type of relationship is being used to benefit people in multitudes of endeavors. In the business world, it's widely understood that having a sponsor can be the difference between success and failure. Those fast-tracking their careers have abandoned the hands-off mentor in favor of the dive-in-with-you sponsor who gives feedback even when it is hard to hear. In *Forbes*, Erica Dhawan, a globally recognized leadership expert, writes of her relationship with her first sponsor in business.

My sponsor and I weren't just the typical adviser-advisee partners; we became what I call "sparring partners." Every time we met, we had really important conversations that shifted the direction of my thinking through deep questioning. I asked her for help getting promotions, debated big decisions with her, and began to gain new opportunities just by the conversations she had with others when I wasn't in the room. Looking back, making the most of my first sponsor relationship changed my life.[74]

Sponsorship in Twelve Step programs is a prototype for how sponsors work most effectively. This isn't just a "figure it out yourself" relationship. Sponsorship is infused with the wisdom and practical knowledge that only comes with hard-won experience, nose-to-the-grindstone commitment, and, ultimately, success in working your own program. Sponsors don't step to the sideline, watch you fall, wait for you to pick yourself up, and by trial and error, hopefully, someday, figure it out. There's too much at stake. In business, it's a career; in recovery, it's a life.

But your Twelve Step sponsor is not a member of your SFR team and does not attend SFR meetings. Sponsors play a specific role in our recovery, and it must remain pure to preserve the integrity of AA, Al-Anon, and other Twelve Step groups. This doesn't mean, however, that your sponsor won't be immensely helpful to you in Structured Family Recovery and can't participate in an occasional SFR meeting for specific purposes, such as leading a discussion on a particular Step. But we need to carefully clarify the role of a sponsor.

Structured Family Recovery supports Twelve Step recovery not the other way around. What we learn and experience in our Twelve Step meetings, the guidance we receive from our sponsor, and what we read in the literature are what we bring back to our Structured Family Recovery meetings and teammates. It's a spiral that keeps moving us upward. The two complement each other, as long as we understand the boundaries.

All Twelve Step meetings make their purpose clear—what they do and don't do—to prevent recovery from morphing into something else that isn't part of their singleness of purpose and, as a result, losing its effectiveness. The AA preamble, which has been adopted by other recovery groups and is read at the beginning of every meeting, clearly states that a Twelve Step group is "not allied with any sect, denomination, political entity, organization, or institution; does not engage in any controversy, neither endorses or opposes any cause."[75] This includes treatment, intervention, therapy, psychology, and, yes, Structured Family Recovery. None of these things is under the auspices of Al-Anon or Alcoholics Anonymous, and we must not blur the lines. But it *doesn't* mean that we're not compatible.

Alcoholics Anonymous writes about sponsorship, which equally applies to other Twelve Step groups including Al-Anon.

> Whether you are a newcomer who is hesitant about "bothering" anyone, or a member who has been around for some time trying to go it alone, sponsorship is yours for the asking. We urge you: Do not delay. Alcoholics recovered in A.A. want to share what they have learned with other alcoholics. We know from experience that our own sobriety is greatly strengthened when we give it away!

Sponsorship can also mean the responsibility the group as a whole has for helping the newcomer. Today, more and more alcoholics arriving at their first A.A. meeting have had no prior contact with A.A. They have not telephoned a local A.A. intergroup or central office; no member has made a "Twelfth Step call" on them. So, especially for such newcomers, groups are recognizing the need to provide some form of sponsorship help. In many successful groups, sponsorship is one of the most important planned activities of the members.

Sponsorship responsibility is unwritten and informal, but it is a basic part of the A.A. approach to recovery from alcoholism through the Twelve Steps. Sponsorship can be a long-term relationship.[76]

It is of the utmost importance that you choose a successful group, or a group that is engaged in enthusiastic recovery, whether it's AA, NA, Al-Anon, or other Twelve Step programs. The key to success is the willingness of members to take the role of sponsorship seriously. If group members don't offer sponsorship, make working the Steps an essential part of recovery, or engage in service by helping the addict or family member, find another group. Remember, a group's lack of engagement is a reflection of its members, not of the Twelve Step program itself. Enthusiastic members make for enthusiastic recovery, which is contagious.

A great way to get a feeling about a group when you first attend is to tell people that you're new and then say, "I'd like to get some feedback on sponsorship, working the Steps, and service positions. I need to better understand what it means to work a program." This is an ideal way to "share" when you first start going to Twelve Step meetings, because it puts you in a position of listening and learning. Pouring out your troubles isn't your priority; learning to work a program is.

Following are some of the benefits of sponsorship in AA or Al-Anon, adapted from *Questions and Answers on Sponsorship.*

1. As a newcomer, there is one person who understands your situation and cares about you in a close, personal way.

2. You can turn to a sponsor, without embarrassment, when you have doubts, questions, and concerns about addiction and recovery.

3. A sponsor is a sympathetic friend who understands recovery when you need one most.

4. A sponsor introduces you to other people in recovery.

5. A sponsor models recovery by the example he or she sets.

6. A sponsor helps you build and work an effective and satisfying program of recovery.

7. A sponsor guides you as you work through the Twelve Steps.

8. A sponsor makes you aware of recovery literature, daily readers, and other publications.

9. A sponsor helps you, as a newcomer, understand the Twelve Traditions and how they preserve the integrity of Twelve Step programs.

10. A sponsor helps you comprehend the scope of the program, beyond the meetings and into your daily life.

11. A sponsor isn't there to criticize, but to support you in using Twelve Step principles as a way to work through problems constructively.

12. A sponsor never tries to impose his or her personal views on you, including religious or political, and does not offer professional services. The only role is to make suggestions based on what works in recovery.

13. A sponsor does not pretend to know all the answers or assume he or she is right all of the time. You do not have to agree with everything a sponsor says.

14. Sponsorship is about working Twelve Step programs and respecting the Twelve Traditions, not about personalities.[77]

Choosing a sponsor is an informal process with only a few guidelines: Choose a sponsor who has what you want, who has his or her own sponsor and has worked through all of the Twelve Steps, who has the time to give you what you need, who is sponsoring you for his own recovery not to take responsibility for yours, and who is of the same gender (those in the LGBTQ community may select sponsors of the opposite gender).

Select someone who demonstrates success in his or her own recovery program. "Stick with the winners," as they say in Twelve Step circles. We don't need someone like ourselves; we need someone who has what we are striving to be. It is one of the foibles of the newcomer to select someone who can't give what is needed, and this can be the start down the road to relapse.

A friend, Stefan, recently told me that when he joined AA, "I didn't know what I needed or who could help me." He asked a fellow who was working a dynamite recovery program to be his sponsor. "The only trouble was that he was very hands off. His philosophy was, 'Call me when you need me.'" Stefan's wife finally told him, after he'd been working with this sponsor for a time, that he didn't act much different than when he was drinking.

"At that moment, I realized I had selected a sponsor that played right into my character defects. I found someone who wouldn't challenge me to open up, because I didn't want to open up." Stefan selected a new sponsor, one who had a more regimented approach to the relationship. "With this fellow, I was forced to engage. After three months of working together, my wife remarked on how much I'd changed," he said. "She told me I exuded gratitude."

A husband in AA told me about his wife's foray into Al-Anon. "She selected a sponsor with two small children and one on the way," he said. She wasn't too excited about Al-Anon and found someone who didn't have much time to give. Once her sponsor's baby was born, they hardly got together anymore. His wife's progress in Al-Anon didn't match his progress in AA, causing marital strife. "Our relationship suffered more in early recovery than when I was drinking and drugging," he said. "We were talking about separation." They saw a marriage therapist who suggested his wife find a more hands-on Al-Anon sponsor. "That's probably the thing that saved our marriage," he said.

When engaged in Structured Family Recovery, we need to be clear with our Twelve Step sponsor about what we are doing as a recovering family. Make a distinct delineation between SFR meetings and our Twelve Step work. Explain how we depend on our sponsor to help us grow, gain wisdom, discuss topics, and make good personal recovery decisions, which we then bring back to our SFR meetings and share with our family recovery team. This in no way impedes on the traditions of Al-Anon, NA, or AA. The wisdom of the program has been shared with family and friends since its inception.

As we'll see in the following chapters, every SFR meeting has a topic that is relevant to Twelve Step recovery. We can bring that topic to our sponsor and our meetings, without bringing Structured Family Recovery into AA or Al-Anon groups. We do not talk about outside professional services, literature, or programs. We do not adulterate Twelve Step recovery meetings with other influences or topics that aren't central to their mission. But all of our topics in Structured Family Recovery are true to Twelve Step recovery. There is no conflict.

Alcoholics Anonymous explains why this is so important. "This we owe to A.A.'s future: To place our common welfare first; to keep our fellowship united. For on A.A. unity depend our lives, and the lives of those to come."[78] We can say the same for all Twelve Step groups.

When we choose a sponsor, we need to explain that our family is engaged in Structured Family Recovery. Our sponsor may not know what that is, so it is incumbent on us to explain. We want our sponsor to know what we are doing to support our recovery and that we understand the boundaries between our SFR meetings and our Twelve Step meetings.

Alcoholics Anonymous co-founder Dr. Bob Smith said, "I spend a great deal of time passing on what I learned to others who want and need it badly." Here are four reasons Dr. Bob gave for sponsoring others in the program. They give us insight as to why people continue to sponsor others throughout all Twelve Step groups.

1. Sense of duty.

2. It is a pleasure.

3. Because in doing so I am paying my debt to the man who took time to pass it on to me.

4. Because every time I do it I take out a little more insurance for myself against a possible slip.[79]

All sponsors lead by example, passing on the pleasures of involvement in Twelve Step recovery. Our sponsors demonstrate that service is our most important spiritual activity. Sponsorship is too important to be left to chance, most recovering people will say, so choosing Twelve Step meetings that actively promote sponsorship is always in one's favor. Twelve Step recovery is simple, but it may not seem that way at first. Our sponsor introduces us to working a program and how to "Keep it simple."

• • •

13

Putting Structured Family Recovery into Place

It's the steps we decide to take that make a difference, not what we think or say. Taking action is the beginning of change. As Napoleon Hill, one of the greatest writers on success, said, "Do not wait; the time will never be 'just right.' Start where you stand, and work with whatever tools you may have at your command and better tools will be found as you go along."

The next two chapters present the information you will need to put Structured Family Recovery into practice. From this point forward, the book becomes a guide for the SFR team. Each new topic is introduced with bold headings, which are numbered, so information is easily accessible and quick to reference. You will encounter some repetition along the way because some points are worth repeating.

1. Family Members Get Underway First. We cannot say it too often: Begin with family members first. It's imperative that by the time you invite the alcoholic to join the team, you can lead by example. You can only do so if you've begun Structured Family Recovery yourselves. Everyone on the team should be able to say they've been to at least one Al-Anon or other Twelve Step family meeting before your addicted loved one is onboard. You need to be comfortable with the format of SFR meetings so the meetings run smoothly. If your team appears disorganized, unsure, or confused, you will send the wrong message to the addict. It isn't necessary, or even possible, to be an expert. You can say to him, "We're all learning about recovery together." But do not disregard team cohesiveness and a certain comfort with SFR meetings. Both create confidence, and your addict will sense it.

2. Preparation. The best way to prepare for Structured Family Recovery is for everyone on the team to read this book. It's designed to give you a solid knowledge base about the disease of addiction, how it affects everyone close to the addicted person, and what it takes to heal the family and create lasting sobriety. It provides a detailed guide that carries you through the earliest days of Structured Family Recovery, to the time the entire team feels a sense of accomplishment in recovery. By following the guidelines closely and consistently, change will happen.

Another reason for reading this book is that gaining a broader understanding of the nature of addiction creates empathy. Anger is no longer a family's modus operandi. Embracing recovery means more than whether the addict drinks or uses other drugs. It's a spiritual journey a family takes together for the betterment of all. It's this higher calling that brings families together. The commitment your family makes in the beginning may be primarily intellectual, mainly in the head, but it eventually travels down to the heart. This is where commitment becomes enduring.

Of course, getting every family team member to read a book can feel like herding cats. Some zip right through it, and others drag their feet or say they can't find the time. Solve this problem before it happens. Employ the idea of tiny tasks. Ask everyone to read for fifteen minutes before going to sleep at night. Let's keep it simple. By asking some people to read an entire book, you're likely to elicit negative reactions, such as, "That sounds too hard. It'll be long and boring. When will I ever fit the time into my schedule?" Make it simple from the start. If not at bedtime, what's their recovery trigger for reading the book a few minutes a day?

It's not unusual for someone in the family to find reading difficult. Think of ways to help that person get the information. For instance, several team members can coordinate a series of short phone calls to provide brief overviews of particular chapters throughout the book. Or sit down and read the book together. With team members taking turns to make these calls, it's a great opportunity to open up discussion and begin positive recovery partnerships.

If you aren't working with an SFR counselor, it is imperative that everyone on the team reads this book. Self-navigating through Structured Family Recovery requires thoroughness and preparation.

3. Select an SFR Counselor or a Chairperson. Working with an SFR counselor, at least initially, will make this startup phase an easier and smoother experience for all. Alcoholics and addicts get a tremendous amount of information while in treatment, whereas families are left mostly in the dark. An SFR counselor is a guide who has all the skills and knowledge a family needs. It's the most powerful and affordable way for a team to get the equivalent of a family treatment program. Use the resource section of this book to find contact information for certified Structured Family Recovery counselors. If your loved one is still drinking and drugging, you'll want to work with an SFR counselor who is also a certified clinical interventionist.

When you are not planning to work with an SFR counselor, select a member of your team to act as the meeting chairperson. Choose someone who is highly respected by everyone on the team, especially the addict. This is a person nobody wants to disappoint and who has the least amount of emotional baggage. Think of the chairperson as the team diplomat. Most families know right away who fits this role. The chairperson is someone who has a cool head and the ability to gently keep people on track. When no one team member fits the role of chairperson, you might consider two people who together meet the criteria to be co-chairs. If even this doesn't work, it may be a sign that family relationships have deteriorated to a point where there is a significant breakdown of mutual respect. In this case, when at all possible, work with an SFR counselor, and if that's not possible, with a local therapist who specializes in addiction and the family, and who is personally familiar with the Twelve Steps, so you can work through the conflicts until there is some cohesion and commitment to working together for recovery.

It's helpful to select a team chairperson even when you are working with an SFR counselor. The two work in tandem, which greatly benefits the family over time. If a team eventually decides to begin working with the SFR counselor on a bi-monthly basis rather than weekly, the chairperson moderates the off-week meetings. When a family team feels working with a professional is no longer necessary, the chairperson takes the role of moderator.

4. Select a Team Secretary. This is the team detail person. The position can rotate among team members, including the addict. It's beneficial for everyone to take a turn, since service positions cultivate a greater sense of team involvement. The secretary is responsible for scheduling weekly meetings, setting up conference calls, and taking the minutes at each meeting. The minutes are a brief overview of the following:

- Names of those who attended and who was absent
- Group decisions
- Goals set for the following week
- Team assignments

The secretary emails the minutes to each team member as well as the SFR counselor, if you are working with one. If someone doesn't have email, fax or mail a copy of the minutes. Your secretary may decide to delegate some of these responsibilities among different team members on a rotating basis.

5. Review the SFR Meeting Format. The meeting format is straightforward and simple to follow. It begins with a team member reading the SFR Meeting Opening Statement, which is a reminder of group expectations (see part III). Then a member reads from a recovery daily reader, having chosen a topic that will correspond to the meeting topic. Readings rotate among team members weekly.

Each meeting is divided into the following segments.

- *Report, Discuss, Plan.* Team members evaluate their recovery program, including progress, blocks, and goals for the week to come.
- *Learn Something New.* Discussion topics are targeted at specific stages of recovery to facilitate advancement and increase satisfaction in the recovery process.

- *Step Work.* The group participates in a thought-provoking insight into one of the Twelve Steps.

- *Working a Recovery Program.* Topics supporting recovery such as understanding emotional sobriety, returning to integrity, kindness, and more are discussed.

- *Assignments.* Team members are given simple assignments that prompt significant experiences.

Meetings are divided into four quarters, with twelve weeks of meetings per quarter. Meetings are closed by reading the SFR closing statement. Everything you need to guide you through the entire process is included in part III of this book.

6. Use Checklists. Checklists are both simple and powerful. They reduce complexity into small steps and then remind us exactly of what we need to do. In an essay on human fallibility, philosophers Samuel Gorovitz and Alasdair MacIntyre identify two reasons why we fail when we are capable of success. First is ignorance. We simply don't have the required knowledge to do the job. Second is ineptitude. We have the knowledge but apply it incorrectly.[80]

Dr. Atul Gawande, an American surgeon and expert on optimizing health care systems, writes in his book *The Checklist Manifesto,* "Checklists seem to provide protection against such failures. They remind us of the minimum necessary steps and make them explicit. They not only offer the possibility of verification but also instill a kind of discipline of higher performance."[81] He goes on to say that bad checklists are imprecise and too long, making them impractical. He recommends checklists that are precise, covering the most important steps without trying to spell out everything. The best checklists are quick and simple to use. Once again, we see simplicity touted as a precursor to success.

There are two types of checklists. First there is the "Do–Confirm" checklist. Once a task is completed, you reference the checklist to determine if you did everything properly. This is a good choice when you are well practiced at a task. The second is the "Read–Do" checklist. This walks you through the essential steps of an endeavor, checking each item off as you go. For beginners, or when engaging in complex activities, this is particularly helpful. Structured Family Recovery uses the Read–Do checklist.

Dr. Gawande found that physicians, on average, take up to seventeen years to adopt new treatments in their practices. Not because of unwillingness, but because "the necessary knowledge has not been translated into a simple, usable, and systematic form . . . distilling the information into its practical essence." I think we can say the same is true for addicts and their families. When it comes to engaging in recovery and achieving lasting sobriety, nobody has ever before translated family recovery into a simple, usable, and systematic form that makes it understandable and doable. Structured Family Recovery does exactly that.

Aviation specialists who create checklists for pilots have refined lists into the most usable form. The recommended number of items on a checklist is five to nine. By adding more, we overtax the limits of our working memory. Language is simple and explicit. They fit on one page. Colors or patterns are a distraction. All of these suggestions are incorporated into SFR checklists.

Dr. Gawande, speaking of the power of using checklists in *The Checklist Manifesto,* says, "Discipline is hard—harder than trustworthiness and skill and perhaps even selflessness. We are by nature flawed and inconsistent creatures. We can't even keep from snacking between meals. We are not built for discipline. We are built for novelty and excitement, not for careful attention to detail. Discipline is something we have to work at." Checklists, he says, can make discipline a norm, something reliable we can depend on. (SFR checklists are located in part IV of this book: Tools, Checklists, and Resources.)

7. Learn to Be Optimistic. After decades of research on learned helplessness and countless peer reviews, Dr. Martin Seligman began studying ways we can enlarge our personal control. He learned that the epidemic of depression that we're facing is linked to three forces. The first is what he calls the *disorder of the "I."* We've made a shift to a culture of individualism, he says, leading people to believe they are the center of the world, and this causes great difficulties in coping with a lack of success.

Dr. Seligman explains further in his book *Learned Optimism: How to Change Your Mind and Your Life,* "Individual failure used to be buffered by the second force, the large 'we.' When our grandparents failed, they had comfortable spiritual furniture to rest in. They had for the most part, their relationship with God, their relationship to a nation they loved, their relationship to a community and a large extended family. . . . [These] have all eroded in the last forty years, and the spiritual furniture that we used to sit in has become threadbare."[82]

The third force, Dr. Seligman says, is a manifestation of the self-esteem movement. Teaching unwarrantedly high self-esteem, as it turns out, causes problems, including people with mean streaks. When confronted with the real world and discovering they aren't as special as they were taught to believe, people lash out. "Boosting self-esteem does not curb depression," according to Dr. Seligman, but instead, "depression and violence both come from this misbegotten concern: how our young people feel about themselves more highly than how we value how well they are doing in the world."

Repeatedly, in my work with alcoholics, addicts, and their families, I have seen depression dissipate when people begin actively working Twelve Step programs of recovery. Is it any wonder? By doing so, we replace the big "I" with the "we." Through involvement in the recovery community and by working the Twelve Steps, we come into possession of comfortable spiritual furniture. The philosophy of AA, NA, and Al-Anon works quite opposite from the self-esteem movement. *If you're going to talk the talk, you better walk the walk.* Twelve Step recovery is all about taking action. Actions change how we feel. Actions create self-worth. Action builds community. Action heals families.

Dr. Seligman notes, ". . . there are grave moral dangers to making an entire generation dependent on drugs for their mood and their productivity," and there are not enough good therapists to treat everyone. When treating alcoholics and addicts, we must remember that addiction is not a mental illness or a psychiatric issue. One reason it may have been lumped into the behavioral health category with psychiatric disorders is out of convenience for insurance and health care providers. The result, in some cases, is the idea that addicts might need to be patients for life.

We have to ask where the resources will come from and what will the quality of life be for people who become dependent on the health care system for treating their addiction rather than learning self-care through a rigorous recovery plan.

The biomedical approach, according to Dr. Seligman, ". . . makes patients out of essentially normal people and makes them dependent on outside forces—pills dispensed by a benevolent physician." It's to be noted that while medications are sometimes needed, there is a growing concern about diagnostic inflation and the resulting overuse of medications. The symptoms of addiction often mimic psychiatric disorders, so in most cases when a mental health problem didn't precede addiction, we must wait until the newly recovering person has time in recovery before we can reliably assess whether the person has a co-occurring disorder and whether a medication is necessary or is the best course of treatment.

A mother called me the other day saying her eighteen-year-old son was just released from treatment on multiple medications. "His father and I were very upset about this," she said. "We didn't want him relying on pills as a recovery from his addiction to pills." Expressing their concerns to the staff of the treatment center, the parents were told, "We can't give your son the treatment he needs because your insurance provider cut off reimbursement. So we're putting him on medications instead."

But this mother's optimism wouldn't let her give up. She knew she could do better for her son. That she had no extra money to spend didn't stop her. She and I together made a decision: Let's not professionalize the problem. Instead, we contacted a young man, age twenty-three, who works a dynamic program of recovery in AA and asked him if he would take this boy to his first meeting. He readily agreed and picked him up for an eight o'clock meeting that night. Since that day forward, the eighteen-year-old has gone to meetings, and the young man from AA who took him to his first meeting is now his sponsor. It all started with a mom who was optimistic enough to keep trying.

Dr. Seligman's research shows that optimism is one of the best predictors of success. Even when optimists fail, they pick themselves up and try again. Optimism is preventive for depression and anxiety. It also improves health. Our immune systems work better when we're optimistic. Pessimists fail more often and are more likely to quit when they do. They are also less healthy.

Dr. Seligman's research shows that, similar to learned helplessness, we are capable of learning to be optimistic, which he teaches in his book on the subject. It's my belief that learned optimism is also a side effect of working Twelve Step programs. Recovering people are optimistic people. It makes sense; they've risen from the depths of despair to reclaim their lives. As a recovering friend of mine says, "It's a beautiful thing."

Family members and alcoholics do well to take a good look at themselves and ask, "Am I a pessimist or an optimist?" If we see the world through the lens of negativity, we will find ourselves on more sinking ships than our optimistic compatriots who are happily sailing past us. Structured Family Recovery creates success by doing what we know works. But it also requires that you head into it with enough optimism— even if you are committed to learn it along the way—that you don't sink the ship.

Action Speaks Loudest

With our first SFR meeting, we take an action that lays the groundwork for family recovery. The structure we lay down now is particularly important for setting us on the right path. We build a recovery program by working a recovery program. We jump in, exactly like our addict, sometimes kicking and screaming, but ultimately, on faith.

Recovery is a learning process. Growth often takes struggle, but it is struggle that leads to satisfaction. Every moment of resistance, doubt, questioning, and resentment that we experience most assuredly coordinates with some struggle our addict is having. It's a marvelous recipe for empathy.

Knowing that it is behavior that creates change, we don't need to rely on our thinking or our feelings but, rather, on moving our feet. It is perfectly acceptable, even normal, to feel reluctance as long as it doesn't stop us from taking our first small step and the one after. Feelings adapt themselves to what we *do*, which is why what we do is so consequential. Like the addict, the world around us changes as we change ourselves.

Before you schedule your first meeting everyone must have a clear understanding that we're talking about a disease. This is the time for us to test ourselves: *Do I really believe addiction is a disease?* Accepting that this is an inherited disease is the beginning of letting go of anger. When we think of it as nothing more than behaving badly, that addicts are just enjoying themselves by getting high, anger grows.

A friend of mine, a former heroin addict with decades of abstinence-based recovery in AA, said the following when I asked him what he thought families most needed to know. "They really, really need to understand it's a disease. Regardless of how their alcoholic or addict behaves, at the very root, they wake up every morning terrified. They live in a constant state of dread. They hate their lives. They see it as nothing more than overcoming one obstacle after another."

Kevin McCauley, in his video *Pleasure Unwoven,* says that when people say they are craving chocolate, they mean they really want chocolate a lot. "Craving for an addict," he explains, "is an intense emotional obsessive experience. The addict wants to think about other things, but his brain is constantly bringing him back to the drug. The addict is up in the middle of the night, can't sleep, his pulse is at 120, and he's thinking over and over again, 'Just one more time.' That's craving, and make no mistake, that is genuine suffering."[83]

The brain is tricked into believing that alcohol or other drugs, above everything else, is the most important thing for survival. To the brain, the drug and survival become indistinguishable. As McCauley makes clear, addicts' behavior can be very bad, but bad acts do not equal bad actors. The degradation of behavior is symptomatic of the disease's disruption of the brain.

With that understanding as our foundation, we are prepared to venture into our first SFR meeting with more confidence and self-possession.

Schedule Your First SFR Meeting

Don't let perfectionism hold you back. Just do it. You're going to be feeling your way along; that's how we learn. Just get a few basics in place: date, time, and who will set up the conference call. Does everyone have a copy of this book to follow? Have they read the book, or at least most of it? If so, get started, and you'll figure out what else you need along the way. Remember, some people might need to experience an SFR meeting before they're motivated to finish the book.

If you're working with an SFR counselor, you'll have a guide. That makes it easier to get started. If not, the team chooses a chairperson using the guidelines already covered. Also, select a team secretary, somebody who likes details. Turn to the first meeting of the first quarter (see Part III) and read over the agenda. Following are some helpful tips.

1. *Materials for Structured Family Recovery.* There are a few things you'll need for SFR meetings. Everyone needs a Twelve Step daily reader. You can buy these at any AA or Al-Anon meeting and at some bookstores. For Al-Anon, *Courage to Change: One Day at a Time in Al-Anon II* is a good choice. In AA, people tend to like *Daily Reflections.* There are many others available. Hazelden publishes an entire line of recovery daily readers. Also, pick up a copy of a book about the Twelve Steps. For AA, the classic text is *Twelve Steps and Twelve Traditions,* informally called the Twelve and Twelve. For Al-Anon, it's *Al-Anon's Twelve Steps and Twelve Traditions.* The addict will also have a copy of *Alcoholics Anonymous,* otherwise known as the Big Book, or *Narcotics Anonymous*—the basic text of NA. If families want to understand AA and NA recovery, these are great books to read. There are a couple of chapters written specifically for families. Keep in mind, the Big Book was written at a time when only a handful of women were members of AA, so the language sounds dated. Make the necessary adjustments in your own head; the message is still as powerful as it was the day it was written. There are other options listed in the resource section in the back of this book. Have a spiral notebook and a pen available. I suggest keeping everything together, in a bag or drawer, so the materials are always easily accessible.

2. *SFR Meeting Opening Statement.* At the beginning of every SFR meeting, begin by reading the SFR Meeting Opening Statement. Ask a different team member to read it each week. This reminds

us of our group expectations, so we all stay on the same page. Group expectations are about mutual respect, trustworthiness, and safety.

3. *Weekly Topic and Daily Reading.* Next, the chairperson announces the topic and introduces the team member who will give the reading. For example, the chairperson could say something like, "Our topic and focus for the week is honesty. Let's see what the program says about honesty in recovery. Peg is going to share an Al-Anon reading with the group." Peg might then use the index in *Courage to Change* and select one of the six readings on honesty, such as the reading on page 175, and share it with the group. "The courage to be honest with ourselves is one quality we can cultivate to help our spiritual growth." When Peg finishes the reading, the chairperson then would typically ask everyone in the group to share their thoughts about it. After this, the chairperson might go on to say, "We alternate our readings between Al-Anon and AA every week. Next week, Tommy is reading from AA's *Daily Reflections.* Looking ahead, I see our topic for next week is 'self-pity.' So Tommy will find a reading on this topic to share with us. Thanks."

4. *Check-in Using the Report, Discuss, Plan Questions.* After the daily reading, we begin our meetings by asking ourselves the Report, Discuss, Plan questions (available in part III) and sharing our answers with the group. These questions help us verbalize to ourselves and others just where we are along the recovery continuum, giving ourselves an opportunity to ask for help or guidance, and then planning our recovery goals for the upcoming week. This is a practical step with a spiritual component. We set up accountability for ourselves, but with the understanding that we are striving for progress not perfection. It isn't about who's winning the race, it's about taking this journey together, learning, sharing, falling, and picking ourselves up. We are not going to do this perfectly, but if we take the next right step, we put trustworthiness into action. We work to support our addict's recovery and suc-

cessful sobriety, but we end up with a family knitting itself back together again.

5. *Report.* "What went well in my recovery this past week? What could be improved? Do I want feedback?" This is a practice of spiritual honesty. "What did I do last week? Was it what I'd planned to do? Do I need to hear from others?" This begins a dramatic departure from the often deteriorated spiritual condition of most addicted families. The unspoken rules are don't talk, don't trust, don't feel. We may not know the rules are in place, but we obey them. We've been silent or explosive. Our feelings are often restricted to fear, anger, resentment, or numbness. But now we're asked to venture onto the precipice of trust. If I tell you, will I be safe? Can I fall down and know you will extend your hand in solidarity? Can I ask for help and be uplifted? Can I share my triumphs and will you rejoice? *If I help you pick up your pieces, will you help me gather mine?* We create safety by practicing this Twelve Step spiritual principle: I share my experience, strength, and hope, and allow you to do the same. When I ask for feedback, you won't tell me what I need to do, but instead share what works for you or that you are having the same problem or you heard someone say something helpful in a Twelve Step meeting. We don't tell—we share. It requires wholehearted listening and coming to a place of empathy before we speak.

6. *Discuss.* "What insights did I gain from my Twelve Step experiences? From last week's SFR assignment?" When we first begin working a program in Al-Anon, AA, or other Twelve Step programs, we don't even know what Twelve Step experiences we're looking for. It helps to remember that Twelve Step programs are built around action and new behaviors. We *go* to a meeting, we *share* in a meeting, we *call* our sponsor, we *read* from our daily reader, we *work* the Twelve Steps, and we *carry out* our weekly SFR assignment. These activities lead to insights and recovery ways of thinking. When we share in SFR meetings, we multiply our insights among the people in our group. When everyone

shares, we have a sundry of insights reverberating through our collective recovery. We strengthen, gain, and delight in insights that everyone shares. We create recovery curiosity.

7. *Plan.* "What new recovery behaviors will I practice this upcoming week?" For example, "I will contact my accountability partner _____ times this week." As the well-worn axiom warns: fail to plan, plan to fail. When we create a simple, doable plan for our recovery for the next week, we want to be specific. What will help me activate my plan for the upcoming week? Remember the concept of simple tasks and triggers. Am I overcomplicating? Do I have a recovery trigger for my plan? How do I make myself accountable? Who is my accountability partner (see below)? Will I contact that partner daily? If not, how often?

8. *Accountability Partner.* Until you have a Twelve Step sponsor, select a member of your SFR team as your accountability partner. This is the person you will call during the week to report on your recovery progress. For example, "I have trouble keeping my commitment to attend meetings, so I will call you before and after each meeting." We all do much better when we promise to be honest with another human being. It gives us a heightened sense of accountability for ourselves when we are accountable to another. Accountability is about working together, being open and honest, staying focused on our goal, and creating trustworthiness. Accountability increases our sense of belonging. When I belong to you, and you to me, we are accountable to one another. Serving as an accountability partner comes with its own set of expectations. I must be accountable before I can talk to you about your accountability. I must create a safe place for you. I must make myself available to you. Each person on the SFR team can act as an accountability partner, working with one teammate at a time. Avoid one or two people taking on this responsibility for the entire SFR team. Keep it simple.

9. *Presenting New Ideas.* Each SFR meeting presents fresh ideas supporting our meeting topics.

a) *Learning Something New* offers information from any number of professional fields that support the principles of Twelve Step recovery. It's helpful to see how these fundamentals work for people in other endeavors.

b) *Step Work* offers a simple idea about one of the Twelve Steps that will offer a new insight. We will cover all Twelve Steps over the course of the four quarters of Structured Family Recovery.

c) *Working a Recovery Program* offers ideas that bolster a more accurate and deeper understanding of what it means to work a program of recovery. The SFR counselor or the team chairperson will ask different team members to read, stopping to discuss each idea before going on to the next. These ideas can fuel thoughts for what team members want to talk about in their Twelve Step meetings or with their sponsors.

d) *Assignments* offer a simple action to take in the upcoming week to bolster recovery progress.

10. *Closing.* We close each meeting with the Promises from Alcoholics Anonymous (see the resources in part IV of this book). It reminds us of what we can achieve working our recovery programs in AA, NA, and Al-Anon.

Create an SFR Recovery Plan

Our Recovery Plans incorporate the Eight Essential Elements, a Relapse Agreement, and a Rapid Relapse Response (see the resource section). All team members create individual recovery plans, asking other team members for feedback. Our plans frame the actions we will take to support lasting sobriety, creating accountability for ourselves. Recovery plans, most importantly, keep everyone in a forward motion, avoiding complacency. Steve Hanna, a Structured Family Recovery counselor with twenty-three years of working with families and addiction, explains:

Complacency is a symptom of the disease of addiction. Defined as a "feeling of quiet pleasure or security that occurs while we are unaware of some potential danger," it's a place we rest between times of crisis. It is not our fault when we slip into recovery complacency, but it is our responsibility to listen to others who recognize that it's happening to us and accept help to pull ourselves out of it.

Responsibility means changing behaviors to free ourselves from the "crisis-complacency" roller coaster ride, which is a reaction to the outside world. Recovery requires consistency in behaviors, which is based upon decisions we make for ourselves guided by the Twelve Steps.

We can't *think* our way out of problems we *behaved* our way into. If change were easy, we wouldn't need help. But change isn't easy. We need help admitting we need help. We need help asking for help. We need help to act on the good suggestions we're given. In SFR, we learn to practice new recovery behaviors while depending upon help and guidance from our team accountability partner and Twelve Step sponsor. In doing so, we practice the "we" of the program.

Begin working on Recovery Plans only after your alcoholic or addict has joined the SFR team. If family members write their Recovery Plans before the addict is onboard, he may feel like the odd man out. When the team is telling the addict to write a Recovery Plan—rather than working on Recovery Plans with him—it gives the impression that the team is telling the addict what to do, leading to resistance or resentment. But when everyone comes together, it's an experience of cooperation and partnership. We ask each other for help, bounce ideas off one another, and work together to individually come up with the best possible plans. The influence of the social group, our family, comes to bear on the desire to do this well. We foster cooperation not coercion.

It is easiest to create our SFR recovery plans while working with an SFR counselor as a guide who can offer insights and directions. If you are unable to work with an SFR counselor even temporarily, until you finish your plans, then begin working on recovery plans only after everyone has a Twelve Step sponsor. A sponsor can't tell you what to put in your plan but can offer plenty of recovery wisdom.

Each SFR Recovery Plan includes a Relapse Agreement (see resource section). Before crisis happens, we decide on our course of action. Family members ask the addict, "What do you want us to do if you have a slip?" We don't expect relapse to ever happen, but we want to be prepared. Again, this is where an SFR counselor can come in handy. If the addict gives an insufficient response to the question of relapse, such as, "I just don't want you talking behind my back," the SFR counselor can guide the process until a first-rate Relapse Agreement is crafted. If working without an SFR counselor, follow the suggestions closely.

In each Relapse Agreement, we're asked to identify positive consequences for recovery behaviors and negative consequences for addiction behaviors. Team involvement is vital. First, each team member comes up with consequences for him- or herself linked to both recovery and relapse. Team members may also have positive and negative consequences to add to the plan.

For instance, Chris, a newly recovering alcoholic, overlooked negative consequences related to his wife, Paulette, and their children if he began drinking again. The team chairperson brought this to his attention by saying, "Chris, I think you and Paulette need to do one more thing together. I think the two of you need to work out a way to prevent addiction from hurting your children again. I don't think anyone wants to see addiction back in your home with your kids. Sober, you're the best dad. But if you stop working your program and relapse, it's my suggestion that you take yourself out of the home until the disease is back in remission."

Chris might readily agree or need additional time to think about it. It's okay to give him time to think. Working a program of recovery, he can bring this to his sponsor and talk about it in his Twelve Step group. He's likely to come to a good decision. If he doesn't, however, then his wife needs to step up and say, "I understand why this is a struggle for you, Chris. You love the kids and our home. While I don't expect you to relapse, I also must tell you that I cannot let the disease live in our house. It's not a question of my love for you, it's about this disease and how harmful it is to the kids. This is my bottom line: no addiction in the house ever again. By working together in recovery—and I'm dedicated to that—we never need to see that day."

Once your alcoholic has attended his first SFR meeting, it's time for everyone to begin working on their Recovery Plans. Here are a few tips:

- Ask for team feedback.
- Work out answers for each of the Eight Essential Elements.
- Have each team member read his or her completed plan to the team.
- Provide copies of everyone's signed SFR Recovery Plan to your team chairperson and SFR counselor, if you are using one.

Our Recovery Plans are sacred promises to ourselves and everyone on our family team. We are pledging to each other that we are committed to recovery and family healing. We inform each other of the specific steps we're taking and how we want to be helped if we're in trouble. It's a simple and straightforward process, resulting in an effective and possibly lifesaving plan.

In the words of Tom Landry, ranked as one of the most innovative coaches in National Football League history, "I don't believe in team motivation. I believe in getting a team prepared so it knows it will have the necessary confidence when it steps on a field and be prepared to play a good game."[84]

Don't Drop Bombs

Living in a family with addiction, we adjust and readjust to the ongoing, worsening problem of addiction, making what is abnormal feel more normal. That's why families can put up with behaviors today that five or ten years ago they'd have said they would never tolerate. We become somewhat immune to crisis. The little troubles that used to get us excited are brushed away without much thought. It now takes crisis on a much grander scale to get us geared up for action. I've worked with families that treated overdose or driving drunk with kids in the car as business as usual. Of course, they would bemoan the general terribleness of it all, but their actions didn't match their words.

It's a way we manage to survive when living in a chronically bad situation. What it can do to us, however, is increase our tolerance to emotional experiences, dulling our connections to normality. As a result, we need more and more drama in our emotional lives. We could even say that we get "hooked" on crisis. It feels exciting and thoroughly engaging. Crisis may be toxic, but it's intoxicating.

This hyper-emotionality, which happens to at least some members of most families where there is addiction, can challenge our progress in recovery. Like the addict chasing the high, family members' brains, accustomed to the excitement of tumultuousness, can at first find recovery lackluster. "This is boring!" But it's not recovery that is boring—or we wouldn't see the huge numbers of people sticking with it—it is our brains needing time to reset. We cannot yet experience the pleasure of a nonchaotic, non-crisis-filled life. So, in the earliest stages of recovery, we often relapse by throwing "bombs" in the middle of the recovery process.

In Structured Family Recovery, we set up a system that helps prevent team members from relapsing in this way. It's called the "Red Light, Yellow Light, Green Light" method of decision making. There are two basic rules.

The first rule is: We do not take it on ourselves to make individual decisions that affect the entire group. We do not surprise our teammates during an SFR meeting with a revelation that has not been previously discussed with appropriate team members *before the meeting*. We can do damage by catching others off guard, creating distrust of the group process.

The second rule is: If we're in conflict with a family member, we need to do an inventory of our own motives with our Twelve Step sponsor. "What's going on with *me*? Did I have a role in causing it or making it worse?" A sponsor assists us in working through angers and resentments that block our peace of mind.

To help sort out what concerns are appropriate for SFR meetings, ask, "Is this concern directly or indirectly related to relapse warning signs or symptoms?" If it is, it's probably within the realm of Structured Family Recovery. If it isn't, then it is likely a problem that needs to be solved elsewhere. But it's not always perfectly clear, so use the following steps to make decisions.

"Red Light" means that, even if the concern is legitimate, it isn't appropriate to bring to our SFR meeting. For Structured Family Recovery to be effective, we must be clear about its purpose—supporting family recovery and lasting sobriety—and what is beyond its domain. Sometimes, the answer isn't always clear, but by getting feedback from appropriate people, we can make the best decision *together.*

LeRoy wanted to use SFR meetings to talk about finances and debt incurred by his wife during her addiction. After all, the topic is related to the consequences of his wife's drug use. But credit counseling isn't what we do in Structured Family Recovery, so what's the right decision here? The SFR counselor or chairperson decided that making this a topic for a meeting wasn't appropriate. It was about looking to the past and not the future. There were no good reasons or benefits for the SFR team to discuss it. What could the group do about it now? So they gave it a "Red Light" and suggested LeRoy work with a financial expert instead.

When LeRoy talked it over with his Al-Anon sponsor, he discovered that his desire to bring this matter up to the SFR team was partially fueled by his anger and wanting to make his wife accountable. Using the Twelve Step principles, he was able to see his own part in the financial crisis: He ignored the addiction, he abdicated his role in the family finances leaving the task all to his wife, and he had been resistant to family members who wanted to get her into treatment years earlier. LeRoy, after having this discussion with his sponsor, sat down and made amends to his wife. "I've been blaming you for our debts, but I've played a major role in it myself. I need to apologize to you," he said. "Let's work together to solve this problem."

"Yellow Light" means the problem is legitimate, but we are not sure if it is or isn't appropriate for an SFR meeting. Since not every topic is clear cut, we prefer to err on the side of caution, taking time to think before making a big deal out of something that may not warrant it. Time alone might solve the problem, or a better course of action may show itself.

Ken and Karen's son wanted to go back to college three months after getting out of treatment. They felt uncomfortable about his readiness and especially living in the dorms. The SFR counselor and team chairperson thought that, by making it a topic in an SFR meeting, the group would give it too much viability at a time when no one was even sure if it was a good idea. Their son would gear up his defenses and position himself against the family team.

When Ken and Karen spoke with their Al-Anon sponsors, they were presented with a series of questions. "Is it an emergency?" No, they said. "For your son, is this a need or a want?" It's a want, they said. "Should he get what he wants when he wants it?" No, that's what it was like in his addiction, they said. Ken and Karen's sponsors didn't make their decision for them but helped clarify their thinking using what they'd learned in their recovery programs.

Sitting down with their son, they told him they understood why he thought going back to college was a good idea. "But first things first," they said, using a recovery slogan that he well understood. "You'll get back to college, but let's do this right. Get solid in recovery and then we'll make plans." Six months later, their son was accepted at a college that had a successful "StepUP" program for college students in recovery. Their son was able to go back to school, and they felt comfortable knowing his recovery would remain a front-burner issue. By using the Yellow Light, they gave themselves time to work out a good solution without creating conflict by elevating the problem to an unnecessary place of importance in Structured Family Recovery.

"Green Light" is when the problem is legitimate and appropriate for Structured Family Recovery. Usually these topics are obviously right for an SFR meeting, but sometimes they require some discussion. "Is it forward-looking? Can we, as a team, offer something worthwhile? How is this related to recovery?" When we decide it's right to use an SFR meeting to discuss a topic related to a particular team member, we must also determine the best way to present the topic in a respectful, dignified manner.

Mia had moved in with her grandparents after treatment. She found a job at a clothing store, was involved in counseling and going to AA, and she had been participating on the SFR team for four months. Everything was going well until she began dating a boy who worked with her. Only five months sober, it was entirely too soon for Mia to date. She began staying out late at night. Her grandparents suspected that she was skipping AA meetings, and by the look of his eyes, they weren't entirely sure that this fellow wasn't using drugs himself.

The grandparents reviewed Mia's wishes on how the team should bring relapse warning signs to her attention. She had written, with the help of her sponsor and the team chairperson, who was her grandfather, the following instructions: "If you see me exhibiting relapse warning signs, I would like Grandmother and Grandfather to sit down and talk to me about it. If I get defensive, it's probably because I know you are right. I will call my sponsor immediately and ask for feedback. After taking these steps, I will bring the issue to an SFR meeting to ask for team feedback and help. I will be honest."

Mia's grandparents sat down with her and asked her to read, out loud, the statement she'd written, giving them permission to talk with her about relapse warning signs. When Mia finished reading, she bristled a little bit and said, "I know what this is about." Her grandfather replied, saying with love, "If you know what this is about, it tells me you have some of the same concerns we have." Mia, true to her word, was honest. She admitted to skipping AA meetings to go to parties with this young man and, yes, he drank and smoked pot. Her grandfather said, "We understand your desire to party, but you have a disease that requires having fun in different ways." Mia began to cry and hugged her grandparents. She called her sponsor and shared in the next SFR meeting. Gathering feedback from everyone, Mia decided she couldn't work with this young man anymore and needed a clean break. She gave her boss her notice and found a job working at a neighborhood coffee shop.

By this point, Mia had been involved with Structured Family Recovery for enough time—witnessing the recovery activities of her mom and dad, aunt, grandparents, and her older brother—and this changed her in significant ways. She wasn't as defiant as she had been just months earlier. Family had a new meaning for her, and it was tied to recovery.

While part of her wanted to be just like everyone else her age, she was comforted by a family who supported sobriety. If she had reacted differently, insisting that she wasn't going to give up the boyfriend, there were also the Eight Essential Elements and her promise to alter her lifestyle to support recovery. She had agreed to negative consequences. If she was doing things that threatened her recovery and refused to make changes, the consequence at the top of the list was moving out of her grandparents' home.

The family team didn't react by becoming punitive. Instead they followed a process that allowed Mia to make better decisions and changes to support her recovery. Written in Mia's SFR recovery plan were decisions that supported recovery in a global fashion. As a result of creating this plan, Mia understood clearly that relapse behaviors came with negative consequences, and recovery behaviors came with positive consequences.

Whenever we feel the need to approach an SFR team member about recovery concerns, we first discuss it with other people: the SFR counselor or team chairperson, and our Twelve Step sponsor. This is a safety lock so we don't cause more damage to a family already battered by the pains of addiction. We make better decisions together than individually.

Conversations about concerns usually start outside the SFR meeting. We are given directions on how to approach team members in their written recovery plans. The person we're concerned about is then encouraged to bring the issue up in an SFR meeting himself. It is much better for the person who needs help to ask for help. There may be exceptions, but this is the preferred approach. Preserving dignity and showing respect maintains relationships and gets better results.

Flexibility preserves dignity. It isn't a sign of wavering on principles but an understanding that people need time. They may need a few days to talk to their sponsor, share in a meeting, and then come to a decision about what they need to do. Of course, if our addicted loved one has relapsed and refuses to follow the relapse agreement in his recovery plan, contact an SFR counselor or clinical interventionist (or someone who is both) and take appropriate action.

* * *

The Heart Triumphs

Ultimately, with all we learn and know, we move onward by way of the heart. It's a bruised heart, no doubt—whether we're the family member or the addict. We're all in tatters after our tenure with addiction. Our hearts may be wounded, but we cannot move forward led by our wounds. We must move forward led by our hearts.

As the Irish playwright George Bernard Shaw wrote, "Those who cannot change their minds, cannot change anything." If we define ourselves by where we are now, how we feel in this moment, believing more in the old fight than in new possibility, it isn't addiction that holds us back, it is ourselves. It's far better to turn to the best in us and gently forgive our worst.

When we come together with Structured Family Recovery, we leave our reasons to fight outside the door. Not that the pain and disappointment and hurt aren't real, they just ultimately are not helpful. They perpetuate the past. The urge to relive these memories over and over again brings nothing new to the table. Better to bring our sufferings to our Twelve Step work as a way to finally leave the pain behind. In Structured Family Recovery we are focusing on how to get to that better place. So, let's unshackle ourselves, stop licking the wounds, stand up straight, and put our focus where it belongs: squarely on ourselves. It's what we do or don't do that creates change.

Begin Structured Family Recovery with compassion for ourselves as well as others.

We Practice the Spirituality of Kindness

A friend of mine recently celebrated twenty years of sobriety. Remembering back to that day, twenty years ago, in detox and very sick, he said, "I woke up and there was a man from AA sitting next to my bed. He gently put his hand on my shoulder and said, 'It's going to be all right.' I didn't believe him at the time, but he's here tonight, all these years later, to help me celebrate." Kindness comes in small packages, little acts that mean so much we never forget them.

True kindness doesn't sit in judgment asking, "Do you deserve me?" Kindness is an identity we choose for ourselves. When we are kind, we have chosen not to be critical. When we are kind, we have chosen not to be angry. When we are kind, we are saying, "You are valuable to me." Small kindnesses are so powerful that when we choose them, we can change a family. Some families, filled with so much hurt, can no longer find kindness in their hearts. But AA has a saying, "Act as if." Act kind, and you will become kind. Aristotle said it, too, "Acting virtuous will make one virtuous."

This doesn't mean we deny and repress feelings of anger or hurt. It simply means we choose to act on our positive feelings and values with each other. We've been battered enough; bringing more anger to the family does not help us. It's far better to take responsibility for our hurts and harms by working through them in a setting where they can be processed and healed. That's what the Fourth through the Tenth Steps are for, and we should lose no time in working through these Steps with our sponsor after completing the first three Steps.

David Brooks, columnist for the *New York Times,* wrote, "The manners and mores of a community are a shared possession. When you violate social norms, you are not only being rude to people around you, but you are making it more likely that others will violate the norms in the future. You are tearing the social fabric."[85] Verbal slights and discourteous remarks, which accelerate when addiction inhabits a home, tear at the fabric of our families, too. If we believe that the manners and mores of a family are a shared possession, wouldn't it then be terribly wrong to trample over them? If kindness belongs to everyone, do I have the right to extinguish it with unkindness?

During active addiction, much is not beautiful and many things hurt us and we, in all likelihood, hurt others. Kindness is hard won after so much injustice and pain. It's born of an experience that offered us little hope. Yet once we're delivered into recovery, we are given the opportunity to repair and strengthen the fabric of our families. It takes working together, and that cannot happen without kindness.

Poet Naomi Shihab Nye, in her poem "Kindness," writes, "Before you know what kindness really is you must lose things, feel the future dissolve in a moment like salt in a weakened broth. What you held in your hand, what you counted and carefully saved, all this must go so you know how desolate the landscape can be between the regions of kindness. . . . Then it is only kindness that makes sense anymore, only kindness that ties your shoes and sends you out into the day to mail letters and purchase bread, only kindness that raises its head from the crowd of the world to say, *It is I you have been looking for,* and then goes with you everywhere like a shadow or a friend."[86] Living in the aftermath of addiction, kindness makes perfect sense.

We Conduct Ourselves with Gentleness during SFR Meetings

Funny thing about our brains—they don't take constructive criticism well. Someone once said, "First we're ticked off, and then we're enlightened." Neuroscientists tell us our brains are naturally defensive. Don't be defensive, we say, but our brains just are. One of the most important functions our brains have is to use the built-in defense mechanisms to protect us from harm, both physical and psychological. When we feel criticized, our brains often protect us by resisting negative information even when it is constructive. We change the information rather than change ourselves.

AA and other Twelve Step programs have bypassed this particularity of the brain by discouraging cross talk—giving each other advice or feedback. In Twelve Step meetings, people share their experience, strength, and hope. Others take what they like and leave the rest. It's a great system that doesn't summon the defensive brain to the rescue.

In SFR meetings, we follow AA's lead for the most part, sharing about ourselves, not talking about others. We are doing recovery not family therapy. In fact, family therapy at this juncture can be unhelpful, unless the family is so broken that members are unable to work together in an SFR setting. The risk is that the addicted loved one will begin focusing on relationships—code word for other people—rather than himself and his recovery. There are so many hurt feelings due to the addiction that stirring the pot just pulls up resentments, poisoning the waters. Much better to use the Twelve Steps to rid ourselves of resentments, get into a place of positive spirituality, build sturdy sobriety (emotional sobriety for the family), learn to focus on ourselves, and build some trust. By doing these things, most family problems fall away. After a year of good, strong recovery, if relationship problems linger, then contemplate family therapy *unless there is a compelling reason to do so earlier.*

Of course, our impulse is to do the opposite. We need to get to the bottom of our problems, air things out, tell each other exactly how we feel, and get things off our chest. "Whew, I feel better now," we say after telling everyone exactly what we think—but it's usually a fleeting feeling of relief. Feeling better in the moment doesn't mean we're better off. Too often it's a lot of talk (mostly about our reactions to other people) and very little action, and it doesn't offer much in the way of making change. A far more effective way to change our attitude is to work a Twelve Step program to change our behavior. In the words of the thirteenth-century Sufi mystic and poet Rumi, "Yesterday I was clever, so I wanted to change the world. Today I am wise, so I am changing myself."

Our struggles start making sense when we understand that our brains are built so that we are prone to remember our negative experiences more strongly and in more detail than our positive experiences. We judge our families with a brain that zeroes in on the negative. We even process negative and positive experiences in different hemispheres of the brain. In a *New York Times* article, "Praise Is Fleeting, but Brickbats We Recall," Alina Tugend writes, "Negative emotions generally involve more thinking, and the information is processed more thoroughly than positive ones . . . we ruminate more about unpleasant events." In other words, bad events wear off more slowly than good events.[87]

This may be evolutionary—a way of remembering events that threaten survival and reduce the likelihood of passing on one's genetic material. But this adaptation of nature has its drawbacks. As George Vaillant, MD, writes in his book *Spiritual Evolution,* "Negative emotions are often crucial for survival—but only in time present. The positive emotions are more expansive and help us broaden and build. . . . They help us to survive in time future." Dr. Vaillant explains that our negative emotions are in service of the "I," whereas our positive emotions are supportive of the "we."[88] This raises our understanding of why Twelve Step recovery focuses on freeing ourselves from negative, isolating emotions and increasing positive emotions that establish human connection.

So, we must be cognizant of the fact that our brains aren't always trustworthy. All that bad stuff—and no one is denying that there's bad stuff—is likely to be remembered more strongly and keeps circling around in our brains, while the good stuff is often bleached out over time. We seem to be built to fret, which prevents us from giving each other a fair shake, and forgiveness often seems impossible. Lasting negative emotions serve to isolate us rather than unite us. Understanding this helps make sense of why heaping our complaints on others keeps the circle of pain going. We can reliably predict that the recipients of the unburdening of our negative feelings are bound to react strongly to our criticism, ruminating about what was said and having difficulties forgetting it, creating an endless cycle of hurt and retribution.

Does this mean we never bring up anything negative? Can we approach difficult issues such as relapse warning signs in our addicts or family members without tripping the cerebral wire that closes the door to criticism? Do we just give up and, as some suggest, never use any form of intervention when we see our loved ones veer off the rails, lest we appear confrontational? Do we restrict ourselves instead to a neutral position with questionings such as, "How is that working for you?" We need to understand that criticism doesn't always have to be critical.

Let's begin by neutralizing criticism without neutering it. *Criticism* is how we define the merit of something, through serious examination and review. "Is my involvement in my recovery program substantial enough to support lasting sobriety, or do I need to do something more?" *Critical* is an inclination of finding fault and calling attention to flaws in something. "I'm always being told I'm not doing it right, but I don't see how you're much better." It's easy to see the benefit of one over the other. When criticism is used as evaluation and is about the event, rather than the person, it can be very helpful. When an entire team is working toward success, open to group evaluation of the recovery process—believing in progress not perfection—criticism is welcomed as something supportive and helpful. Then the message becomes, "What more do I need to know or do, and how can you help me?"

So how do we talk to one another when we need to say we're worried or scared? When we see something that doesn't look like recovery but rather the return of the insidious beast of addiction? How do we point out behaviors that have the air of recovery sabotage? We are uncomfortable with offering criticism just as we are with receiving it. We worry that if we bring up anything negative, we'll be seen as being critical of the person. As the old maxim goes, the head of the messenger rolls.

In our old way of doing things, we addressed *behaviors caused by the addiction,* person, or event, but not *the addiction itself.* We focused almost exclusively on past behaviors, whether yesterday, last week, or last year. We would point out how bad the addict behaved, how upset we were, and why it better not happen again. We left the addict with the job of figuring out how to straighten up, which was a surefire way to get to the next fiasco. We'd throw in a variety of threats for good measure, most of which we never followed through on. After all, making good on our threats meant we'd lose something, too. "If you stay out all night again, I'm getting a lawyer!" Of course, we didn't really want all the losses that come with divorce. We just wanted things to get better. It's no wonder they didn't.

Structured Family Recovery focuses on the future and on recovery. We're interested in how we can work together to meet our goals. We don't label the addict the bad guy and ourselves the good guys anymore, and vice versa—the addict stops blaming the family. We're a family coping with a chronic illness. By working a Twelve Step program, we grow along spiritual lines so we might offer something transformative to our family.

When we speak to one another, we *converse*. By sharing our own experiences in recovery, we add value to the conversation. We listen to others. We ask how we can help. We acknowledge that we're imperfect, each of us in our own way. We share accountability. We recognize our gifts as well as our shortcomings. By making it safe, we can, when necessary, give important feedback to any one of us whose recovery is in a slump.

Before anybody is having problems or is sliding into relapse, we ask each member of our SFR team, "What would you like us to do if we thought your recovery was in jeopardy?" Each gives the others permission to offer feedback. We tell each other exactly how to go about it. For example, someone might say, "If anyone sees me slipping, go to Jack with your concerns. I take feedback from him far better than anyone else. And, Jack, I'd like you to call me first, before the next SFR meeting. After you and I talk, I'll bring it to the group myself and explain what we worked out. Then I'll ask the rest of the team for their support."

Since our brains go on the defensive, we want to be honest about what's going on with us when we're receiving feedback. The family member in the above example can say, "Jack, I hear what you're saying, but my brain is doing its thing right now, getting sort of defensive. I know it's a normal reaction and has nothing to do with the value of what you are telling me. Let me take a minute for the defensiveness to die down, so I can respond to you honestly and openly."

Because we regularly attend SFR meetings, problems are unlikely to grow out of proportion before anyone notices. Most challenges will be small and self-reported. For example, "I put recovery at the bottom of my list this past week and skipped my Al-Anon meeting. I need some feedback on how others are keeping their priorities straight." Of course, a team member could be untruthful about his or her recovery activities, but a group can usually sniff out dishonesty because of its dissonance with recovery goals and values. Recovery and dishonesty project distinctly different feelings. If we're concerned about someone but we're not able to put our finger on it, talk to the SFR counselor or the team chairperson. We want to speak up sooner rather than later if something seems wrong.

In the business world, crowdsourcing is a positive feedback trend that's gained a big following. It allows employees to give immediate kudos to colleagues while work is in progress. The Harvard Business Review Blog explains, "Social recognition is the epitome of effective reviews: they're truly inspired, not forced by antiquated performance review processes."[89]

In Structured Family Recovery, we do something similar called *team-sharing*. Rather than just saying "good job" to our teammates, however, we contact each other to share something about recovery that we find truly inspiring or has challenged our way of thinking. An alcoholic might call his sister and say, "I was reading my AA meditation book this morning and had such an a-ha! moment. For the first time, I realized that not having to take a drink today is a freedom, not a struggle. I wanted to share that with you." Team-sharing isn't scheduled or expected; it's something we're moved to do. We share something we find meaningful with someone else. It's an intimate connection that allows us to interact on a spiritual level.

Since our brains tend to react more strongly to the negative than the positive, we need to create more positives in recovery to overcome the negatives we lived with during the addiction. According to researcher Roy Baumeister of Case Western Reserve University, good events can overcome the psychological impact of bad events. It's estimated that it takes five goods to every bad.[90] "That's a good reminder that we all need to engage in more acts of kindness—toward others and ourselves—to balance out the world," notes Alina Tugend in her article for the *Times*.[91]

We Cultivate Trustworthiness

Scottish author and poet George McDonald wrote, "To be trusted is a greater compliment than being loved." Addiction preys on trust. It is by the misuse of trust that it survives. It gets its way through lies and subterfuge, using for its purposes the sweetest and dearest qualities of the person whose body, mind, and spirit it has invaded. When that doesn't work, it turns to wrath.

When alcoholics and addicts gain the smallest foothold in recovery, and the fog lifts and the brain begins to clear, they realize they've lost their most precious possession: the trust of others. Without it, it's difficult to receive and give love. Civility is at its lowest ebb. Acts of compassion dry up. When no one trusts them, no one has faith in them.

Immediately, they want to know how to get it back. When I worked with alcoholics and addicts in treatment, it was one of the first questions they'd ask me. "How do I get my family to trust me again?" They urgently want to find a way back into the fold, because living without trust is painful. But trust can no longer be reclaimed by apology or promise; it must be earned.

Alcoholics and addicts must realize that they no longer have the right to ask, "Do you trust me?" The only question they can properly ask is, "Am I being trustworthy today?" Being trustworthy in recovery is evidenced by specific daily actions: working a recovery program, demonstrating honesty, treating others with courtesy and kindness, and remaining sober. When falling short of the mark, a recovering person makes amends and goes on. Taking responsibility for shortcomings is an act of trustworthiness.

Trust in recovery is measured in twenty-four-hour increments. *Am I being trustworthy today?* As time progresses and the addict stays true to his program of recovery, people in his life come to believe that the answer to that question, day after day, will be yes. But with early recovery comes a warranted uncertainty. Each day must speak for itself. The disease is close to the surface and recovery is fledgling. If a newly recovering person strays from the program, or holds on to dishonesty, trustworthiness isn't earned. The disease waits for those moments. It can reassert itself whenever trust is breached.

Paradoxically, a trustworthy addict knows that he can't be trusted on his own to maintain sobriety. He's aware that the disease is always in the wings waiting. Protection comes not from the addict's thinking, but from the wisdom of the greater recovery community. As it's said in AA, "My head is like a dangerous neighborhood; I should never go in there alone."

The question families usually ask is, "How do we know he won't relapse?" What they are really asking is, how can we trust again? Families stay focused on the addict's every move, trying to determine at what point in time he becomes trustworthy.

Families often fixate on how little trust they have for the addict, reminding him at every opportunity. This is never helpful. The lack of trust should not be articulated in a way that is punitive or humiliating. We're better served supporting recovery and setting appropriate limits. The addict needs limits to know what it takes to move beyond them. Families need limits to protect themselves from the disease. These actions are best guided by empathy, always remembering the addicted person is suffering from a disease and the family suffers from the secondhand effects.

Catherine, a young heroin addict, was no longer allowed in her parents' home after she stole from them repeatedly. She survived the cold Vermont winter living in an abandoned house. When she finally agreed to treatment, she thought she'd be welcomed home, but her parents remained firm. They knew it took more than treatment to stay sober, so they helped her move into professionally supervised transitional housing, where she would live and work for the next eighteen months. When Catherine celebrated a year of sobriety, her parents invited her home for a visit. She was bubbling over with delight. She knew what it meant to earn the right to go home for a few days and spend time with her parents. It made her proud of her recovery. By learning to live within a structure imposed by her mother and father, she learned what she needed to do to grow beyond those limitations.

Catherine's parents didn't wrestle with how much they could or couldn't trust their daughter. Instead they asked themselves an important question. "Can Catherine trust us?" If they allowed themselves to be fooled by false hopes or empty promises, the answer was no. But they made tough decisions, setting necessary limitations *with love,* so the answer to their question was yes. Being trustworthy parents required supporting only their daughter's recovery. They endured emotional tantrums and abusive language from her in the beginning but stood firm. When she reached one year of sobriety, they celebrated this important milestone with her, but they also understood that it was still just a beginning.

We Have Fun in Recovery

Play lights up our brains. It generates many positives most alcoholic families can use more of: optimism, empathy, a sense of belonging. According to Dr. Stuart Brown, the pioneer of innovative studies on play, "If you want to belong, you need to engage in social play."[92] Play signals are the basis for building trust among humans.

Throughout neurophysiology and developmental and cognitive psychology, there is significant research on play. Researchers have found that the brain doesn't develop normally when it suffers from play deprivation. It begins to atrophy. Interestingly, Dr. Brown tells us it isn't work that's the opposite of play; it's depression. Play has a biological place in our lives, he says, just like sleep and dreams.

In addicted families, there hasn't always been much fun, but we experienced plenty of negatives. We need to create more play in our families to replace that negativity with positive experiences. Play helps heal relationships. By playing, we feel closer to one another, experience greater empathy, increase our sense of belonging, and have healthier immune systems (rebuilding what stress has damaged). Families in recovery desperately need to enjoy themselves.

Play refreshes our relationships, especially when we're willing to try new and novel ways of having fun. It activates our reward center and creates an altered state of mind, says Dr. Brown. Play activates good brain chemistry, which is what an addict needs after having a drug-soaked brain for so long. Families need to recondition brains that have been assaulted with unrelenting stress.

Recovery needs to be fun so we learn to enjoy each other's company again. It's also essential in preventing relapse. If the addict is bored out of his mind, he's more likely to drink. If family members feel their relationships are stale, they're less likely to bond. Fun changes all of that, and as human beings, we are designed to play throughout our lives.

So be creative. Sing. Dance. Play games. Bicycle. Picnic. Swim. Make popcorn and watch old movies. Go bowling. Make an apple pie. Go to the zoo. Check out the free things to do in town. Make cookies and package them for friends. Have soup night and invite the whole family over. Play charades. Go sledding or make a snowman. Make paper snowflakes.

Take a tour of an art museum. Plant something. Make an old family recipe together. Start a family book club. Look at old family photos or videos. Shoot hoops. Visit garage sales. Take a field trip to an interesting part of town. Write and direct movie shorts on your video camera or smartphone. Go thrift shopping. Eat dinner at home and then go out for a dessert splurge. Watch comedies. Cuddle. Learn something new together. Visit small farms to pick berries or apples. Go to a park or a conservatory. Attend an auction. Fly a kite. Make a fort. Help at a soup kitchen. Start a family photography club. Read a book out loud. Go out and look at the stars.

Do something, anything that is new, different, fun. And laugh.

Eric Clapton writes in his autobiography, *Clapton,* about his life in sobriety. "The last ten years have been the best of my life. They have been filled with love and a deep sense of satisfaction. . . . I have a loving family at my side, a past I am no longer ashamed of, and a future that promises to be full of love and laughter. . . . If I were anything but an alcoholic, I would gladly say that [my family is] the number one priority in my life. But this cannot be, because I know I would lose it all if I did not put my sobriety at the top of the list."

As is true with any other alcoholic or addict who achieves lasting sobriety, Clapton explains, "I continue to attend Twelve Step meetings and stay in touch with as many recovering people as I can. Staying sober and helping others to achieve sobriety will always be the single most important proposition of my life."[93]

I go back to these words again and again, drawn to the power of them. Here is a man of great success, talent, and wealth. One doesn't often reach such pinnacles without also being smart and savvy. Yet, for him and his family, recovery comes first. He understands most clearly that, without it, all else is lost. If recovery comes second or third on his list of priorities, he will no longer be "going to any lengths" for recovery and will slide back into the disease, taking his family with him.

Make recovery as important for your family. Claim your right to the gifts that come with sobriety. Begin now and take it one day at a time. Schedule your first meeting for Structured Family Recovery and follow the guidance for weekly meetings. Get professional help if you need it or if you feel better having it. Move forward in a direction that takes you to a place worth going. We will no longer follow the disease of addiction; we are all worth more than that.

Two years after Bill Wilson and Dr. Bob Smith began Alcoholics Anonymous, they sat in Bob's living room with his wife, Anne, and counted the number of alcoholics who had thus stayed bone dry. This is how Bill describes the conversation that followed.

> As we carefully rechecked this score, it suddenly burst upon us that a new light was shining into the dark world of the alcoholic . . . a benign chain reaction from one alcoholic carrying the good news to the next, had started outward from Dr. Bob and me. Conceivably it could one day circle the whole world. What a tremendous thing that realization was! At last we were sure. There would be no more flying totally blind. We actually wept for joy. And Bob and Anne and I bowed our heads in silent thanks.[94]

Fourteen years later, Lois Wilson, Bill's wife, did the same for families of alcoholics. At sixty years of age, preferring to spend her days tending her garden and involving herself in artistic projects, she was called on to begin a program for families using the principles of AA. She agreed only because she knew the need was so great. In 1951, working with a nearby friend whose husband was a recovering alcoholic, and eighty-seven family members from around the country who had written looking for help, Lois began Al-Anon. Today, the group has spread worldwide.

As Aldous Huxley once said, "When the history of the twentieth century is finally written, the greatest achievements America will be known for giving the world will be Alcoholics Anonymous and Al-Anon."[95]

● ● ●

The Hero's Journey

Joseph Campbell, American mythologist, writer, and lecturer, discovered in his studies that myth, storytelling, and religions around the world all share a fundamental narrative that he calls the *monomyth,* or the Hero's Journey.

Campbell describes this journey in his book *The Hero with a Thousand Faces:* "A hero ventures forth from the world of common day into a region of supernatural wonder: fabulous forces are there encountered and a decisive victory is won: the hero comes back from this mysterious adventure with the power to bestow boons on his fellow man."[96]

Every person who enters into recovery from the disease of addiction, I believe, embarks on the Hero's Journey. He begins an ordinary life, thinking nothing threatening or life-altering lies ahead. He goes about his business—home and family, work, and friends—unaware that something is brewing.

Once addiction begins creating a negative pressure on his life, he is already standing on the extremity of change. Both from external forces and deep internal disruptions, he is being coerced to pay attention. He will be changed one way or another, and he now must make a choice.

But, as the hero faces the unknown, he refuses the call. He turns away from the adventure he is meant to take. But, as his world continues to crumble, he comes upon a mentor who shares his wisdom, teaching the hero courage and good judgment. It is only then that he agrees to leave his ordinary world and cross into this new, unfamiliar territory of sobriety.

Once in the new world, it isn't easy for the hero. He second-guesses himself. He is tested and feels the cold breath of fear on his face. He can turn back or push forward. He must decide.

By providence and good fortune, his new allies stand by his side, preparing him to rise to the challenge. This is the time in which the hero must confront his greatest trials and tribulations. He must be willing to go beyond what he believes is possible. Out of this ultimate struggle, like the Phoenix rising from the ashes, comes a new life.

This is when the hero discovers his treasure—recovery—that he knows he must bring home. The road to home isn't an easy one, with much to overcome along the way. But when he finally arrives, it is as a transformed man, bringing with him a power that changes the world from which he began.

As family, we go with our addict on this hero's journey. We are tested all along the way. But, together, we find the treasure, and we bring it home.

● ● ●

PART III

Structured Family Recovery Weekly Meetings

INCLUDED IN THIS SECTION are the opening and closing statements for your SFR weekly meetings and templates with suggested topics for a full year, broken out into four quarters with agendas and topics for each week.

Opening and Closing Statements

for Structured Family Recovery Weekly Meetings

Rotate the reading of the opening and closing statements among team members.

Opening Statement

1. Our team meetings are confidential. We are bound not to disclose what is said here to nonparticipating family members, friends, or other persons. Observing confidentiality, we create an atmosphere of trust and safety.

2. We join and start conference calls on time. By doing so, we show respect for team members and their schedules. If someone is late, we do not stop to go back and explain what was missed. We continue with our agenda.

3. We speak only about ourselves, using "I" statements. We do not use "I" statements as thinly veiled "you" statements. We do not tell others how they feel or think, or what they should do. By keeping the focus on ourselves, we learn what is within our power to change. *myself.*

4. Negative emotions often linger well into early recovery. Turning anger, resentment, or blame on our family members results in multiplying our problems. It is best to work through negative emotions with our Twelve Step sponsor and during Al-Anon, AA, or other Twelve Step meetings.

5. We follow the "Red, Yellow, Green Light" protocol when we believe a serious issue needs to be addressed. We don't drop unexpected issues or "bombs" into the middle of SFR meetings. We contact our SFR counselor or chairperson *before a meeting* to decide how to proceed properly or at all.

6. We are active listeners. We treat one another as we would like to be treated. We are tolerant of others' limitations and honest about our own. We celebrate our successes. We remember that none of us is perfect, but we are all deserving of love.

7. This is our group and our time. We use it wisely for our mutual benefit. We focus on how the Twelve Steps are implemented in all our affairs.

Closing Statement: The Promises

1. If we are painstaking about this phase of our development, we will be amazed before we are half way through.

2. We are going to know a new freedom and a new happiness.

3. We will not regret the past nor wish to shut the door on it.

4. We will comprehend the word serenity, and we will know peace.

5. No matter how far down the scale we have gone, we will see how our experience can benefit others.

6. That feeling of uselessness and self-pity will disappear.

7. We will lose interest in selfish things and gain interest in our fellows.

8. Self-seeking will slip away.

9. Our whole attitude and outlook upon life will change.

10. Fear of people and of economic insecurity will leave us.

11. We will intuitively know how to handle situations which used to baffle us.

12. We will suddenly realize that God is doing for us what we could not do for ourselves.

Are these extravagant promises? We think not. They are being fulfilled among us—sometimes quickly, sometimes slowly. They will always materialize if we work for them.[97]

First Quarter

The first twelve SFR meetings are defined by the slogan "Progress not perfection." We are learning how to do recovery, keeping it simple, and making a shift to thinking about recovery as something we do together. It begins as a way to help free the addict from the subjugation of addiction but culminates in bringing people together in ways we never expected.

At this beginning point in recovery, we don't know where this journey will take us, so we need to step out on faith. It's not enough for the addict to stop using or to work a recovery program on his own. For lasting sobriety, we need cooperation from the people who love each other most. Putting this disease into remission is not the same thing as healing a family. To heal is to make whole. Addiction pulled us apart; *family* recovery makes us whole again.

WEEK 1: STRUCTURED FAMILY RECOVERY

Date: _____

Topic: Why Al-Anon?

Opening

The chairperson asks a team member to read the SFR Opening Statement.

Daily Reading

A team member reads aloud from a Twelve Step daily reader, then reads each of the following discussion points, allowing time for team sharing.

Report, Discuss, Plan

1. What went well in my recovery this past week? What could be improved? Do I want feedback?

2. What insights did I gain from my Twelve Step experiences? From last week's SFR assignment?

3. What new recovery behaviors will I practice this upcoming week? I will contact my accountability partner _____ times this week.

Learn Something New

It's well understood that human beings do not like to give up something we're used to, even when it no longer serves its original purpose. Researchers find that we suffer from loss aversion. We struggle to let go of anything we perceive as ours. This can be extended to behaviors, even those that no longer work. We can become so invested in unproductive behaviors that we believe they are still working for us. Admitting that these behaviors don't work triggers an innate sense of loss and, thus, a desire to hang on to them. In our Twelve Step work, we can admit to behaviors that don't help us move forward in recovery. Once we make this admission, we can open ourselves up to what works.

Step One

We admitted we were powerless over alcohol—
that our lives had become unmanageable.

Step One is about acceptance. We recognize that our many past attempts at controlling addiction didn't bring us the results we'd wanted. Paradoxically, this frees us to move out of the problem and into the solution. By admitting that we can't control outcomes, especially with other people, we can concentrate on the thing we can change: ourselves. We can move toward being in control of our own actions, and by changing our own behaviors we model positive recovery for the person we're concerned about.

Working a Recovery Program

Family members are often surprised to learn that they need to play an active role in recovery because addiction doesn't feel like their problem. Calling it a family disease might seem somewhat contrived. How is it our disease? But addiction is pervasive, significantly affecting those who have close emotional bonds with the addict. Family members, much like the addict, often cannot see how the disease has changed them. Al-Anon helps lift the blinders so we might see what needs repair—emotional, spiritual, and physical—and then shows us how to heal. This is similar to what AA and NA do for the addict, who has also been blinded by the disease.

Assignment

Family members, like the addict, are often resistant to the idea of attending Twelve Step meetings. Reluctance is based on fear or uncertainty, or an inability to see why it's necessary. The response to this common hesitation to attend meetings is "Take it a step at a time." Attend an Al-Anon meeting and ask for feedback on why this piece of advice is so powerful when put into practice. Journal the responses you receive.

Closing

The chairperson asks a team member to read the SFR Closing Statement.

Date: _____

Topic: Anger

Opening

The chairperson asks a team member to read the SFR Opening Statement.

Daily Reading

A team member reads aloud from a Twelve Step daily reader, then reads each of the following discussion points, allowing time for team sharing.

Report, Discuss, Plan

1. What went well in my recovery this past week? What could be improved? Do I want feedback?

2. What insights did I gain from my Twelve Step experiences? From last week's SFR assignment?

3. What new recovery behaviors will I practice this upcoming week? I will contact my accountability partner _____ times this week.

Learn Something New

Anger is an emotion usually tied to social interactions: when we feel trespassed against or violated in some manner. Addiction certainly does both. We hold certain expectations of people closest to us, and addiction pays no heed to these expectations. Our anger grows in proportion to the progression of the disease. As addiction worsens, so do negative behaviors. Anger is usually the core feeling of family members, even though they often outwardly exhibit helplessness. Social scientists suggest cognitive restructuring—changing the way we think about things—as a solution to persistent anger. Recovery helps us with cognitive restructuring.

Step One

We admitted we were powerless over alcohol—
that our lives had become unmanageable.

When coping with addiction in the family, justifiable anger is common. Whenever we are disturbed by anger, resentments, or other negative emotions, it is almost always a Step One issue. We have expectations of others that are not being met. Step One can be adapted to say, "I'm powerless over people, places, and things." We find our power in how we choose to respond. When we accept this paradox, our lives become more manageable.

Working a Recovery Program

We often don't see our own anger. It may reside below the surface, fueling our responses and behaviors. Other times it's explosive, triggered by every slight and injustice. Chronic anger damages relationships, health, and overall quality of life. Working the Twelve Steps gives us a way to resolve anger and resentments of the past and handle new situations. Anger keeps us stuck in the problem. Working a Twelve Step program moves us from anger to action.

Assignment

Read page 167 in the Al-Anon book *Courage to Change*. Underline meaningful passages or write your insights in a journal. Ask yourself, *What triggers my anger? How would I prefer to act?* Share answers in a Twelve Step meeting and ask others to share their experiences on the topic. Journal any other further insights gained.

Closing

The chairperson asks a team member to read the SFR Closing Statement.

Date: _____

Topic: Resentments

Opening

The chairperson asks a team member to read the SFR Opening Statement.

Daily Reading

A team member reads aloud from a Twelve Step daily reader, then reads each of the following discussion points, allowing time for team sharing.

Report, Discuss, Plan

1. What went well in my recovery this past week? What could be improved? Do I want feedback?

2. What insights did I gain from my Twelve Step experiences? From last week's SFR assignment?

3. What new recovery behaviors will I practice this upcoming week? I will contact my accountability partner _____ times this week.

Learn Something New

Resentment is anger recycled over and over again. Resentments left unresolved can develop into difficulty trusting people, stunted emotional growth, and pessimism, all barriers to healthy relationships. Resentment stems from an inability or refusal to forgive. As an anonymous writer explains, "The moment you start to resent a person, you become his slave. He controls your dreams, absorbs your digestion, robs you of your peace of mind and goodwill. . . . You cannot take a vacation without his going along. He destroys your freedom of mind and hounds you wherever you go. There is no way to escape the person you resent. . . . So if you want to be a slave, harbor your resentments!"

Step One

*We admitted we were powerless over alcohol—
that our lives had become unmanageable.*

Resentments are an addictive state of mind. Living with resentments confuses the present with the past. In Twelve Step circles, it's said that resentment is akin to taking poison and expecting the other fellow to die. Step One teaches us that we are powerless to change the past. We regain personal power by staying in the moment, understanding that we can't change yesterday and cannot predict tomorrow.

Working a Recovery Program

The Serenity Prayer is used in Twelve Step meetings to remind us how we create manageability in our lives. "God, grant me the serenity to accept the things I cannot change, courage to change the things I can, and wisdom to know the difference." Once we understand that we can only change *ourselves,* we are less likely to create more resentments.

Assignment

Read page 178 in *Courage to Change.* What resentments am I holding onto? Ask yourself, *How does my response to others cause me to feel resentful? What price do I pay?* Share insights in a Twelve Step meeting and ask others to share their experiences. Journal your insights.

Closing

The chairperson asks a team member to read the SFR Closing Statement.

WEEK 4: STRUCTURED FAMILY RECOVERY

Date: _____

Topic: Forgiveness

Opening

The chairperson asks a team member to read the SFR Opening Statement.

Daily Reading

A team member reads aloud from a Twelve Step daily reader, then reads each of the following discussion points, allowing time for team sharing.

Report, Discuss, Plan

1. What went well in my recovery this past week? What could be improved? Do I want feedback?

2. What insights did I gain from my Twelve Step experiences? From last week's SFR assignment?

3. What new recovery behaviors will I practice this upcoming week? I will contact my accountability partner _____ times this week.

Learn Something New

Forgiveness may benefit those who forgive even more than the forgiven. Research shows that forgiveness is linked to our physical, mental, and spiritual health. It also plays a major role in the health of families. The International Forgiveness Institute has developed a forgiveness intervention to increase forgiveness, which then reduces anger, anxiety, and grief. Studies find that forgiveness lowers blood pressure and heart rate. It appears that forgiveness isn't something that comes naturally to us but is something we learn. Twelve Step programs help us learn to forgive.

Step One

We admitted we were powerless over alcohol—
that our lives had become unmanageable.

When we understand that addiction is a genetically based disease, we recognize that the addict was powerless over alcohol or other drugs. We begin to see that we've all been living with symptoms of a disease. Much like Alzheimer's changes the behavior of the person suffering from it, so does addiction. Separating the disease from the person helps us forgive. It also helps the addict to forgive himself and his family.

Working a Recovery Program

Forgiveness is the key to healing resentment. Resentment keeps everyone disconnected; forgiveness brings us back together. Working the Twelve Steps converts us into people capable of forgiving. In homes ravaged by addiction, we all need to be forgiven for something, and we all need to forgive. This is how we create new beginnings in our families.

Assignment

Forgiveness doesn't absolve the wrong but rather cleans up our reaction to it. Making amends, which the addict and family will be doing systematically in Steps Eight through Ten, doesn't guarantee forgiveness, only that we are righting a wrong. Discuss struggles with forgiveness in a Twelve Step meeting. Journal your insights.

Closing

The chairperson asks a team member to read the SFR Closing Statement.

WEEK 5: STRUCTURED FAMILY RECOVERY

Date: _____

Topic: Relapse Warning Signs

Opening

The chairperson asks a team member to read the SFR Opening Statement.

Daily Reading

A team member reads aloud from a Twelve Step daily reader, then reads each of the following discussion points, allowing time for team sharing.

Report, Discuss, Plan

1. What went well in my recovery this past week? What could be improved? Do I want feedback?

2. What insights did I gain from my Twelve Step experiences? From last week's SFR assignment?

3. What new recovery behaviors will I practice this upcoming week? I will contact my accountability partner _____ times this week.

Learn Something New

Terence T. Gorski, noted relapse specialist and author, writes, "[Family members'] attitudes and behaviors can become such complicating factors in the addict's recovery that they can contribute to the process of relapse and even 'set-up' the addict's next episode of use. On the other hand family members can be powerful allies in helping the addict prevent fully engaging in the relapse process."[98] Gorski has identified the most common signs of relapse in both the addict and in the family. Relapse always begins in our thinking process. For the addict, it leads to the next drink or drug. For the family, it leads to the loss of emotional sobriety.

Step Two

*Came to believe that a Power greater than ourselves
could restore us to sanity.*

Step Two is about looking for help outside ourselves. Our insanity comes from thinking we have all the answers. We experience a return to sanity by having the faith that answers will come from sources outside ourselves: recovering people, Twelve Step meetings, sponsors, our SFR team, and a power greater than ourselves. People find this greater power in several places: in the larger recovery community and its literature, universal love, good orderly direction, or in the God of our understanding. The help of others is what safeguards us from relapse.

Working a Recovery Program

Relapse prevention requires that we know our relapse warning signs. When we or others begin to see symptoms early, we can make changes to our behavior to avoid relapse. Working a strong program of recovery and spending time with our sponsor is the best way to prevent relapse. Once we begin to exhibit relapse warning signs, it means our program is slipping. Either we're not engaging in recovery activities fully, or we are not being honest, open, and willing. If we stop taking care of ourselves, we also risk relapse. We can take the H.A.L.T. quiz: Am I hungry, angry, lonely, or tired? If we answer yes to any of the questions, we need to take appropriate actions to restore balance in our lives. Get some rest, eat something nutritious, pick up the phone, and talk to another recovering person.

Assignment

Find the relapse warning checklists in the resource section of this book for the family and addict. Check off your relapse warning signs. Share them during the next SFR meeting and with your Twelve Step sponsor. Add your relapse warning signs to your Recovery Plan. Journal your insights.

Closing

The chairperson asks a team member to read the SFR Closing Statement.

WEEK 6: STRUCTURED FAMILY RECOVERY

Date: _____

Topic: Check Up

Opening

The chairperson asks a team member to read the SFR Opening Statement.

Daily Reading

A team member reads aloud from a Twelve Step daily reader, then reads each of the following discussion points, allowing time for team sharing.

Report, Discuss, Plan

1. What went well in my recovery this past week? What could be improved? Do I want feedback?

2. What insights did I gain from my Twelve Step experiences? From last week's SFR assignment?

3. What new recovery behaviors will I practice this upcoming week? I will contact my accountability partner _____ times this week.

Learn Something New

Our brains create patterns, a normal way of doing things. These patterns are so ingrained that they are easy to perform without much thought or effort. When we ask our brains to change, according to neuroscientists, it is comparable to telling them something is wrong. This activates the emotional center of our brains, which then sends out a signal that there's an error or hazard. This is why change can feel threatening, and why we respond with reluctance. When we tell ourselves that change is good, and it will make our lives better, we help our brains to become accepting.

Step Two

*Came to believe that a Power greater than ourselves
could restore us to sanity.*

Change isn't as daunting when we ask for help. A positive spirituality means we leave isolation behind and reach out to others. It's in accepting help that sanity returns. Being overly self-reliant hasn't solved our problems in the past. How have we been reluctant to reach out for help from others in the program? How can we override our brain's resistance to change?

Working a Recovery Program

Where am I in my recovery today? Do I have a sponsor, a home group, a service position? Am I using my recovery checklist? Do I use an accountability person? Have we, as a team, completed our Recovery Plans? What actions do I need to take this week to make positive changes?

Assignment

Use your recovery checklist daily to complete any actions left undone. Talk to your accountability person or sponsor daily for support.

Closing

The chairperson asks a team member to read the SFR Closing Statement.

WEEK 7: STRUCTURED FAMILY RECOVERY

Date: _____

Topic: Humility

Opening

The chairperson asks a team member to read the SFR Opening Statement.

Daily Reading

A team member reads aloud from a Twelve Step daily reader, then reads each of the following discussion points, allowing time for team sharing.

Report, Discuss, Plan

1. What went well in my recovery this past week? What could be improved? Do I want feedback?

2. What insights did I gain from my Twelve Step experiences? From last week's SFR assignment?

3. What new recovery behaviors will I practice this upcoming week? I will contact my accountability partner _____ times this week.

Learn Something New

John Jay McCloy, former president of the World Bank, said, "Humility leads to strength and not to weakness. It is the highest form of self-respect to admit mistakes and to make amends for them."[99] Humility is a relaxed form of self-assurance. It's accepting the truth about ourselves, both strengths and weaknesses. With humility we are able to welcome positive criticism and feedback from others. When we succeed, we give credit to those who helped us. We are quick to recognize the strengths of others. Humility brings balance to our sense of self.

Step Two

*Came to believe that a Power greater than ourselves
could restore us to sanity.*

Admitting we need help from others requires humility. We experience more spiritual growth by learning to accept help than by giving it. In Twelve Step groups, when we allow others to help us, we give them an opportunity to practice their program of recovery. It's a two-way gift.

Working a Recovery Program

Recovery from addiction is not a self-help program. It is a *mutual*-help program. It requires we each are willing to accept help and give help. Whichever we do, we are doing both, because every time we accept help, we give help, and vice versa. Recovery is a spiritual two-way street. It's defined by the ability to extend ourselves to others.

Assignment

This week, find a place of humility through your gratitude for others. You will be thankful for those willing to help you, and the connection you make when you accept help.

Closing

The chairperson asks a team member to read the SFR Closing Statement.

WEEK 8: STRUCTURED FAMILY RECOVERY

Date: _____

Topic: Honesty

Opening

The chairperson asks a team member to read the SFR Opening Statement.

Daily Reading

A team member reads aloud from a Twelve Step daily reader, then reads each of the following discussion points, allowing time for team sharing.

Report, Discuss, Plan

1. What went well in my recovery this past week? What could be improved? Do I want feedback?

2. What insights did I gain from my Twelve Step experiences? From last week's SFR assignment?

3. What new recovery behaviors will I practice this upcoming week? I will contact my accountability partner _____ times this week.

Learn Something New

We become honest, not by fear of punishment, but by learning the value of honesty. Researchers have found that when people are told stories about liars being punished, lying behaviors stay the same or get worse. But when they are told stories emphasizing the rewards of honesty, honesty increases. This demonstrates the power of social norms. Twelve Step recovery groups abound with stories of the rewards of honesty.

Step Two

*Came to believe that a Power greater than ourselves
could restore us to sanity.*

When addiction takes hold of a family, an illusion of control develops. The addict uses dishonesty and the family uses enabling (which employs dishonesty) to maintain the illusion. This is a form of insanity. A power greater than ourselves restores us to sanity by returning us to honesty. As a member of Al-Anon said, "The disease of addiction had profoundly affected me, but I couldn't see the insanity in my life. I needed a place where people understood alcoholism to help me open my eyes."

Working a Recovery Program

Working a program of recovery is the beginning of change. The negative chatter in our heads doesn't matter as long as we move our feet in the right direction. *Behavior changes attitude.* When we are honest about our feelings of reluctance, but take action nonetheless, we create positive social norms and behavioral expectations. Both set an example that helps the entire family move forward in recovery.

Assignment

Focus on the spiritual practice of being honest. How is honesty linked to simplicity, trustworthiness, and peace of mind? Discuss this at a Twelve Step meeting. Journal your insights.

Closing

The chairperson asks a team member to read the SFR Closing Statement.

WEEK 9: STRUCTURED FAMILY RECOVERY

Date: _____

Topic: Twelve Step Slogans

Opening

The chairperson asks a team member to read the SFR Opening Statement.

Daily Reading

A team member reads aloud from a Twelve Step daily reader, then reads each of the following discussion points, allowing time for team sharing.

Report, Discuss, Plan

1. What went well in my recovery this past week? What could be improved? Do I want feedback?

2. What insights did I gain from my Twelve Step experiences? From last week's SFR assignment?

3. What new recovery behaviors will I practice this upcoming week? I will contact my accountability partner _____ times this week.

Learn Something New

As a recovering alcoholic wrote in her blog, *The Wild Life*, "The thing about the corny slogans is they're actually little parables that express a deeper truth."[100] No one knows the origins of the slogans, but it's assumed the earliest ones—"Easy does it," "Live and let live," and "First things first"—originated with Bill Wilson and the first AA members. The others were passed down orally from one recovering person to the next. As an Al-Anon group describes them, "Slogans serve as gentle, calming reminders that our circumstances might not be as impossible or as desperate as they first appear . . . a simple slogan can put the entire situation in perspective."

Step Three

Made a decision to turn our will and our lives over
to the care of God as we understood Him.

This is a decision Step: "I am willing to open myself up to guidance."
Some find the God-word troublesome, but remember, each person
chooses his or her Higher Power. By working this Step, we abandon
"Self-will run riot," and allow ourselves to let go of controlling behaviors. The slogan "Turn it over" reminds us to relinquish the things we
have no control over to our Higher Power. We always have control over
choices we make for ourselves, but we can ask for guidance to help us
make better choices.

Working a Recovery Program

Slogans and other recovery sayings are packets of wisdom easy to access and digest. In a flash, they can right our attitude or put our actions
back on track. Slogans are the epitome of simplicity. "Easy does it . . . but
do it" reminds us that when we're overwhelmed we don't have to do
everything at once; by calming down we are better able to meet our ob-
ligations. "Let go and let God" reminds us that we once expected happiness to originate from things outside ourselves, and, as a result, we tried
to control what we had no control over. It was a recipe for anger, blame,
and resentment. We can find a slogan to fit just about any situation we
might face in recovery.

Assignment

Reference a list of slogans from your Twelve Step meetings. Check off two
or three that most resonate with you, and discuss one in your home group.
What slogans are most common among SFR team members? Choose one
as the SFR team slogan. Take a vote during the next SFR meeting. (The
SFR secretary can coordinate tallying the top slogan choices before the
next meeting.)

Closing

The chairperson asks a team member to read the SFR Closing Statement.

WEEK 10: STRUCTURED FAMILY RECOVERY

Date: _____

Topic: Higher Power

Opening

The chairperson asks a team member to read the SFR Opening Statement.

Daily Reading

A team member reads aloud from a Twelve Step daily reader, then reads each of the following discussion points, allowing time for team sharing.

Report, Discuss, Plan

1. What went well in my recovery this past week? What could be improved? Do I want feedback?

2. What insights did I gain from my Twelve Step experiences? From last week's SFR assignment?

3. What new recovery behaviors will I practice this upcoming week? I will contact my accountability partner _____ times this week.

Learn Something New

The term *Higher Power* was used by AA as early as the 1930s. We also hear people use "a power greater than ourselves." As some newcomers in AA say, "I'm not sure yet who my Higher Power is, but I'm pretty sure it's not me." According to a 2010 Gallup Poll, 80 percent of Americans, when asked, say they believe in God. Twelve percent believe in a universal spirit, and 6 percent don't believe in either. One percent believes in something described as "other," and another 1 percent have no opinion. Among AA members, there are representatives from across the spectrum of belief.[101]

Step Three

*Made a decision to turn our will and our lives over
to the care of God* as we understood Him.

They key to Step Three is making a decision, in everything regarding addiction and recovery, to accept guidance from a power greater than ourselves. Most of us already know or have an idea of who our Higher Power is, and for those who don't, members of the recovery community give us a starting point. The "we" of the program is more powerful than the "I." As a recovering addict said, "I didn't know what God's will was for my life, but I was quite sure what God's will for me was *not*."

Working a Recovery Program

Twelve Step meetings give us a perfect opportunity to find guidance from outside of ourselves. Leaning on the experience, strength, and hope of other recovering people is a way of practicing Step Three. This helps us in our daily lives. When we find ourselves falling back into old ways of thinking or behaving, Step Three allows us to turn ourselves over to the care of a Higher Power. We can take a variety of action steps, such as to call our sponsor or a member of the SFR team, use a slogan, or say a prayer: "Your will be done, not mine."

Assignment

In your journal, write down the definition of your Higher Power. How has your belief in God or a Higher Power been helpful to you in the past? In Twelve Step meetings, ask others to share their experiences with Step Three. Journal your insights.

Closing

The chairperson asks a team member to read the SFR Closing Statement.

WEEK 11: STRUCTURED FAMILY RECOVERY

Date: _____

Topic: Trusting the Process

Opening

The chairperson asks a team member to read the SFR Opening Statement.

Daily Reading

A team member reads aloud from a Twelve Step daily reader, then reads each of the following discussion points, allowing time for team sharing.

Report, Discuss, Plan

1. What went well in my recovery this past week? What could be improved? Do I want feedback?

2. What insights did I gain from my Twelve Step experiences? From last week's SFR assignment?

3. What new recovery behaviors will I practice this upcoming week? I will contact my accountability partner _____ times this week.

Learn Something New

A man spent more than an hour watching a butterfly struggle to free itself from its cocoon without success. It had made a small hole, but its body was much too large to squeeze through. Finally, the butterfly stopped struggling and lay inside the cocoon motionless. The man became concerned and decided to cut open the cocoon. The butterfly crawled out, but its body was shriveled and its wings crumpled. The man watched, hoping the butterfly would eventually spread its wings and fly. But it never did. What the man didn't realize was that nature intended the butterfly to squeeze through that small hole. It would strengthen its wings. By not trusting the process, the man took away the butterfly's necessary struggle and its chance to fly.

Step Three

Made a decision to turn our will and our lives over
to the care of God as we understood Him.

Trusting the process means we need to have faith and patience. We didn't get here overnight, and the solutions are going to take time. When we see our loved ones struggle—especially the addict—we may want to step in and begin working his program. But we have to stop to remember that our loved ones must go through their own struggles so they can mature and grow. When we are tempted to "help" that is when we need to think of Step Three and say, "My loved ones have their own Higher Power, and it is not me."

Working a Recovery Program

In Twelve Step circles, a popular slogan is "Time takes time." We get into recovery, and in short order we want everything fixed. But recovery is a process of growth, and growth takes time. We need to work our programs, "One day at a time," to collect the experiences that eventually bring us long-term results. As we continue, we learn to trust the process and worry less.

Assignment

This week think of your recovery as planting a garden. Once the seed goes into the ground, you have to wait for the roots to take hold before the plant grows, the leaves sprout, and the flowers bloom. Along the way, you must do your part, watering the plant, weeding the garden, and fertilizing the soil. Most importantly, you must have patience. Journal your thoughts and insights about working a recovery program.

Closing

The chairperson asks a team member to read the SFR Closing Statement.

WEEK 12: STRUCTURED FAMILY RECOVERY

Date: _____

Topic: Choices

Opening

The chairperson asks a team member to read the SFR Opening Statement.

Daily Reading

A team member reads aloud from a Twelve Step daily reader, then reads each of the following discussion points, allowing time for team sharing.

Report, Discuss, Plan

1. What went well in my recovery this past week? What could be improved? Do I want feedback?

2. What insights did I gain from my Twelve Step experiences? From last week's SFR assignment?

3. What new recovery behaviors will I practice this upcoming week? I will contact my accountability partner _____ times this week.

Learn Something New

Daily we make hundreds of choices. How do we find the guidance to make the best choices in the most important areas of our lives? When we are living in the crisis or aftermath of addiction, stress creates tunnel vision. We're less able to absorb all the information available to us. Worry, anxiety, and fear distort choices, and our brains suffer from decision fatigue. Structured Family Recovery avoids these pitfalls by writing Recovery Plans to make decisions in advance, utilizing checklists, making commitments not decisions, simplifying recovery, and using triggers to spark behaviors.

Step Three

*Made a decision to turn our will and our lives over
to the care of God as we understood Him.*

In AA's *Twelve Steps and Twelve Traditions* it says, "Practicing Step Three is like opening a door which to all appearances is still closed. All we need is a key, and the decision to swing the door open."[102] The key, of course, is willingness. Once we are willing, making the choice to open the door is easy. This Step is asking us to make a *decision* to turn our lives and will over to the *care* of a power greater than ourselves. Our will is our thinking and our life is our actions. By making this choice, we prepare ourselves for the Steps to come.

Working a Recovery Program

Once the disease has found its way into our family, the way out is working a program of recovery. It can be a hard personal choice for both family and addict to make a lasting commitment to recovery. But when we think about recovery in the same way we think about our jobs, it's easier. We don't always consciously make a daily choice about whether we're going to work. Work is a commitment—we know we are going and when we need to be there. We go to work for the positive rewards, to provide for ourselves and our family, and to avoid negative consequences, such as dismissal. The same is true of recovery. It's a commitment. We don't have to make a new decision every day, we just do it.

Assignment

Are you still making daily choices about your involvement in recovery or have you made a commitment? How does commitment simplify recovery? Talk to your Twelve Step sponsor about commitment. Journal your insights.

Closing

The chairperson asks a team member to read the SFR Closing Statement.

Second Quarter

The next twelve weeks focus on issues common to this stage of recovery. By this time, members of the recovery team are working a Twelve Step program of recovery and understand that recovery is more than keeping the addict abstinent. By following the directions, we are beginning to see some results by now. Even though we are still in the earliest stage of recovery, working a program of recovery has given us a constructive role to play.

We expect that team members have a home group, a sponsor, and have begun working the Twelve Steps. We move ahead based on what we need to help us through the next phase of recovery. We will begin working the action Steps: Steps Four and Five. For the addict, these are the first Steps toward physical and emotional sobriety. For the families, these Steps are about achieving emotional sobriety. Actively work with your Twelve Step sponsor on these Steps while following the guidance of your SFR meetings. This ushers in a period of recovery that increases comfort and willingness.

WEEK 13: STRUCTURED FAMILY RECOVERY

Date: _____

Topic: Open and Willing

Opening

The chairperson asks a team member to read the SFR Opening Statement.

Daily Reading

A team member reads aloud from a Twelve Step daily reader, then reads each of the following discussion points, allowing time for team sharing.

Report, Discuss, Plan

1. What went well in my recovery this past week? What could be improved? Do I want feedback?

2. What insights did I gain from my Twelve Step experiences? From last week's SFR assignment?

3. What new recovery behaviors will I practice this upcoming week? I will contact my accountability partner _____ times this week.

Learn Something New

Gaylord Nelson, former U.S. senator and governor, said, "The ultimate test of man's conscience may be his willingness to sacrifice something today for future generations whose words of thanks will not be heard." Working the Twelve Steps requires that we do some rigorous inside work. When a family does this work together, it's transformative on a larger scale, changing the very legacy of a family. The recovery work we do today is an inheritance for the generations to come. We pass on—not the behaviors molded by addiction, a kind of spiritual illness—but an emotional stability that provides an ability to regulate behaviors. In the words of Bill Wilson, it results in "easy, happy, and good living."

Steps Four and Five

Made a searching and fearless moral inventory of ourselves.

Admitted to God, to ourselves, and to another human being
the exact nature of our wrongs.

Steps Four and Five are simply about taking an inventory of ourselves. For most of us, the addiction has been our primary focus; these Steps help us put the focus back where it belongs, on us. It requires using the HOW of the program: being honest, open, and willing. We can experience reluctance at the idea of taking a personal inventory. By using Steps One, Two, and Three, we find the courage to take a fearless look at ourselves.

Working a Recovery Program

The founders of AA stated that failure to do a thoroughly honest Fourth and Fifth Step is one of the primary causes of relapse. This is as true for families as for alcoholics. With the guidance of our sponsor, we write our Fourth Step inventory on paper. Being honest about ourselves is as liberating as it is frightening. We do a Fifth Step by reading our inventory to our Twelve Step sponsor or someone experienced at hearing Fifth Steps, such as a pastor or an addictions counselor. As it is said in the Big Book, "We pocket our pride and go to it, illuminating every twist of character, every dark cranny of the past. Once we have taken this step, withholding nothing, we are delighted. We can look the world in the eye. We can be alone at perfect peace and ease."[103]

Assignment

In this upcoming week, begin talking with your sponsor about doing Steps Four and Five. Read about the Steps in your *Twelve and Twelve* book.

Closing

The chairperson asks a team member to read the SFR Closing Statement.

Date: _____

Topic: Secrets

Opening

The chairperson asks a team member to read the SFR Opening Statement.

Daily Reading

A team member reads aloud from a Twelve Step daily reader, then reads each of the following discussion points, allowing time for team sharing.

Report, Discuss, Plan

1. What went well in my recovery this past week? What could be improved? Do I want feedback?

2. What insights did I gain from my Twelve Step experiences? From last week's SFR assignment?

3. What new recovery behaviors will I practice this upcoming week? I will contact my accountability partner _____ times this week.

Learn Something New

Holding in secrets takes a lot out of us. *It's eating me up alive.* When we're hanging on to secrets and resentments we hedge ourselves in, and it takes its toll on us. Depression and anxiety often increase as do body aches and pains. Appropriately letting go of secrets and harbored resentments is correlated with better mental and physical health. Neuroscientists tell us that secrets cause the brain to fight with itself, whereas just the act of writing secrets down on paper can release the stress.

Steps Four and Five

Made a searching and fearless moral inventory of ourselves.

Admitted to God, to ourselves, and to another human being the exact nature of our wrongs.

Steps Four and Five are often the first tools of the program that help us come to a point of feeling okay about ourselves at a deep level. All the little secrets and hidden feelings that drag us down are brought to light. As they say in Twelve Step groups, "We're only as sick as our secrets." Working these Steps with our sponsor, clergyperson, or counselor gives us a safe and appropriate place to reclaim parts of ourselves that were buried by secrets and disturbed emotions. It's much easier to live with ourselves once we've cleaned house.

Working a Recovery Program

These two Steps bring us to a place of complete honesty. The addict for the first time is taking account of the havoc the disease had on his life and the lives of others. Family members, through this inventory process, are able to identify the role they played in the saga of the family disease. When everyone completes a personal Fourth and Fifth Step, the family can begin to do away with the hierarchy of relationships within it—who is better and who is worse. These two Steps are the great equalizers. By taking our own inventory, we are less likely to sit in judgment of one another. Instead, we have a common bond in recovery.

Assignment

With your sponsor's continued guidance, ask for feedback at Twelve Step meetings about doing a Fourth and Fifth Step. Journal your insights.

Closing

The chairperson asks a team member to read the SFR Closing Statement.

WEEK 15: STRUCTURED FAMILY RECOVERY

Date: _____

Topic: Character Defects

Opening

The chairperson asks a team member to read the SFR Opening Statement.

Daily Reading

A team member reads aloud from a Twelve Step daily reader, then reads each of the following discussion points, allowing time for team sharing.

Report, Discuss, Plan

1. What went well in my recovery this past week? What could be improved? Do I want feedback?

2. What insights did I gain from my Twelve Step experiences? From last week's SFR assignment?

3. What new recovery behaviors will I practice this upcoming week? I will contact my accountability partner _____ times this week.

Learn Something New

Character defects are patterns we've developed that don't work for us anymore. We developed many of these patterns of thought and behavior, which made perfect sense in the short run, to cope with the ongoing crisis of addiction. But as our lives filled with crisis—or the threat of crisis—these patterns became ingrained habits. We're not even cognizant of doing them. They sometimes developed to protect us and serve a purpose, but now they block healthy relationships and spiritual growth. The next step in our recovery is simply to identify our patterns and share them with our sponsor.

Steps Four and Five

Made a searching and fearless moral inventory of ourselves.

Admitted to God, to ourselves, and to another human being the exact nature of our wrongs.

Taking an inventory of the ways we've been coping (making sure we refrain from taking the inventory of others), we consider these common patterns and discuss them with our sponsor or trusted Fifth Step counselor:

anger	dishonesty	controlling behavior
resentment	impatience	people-pleasing
self-pity	false pride	aloofness
fear	perfectionism	irritability
self-justification	intolerance	criticizing
self-condemnation		

Whichever we relate to, we must remember that these began as ways to create a safe place for ourselves and others. They no longer work for us because survival skills have an expiration date, after which they go bad. Used habitually, they start causing problems, signaling that we must make changes in our lives. That we've needed them for so long in the face of addiction isn't our fault.

Working a Recovery Program

Sponsors help us by sharing their personal experience working the Steps. They aren't asking us to do anything they haven't done. Sponsors tell us how they did it, what helped them, and how they would like us to do it. We are not alone in this process; we just need to follow the directions. Many a sponsor, when asked the best time to start a Fourth and Fifth Step, replies, "When you want to stop hurting."

Assignment

Take time this week to consider which defects listed above you relate to. Ask for feedback from others in your Twelve Step meetings and journal your insights.

Closing

The chairperson asks a team member to read the SFR Closing Statement.

WEEK 16: STRUCTURED FAMILY RECOVERY

Date: _____

Topic: Gentleness

Opening

The chairperson asks a team member to read the SFR Opening Statement.

Daily Reading

A team member reads aloud from a Twelve Step daily reader, then reads each of the following discussion points, allowing time for team sharing.

Report, Discuss, Plan

1. What went well in my recovery this past week? What could be improved? Do I want feedback?

2. What insights did I gain from my Twelve Step experiences? From last week's SFR assignment?

3. What new recovery behaviors will I practice this upcoming week? I will contact my accountability partner _____ times this week.

Learn Something New

Be gentle first with yourself if you wish to be gentle with others.
—Lama Yeshe

Moving through Steps Four and Five, we must first be gentle with ourselves. In doing so, we temper negative feelings we have toward ourselves. When we come with gentleness, we bring patience and kindness.

Steps Four and Five

Made a searching and fearless moral inventory of ourselves.

Admitted to God, to ourselves, and to another human being the exact nature of our wrongs.

George Mann, MD, founder of The Retreat, in the video *Touch Life Gently,* describes Step Four as critical for the development of a good self-image. As a *fearless* and *searching* inventory, we aren't called to log just the negative but also positive attributes. Dr. Mann says, "We need to look at our positives too and say, 'This is who I am!'" What made the difference for him in doing a Fourth Step, he said, was realizing he was a good person. "Goodness is an inherent quality. . . . I can make mistakes and do dumb things, and I can take wrong turns. But my basic goodness is an ongoing characteristic."[104]

Working a Recovery Program

Some find taking an inventory of their positive characteristics more difficult than the negatives. When we attend a Twelve Step meeting, we hear others share about overcoming negative characteristics by turning them into positives. The perfectionist, for instance, becomes a person who strives for excellence but understands that this requires allowing for mistakes. Positive characteristics include:

being honest	forgiving	enthusiasm
having integrity	taking personal	creativity
fairness	responsibility	gratitude
cooperation	pursuing excellence	joyfulness
tolerance	having self-respect	reliability
empathy	being accountable	sincerity
humility	demonstrating	sobriety
respect for others	courage	trustworthiness
having patience	commitment	engaging in service

Assignment

Sit with your eyes closed in a quiet place and ask yourself, "What are my positive qualities, the parts of me that are inherently good?" Circle positives you relate to from the list above. Write these in your journal and share with your sponsor.

Closing

The chairperson asks a team member to read the SFR Closing Statement.

WEEK 17: STRUCTURED FAMILY RECOVERY

Date: _____

Topic: Empathy

Opening

The chairperson asks a team member to read the SFR Opening Statement.

Daily Reading

A team member reads aloud from a Twelve Step daily reader, then reads each of the following discussion points, allowing time for team sharing.

Report, Discuss, Plan

1. What went well in my recovery this past week? What could be improved? Do I want feedback?

2. What insights did I gain from my Twelve Step experiences? From last week's SFR assignment?

3. What new recovery behaviors will I practice this upcoming week? I will contact my accountability partner _____ times this week.

Learn Something New

Empathy is experiencing what another person is facing or going through from that person's perspective. Isn't this what we all want from others? When a family has been coping with addiction, each member—including the addict—scrambled to find ways to survive the destructive nature of the disease. Often we can more easily see the harmful patterns in others' lives than in our own. Let's begin by understanding the attempt to survive from the perspective of each member of our family. How is it different from the viewpoint we've taken in the past?

Steps Four and Five

Made a searching and fearless moral inventory of ourselves.

Admitted to God, to ourselves, and to another human being the exact nature of our wrongs.

Since our brains experience the negative more intensely than the positive, let's challenge our unfavorable thinking toward our family. What positive qualities are true of our family and its members? Here are some examples to help us take this inventory:

We are committed to the well-being of each one of us

We make an effort to spend time and do things together

We're willing to go the extra mile for each other

We communicate with positive emotions

We express appreciation

We have clearly established values that guide our behaviors

We engage in problem solving together

We show flexibility and tolerance toward each other

We value learning

We treat each other kindly and delight in each other

We have balance in our lives inside and outside of family

We can show and accept love

We are willing to work together to strengthen and improve our family

Working a Recovery Program

By working a program of recovery, we begin to let go of fear. Finally able to raise our heads out of the foxhole, we can afford to feel empathy. Everyone is on the same team; it was the chaos of addiction that separated us. Attending Twelve Step meetings, we know our family is not alone. Others have experienced what we have and worse, and they gladly share what worked for them. Empathy is our way out of spiritual isolation.

Assignment

To increase empathy, challenge preconceived notions, listen carefully to others, imagine living another's life, identify your blocks to empathy, heal past hurts, pay attention to what you have in common with others, and increase pleasant family encounters. Select two of these empathy builders, incorporating them regularly. Discuss with your sponsor. Journal your ongoing insights.

Closing

The chairperson asks a team member to read the SFR Closing Statement.

WEEK 18: STRUCTURED FAMILY RECOVERY

Date: _____

Topic: Patience

Opening

The chairperson asks a team member to read the SFR Opening Statement.

Daily Reading

A team member reads aloud from a Twelve Step daily reader, then reads each of the following discussion points, allowing time for team sharing.

Report, Discuss, Plan

1. What went well in my recovery this past week? What could be improved? Do I want feedback?

2. What insights did I gain from my Twelve Step experiences? From last week's SFR assignment?

3. What new recovery behaviors will I practice this upcoming week? I will contact my accountability partner _____ times this week.

Learn Something New

When we have patience, we are better able to endure hardship. It shows itself as perseverance even when we don't know the outcome of our efforts. Patience is how much we can tolerate before our negative thinking sets in. Cognitive neuroscience has identified patience as a decision making process. In recovery, we choose the valuable rewards that come with steadfastness over immediate gratification. Our natural inclination, however, is to take the less valuable reward of immediate gratification. Perhaps this is why patience is one of the highest virtues in world religions.

Steps Four and Five

Made a searching and fearless moral inventory of ourselves.

*Admitted to God, to ourselves, and to another human being
the exact nature of our wrongs.*

When we begin identifying character defects—our unhelpful patterns of behavior—we want them gone instantly. But they are well practiced and have created stable pathways in our brains. Some of them, we may find, we're not yet ready to give up. For now, we will practice patience. We are called only to identify our character defects and admit their exact nature to ourselves, our Higher Power, and another human being.

Working a Recovery Program

A Twelve Step slogan, "Live and let live," helps us remember patience. It tells us we do not need to tie ourselves into knots thinking about what others need to do. When we find ourselves becoming impatient with another person, it's usually because that person isn't doing what we want. This popular slogan reminds us, just as we want to live free of others' controlling behaviors, we can't micro-manage another's life or recovery. As we each work our own program, our rate of personal growth will vary, but with patience and right behavior, results come.

Assignment

Unrealistic expectations are often a source of impatience. Make patience the goal for the next week. Slow down. Take time to think about your expectations. Delay gratification. Take walks when agitated. Call your sponsor when impatience takes over and discuss patience in your Twelve Step group. Journal your insights.

Closing

The chairperson asks a team member to read the SFR Closing Statement.

WEEK 19: STRUCTURED FAMILY RECOVERY

Date: _____

Topic: Fear

Opening

The chairperson asks a team member to read the SFR Opening Statement.

Daily Reading

A team member reads aloud from a Twelve Step daily reader, then reads each of the following discussion points, allowing time for team sharing.

Report, Discuss, Plan

1. What went well in my recovery this past week? What could be improved? Do I want feedback?

2. What insights did I gain from my Twelve Step experiences? From last week's SFR assignment?

3. What new recovery behaviors will I practice this upcoming week? I will contact my accountability partner _____ times this week.

Learn Something New

I must say a word about fear. It is life's only true opponent. Only fear can defeat life. It is a clever, treacherous adversary, how well I know. It has no decency, respects no law or convention, shows no mercy. It goes for your weakest spot, which it finds with unnerving ease. It begins in your mind, always . . . so you must fight hard to express it. You must fight hard to shine the light of words upon it. Because if you don't, if your fear becomes a wordless darkness that you avoid, perhaps even manage to forget, you open yourself to further attacks of fear because you never truly fought the opponent who defeated you.

—Yann Martel, *Life of Pi*

Steps Four and Five

Made a searching and fearless moral inventory of ourselves.

*Admitted to God, to ourselves, and to another human being
the exact nature of our wrongs.*

When living with addiction, fear becomes the governing force in our lives. Ever-present, we may no longer recognize it as our constant companion. Fear is behind most of our character defects. If we peek behind anger, we're likely to find fear. Look at the root of perfectionism, you'll probably find fear. Certainly controlling behavior is a way to keep us safe from what we fear. Self-pity, dishonesty, negative thinking—all can have their roots in fear. It's promised that one of the results of doing a Fifth Step is "Our fears fall from us."

Working a Recovery Program

Fear tells us what we can't do, fear tells us good things won't last, fear tells us we don't have what it takes, fear finds faults in our loved ones, fear predicts the worst possible future. But we can overcome fear by staying in the now, doing the next right thing, and being actively involved with other people in the recovery community. When others share their experience, strength, and hope, they help to extinguish our fears, reminding us everything is really all right. In Steps Four and Five, it is important to take an inventory of when fear stopped us from doing what we needed to do, so we understand how fear undermines us.

Assignment

Ask in a Twelve Step meeting how people have dealt with fear. Journal your insights.

Closing

The chairperson asks a team member to read the SFR Closing Statement.

WEEK 20: STRUCTURED FAMILY RECOVERY

Date: _____

Topic: Self-Centeredness

Opening

The chairperson asks a team member to read the SFR Opening Statement.

Daily Reading

A team member reads aloud from a Twelve Step daily reader, then reads each of the following discussion points, allowing time for team sharing.

Report, Discuss, Plan

1. What went well in my recovery this past week? What could be improved? Do I want feedback?

2. What insights did I gain from my Twelve Step experiences? From last week's SFR assignment?

3. What new recovery behaviors will I practice this upcoming week? I will contact my accountability partner _____ times this week.

Learn Something New

Bill Wilson wrote in the Big Book, "Selfishness—self-centeredness! That, we think, is the root of our troubles."[105] Self-centeredness keeps us iso lated from others and a power greater than ourselves. At the core of self-centeredness is fear. Self-centeredness goes along with a lack of trust, often based on hard experience. In recovery we move past self-centeredness by working closely with a sponsor and other recovering people until we can trust the process.

Steps Four and Five

Made a searching and fearless moral inventory of ourselves.

Admitted to God, to ourselves, and to another human being the exact nature of our wrongs.

The inventory process provides a method for identifying and rooting out our selfish and self-centered behaviors. By taking a close look at these defects, we can come to understand the underlying fears that motivate them. Often, our sponsor or counselor can provide additional insight and guidance in the Fifth Step process. We must root out self-centered behaviors if we hope to maintain physical and emotional sobriety.

Working a Recovery Program

In the past, self-centeredness has been a cocoon used for protection. In recovery, we can take the risks of creating more authentic relationships based on our common welfare. The greatest relief from self-centeredness always comes from working with others. This is the paradoxical magic of the Twelve Step program. By extending ourselves to others, we find relief from the demands of the big "I." A recovering friend, sober more than twenty years from heroin addiction, said, "I'd followed the directions for the first time and worked with my sponsor to do a thorough Fourth and Fifth Step. It was a rite of passage and a great relief. I'd never felt more a part of the fellowship of AA."

Assignment

Take time after your next Twelve Step meeting to reach out to someone who shared something that resonated with you. Take a few moments to talk and to offer thanks. Journal about this interaction.

Closing

The chairperson asks a team member to read the SFR Closing Statement.

Date: _____

Topic: Self-Pity

Opening

The chairperson asks a team member to read the SFR Opening Statement.

Daily Reading

A team member reads aloud from a Twelve Step daily reader, then reads each of the following discussion points, allowing time for team sharing.

Report, Discuss, Plan

1. What went well in my recovery this past week? What could be improved? Do I want feedback?

2. What insights did I gain from my Twelve Step experiences? From last week's SFR assignment?

3. What new recovery behaviors will I practice this upcoming week? I will contact my accountability partner _____ times this week.

Learn Something New

"Self-pity is easily the most destructive of the non-pharmaceutical narcotics; it is addictive, gives momentary pleasure and separates the victim from reality," wrote John Gardner, American novelist. Self-pity is a call for others to repeatedly come to our rescue. It requires that we mire ourselves in helplessness and blame. I've heard it said that the recipe for self-pity is misery plus self-obsession. For addicts, self-pity is an especially threatening relapse symptom: "Poor me, poor me, pour me a drink." The antidote for self-pity is gratitude.

Steps Four and Five

Made a searching and fearless moral inventory of ourselves.

Admitted to God, to ourselves, and to another human being the exact nature of our wrongs.

Step Four is when we begin to see the ways self-pity takes a toll on our lives and our relationships as we look to others to validate us. What's less obvious is that this is a symptom of resentment and self-centeredness. Some call self-pity, resentment, and self-centeredness a character defect three-pack. Recovery requires us to use Step Four to squarely face self-pity and the relentless belief that life isn't working out for us. By doing so, we begin taking responsibility for ourselves.

Working a Recovery Program

The more active we are in our recovery—attending meetings, spending time with other recovering people, working the Steps with our sponsor, and doing service work—the less time we have to dwell on ourselves. The ingredients for self-pity—resentment and self-centeredness—begin to wither away as we work an enthusiastic recovery program.

Assignment

Ask in a Twelve Step meeting how people have dealt with self-pity. Journal your insights.

Closing

The chairperson asks a team member to read the SFR Closing Statement.

WEEK 22: STRUCTURED FAMILY RECOVERY

Date: _____

Topic: People Pleasing

Opening

The chairperson asks a team member to read the SFR Opening Statement.

Daily Reading

A team member reads aloud from a Twelve Step daily reader, then reads each of the following discussion points, allowing time for team sharing.

Report, Discuss, Plan

1. What went well in my recovery this past week? What could be improved? Do I want feedback?

2. What insights did I gain from my Twelve Step experiences? From last week's SFR assignment?

3. What new recovery behaviors will I practice this upcoming week? I will contact my accountability partner _____ times this week.

Learn Something New

Earnie Larsen, the late recovery author and lecturer, wrote in his book *Stage II Recovery,* "People-pleasers have learned that their self-esteem is based on never making anyone angry." People-pleasers have difficulty saying no because they fear their loved ones and friends will become angry. Therefore, people-pleasers aren't free to be honest about what they think or how they feel. They don't get what they need and, as a result, harbor hidden resentments. This character defect is marked by fear, resentment, and dishonesty. People-pleasers often use phrases such as "It doesn't matter" when their efforts aren't sufficiently acknowledged or they don't get their way. But of course it does—very much.

Steps Four and Five

Made a searching and fearless moral inventory of ourselves.

*Admitted to God, to ourselves, and to another human being
the exact nature of our wrongs.*

People-pleasers cannot begin taking care of themselves until they name this character defect. Otherwise the fear of making others angry continues as a normal part of life. Steps Four and Five take us out of our comfort zone and make it so people-pleasing—and other defects—are no longer the norm. This moves us toward change.

Working a Recovery Program

Recovering people model honesty and openness. There is no safer place for people-pleasers to begin testing the waters than Twelve Step meetings. Experiencing acceptance when expressing honest thoughts and true feelings is liberating. By completing a Fourth and Fifth Step, they learn that they can be honest about their resentments and fears without being abandoned. Rather, they are readily welcomed into the recovery community. In Al-Anon, they hear other recovering people-pleasers share how they began respecting themselves. Little by little, people-pleasers begin losing their fears, letting go of resentments, and living a more fulfilling emotional life.

Assignment

Earnie Larsen was known for asking, "Who's driving your bus?" Ask yourself, "What defects are driving my bus?" If possible, schedule your Fifth Step with your sponsor or trusted counselor sometime in the upcoming two weeks, if you haven't already done so. It may seem like an insurmountable task, but by following the suggestions of someone experienced in doing Fifth Steps, you'll find that it's much easier than you thought.

Closing

The chairperson asks a team member to read the SFR Closing Statement.

WEEK 23: STRUCTURED FAMILY RECOVERY

Date: _____

Topic: Regret

Opening

The chairperson asks a team member to read the SFR Opening Statement.

Daily Reading

A team member reads aloud from a Twelve Step daily reader, then reads each of the following discussion points, allowing time for team sharing.

Report, Discuss, Plan

1. What went well in my recovery this past week? What could be improved? Do I want feedback?

2. What insights did I gain from my Twelve Step experiences? From last week's SFR assignment?

3. What new recovery behaviors will I practice this upcoming week? I will contact my accountability partner _____ times this week.

Learn Something New

Regret binds us to the past. Recovering people often say, "You can't move forward when you are facing backward." For addicts, the negative consequences of addiction can be devastating. Their life is often in shambles and the heartache is unbearable. The family, too, is grieving many losses. Family members often say, "I wish we had gotten into recovery years ago." But we are powerless to change the past. Self-forgiveness and gratitude for today can close the door on regret. Then we can turn toward the future and move on.

Steps Four and Five

Made a searching and fearless moral inventory of ourselves.

*Admitted to God, to ourselves, and to another human being
the exact nature of our wrongs.*

We write about our regrets in Step Four and share them with our sponsor or counselor in Step Five. Being thoroughly honest and specific about the nature of our regrets, we can rid ourselves of their power over us, bringing about a renewed peace of mind. The Fourth and Fifth Steps are housekeeping for the soul.

Working a Recovery Program

"The past is done and can't be returned. So if we can do a good job this day we are doing the best we possibly can." This quote comes from the pamphlet "A Guide to the Twelve Steps of Alcoholics Anonymous."[106] It reminds us that we have power only over today. The past has let us go; let's let it go. The wisdom that comes from working a daily recovery program will prepare us to address our defects of character.

Assignment

Display the above AA quote about the past someplace where you'll see it every day. Ask members of your Twelve Step group how they moved past their most troublesome regrets. Journal your insights.

Closing

The chairperson asks a team member to read the SFR Closing Statement.

WEEK 24: STRUCTURED FAMILY RECOVERY

Date: _____

Topic: A New Freedom

Opening

The chairperson asks a team member to read the SFR Opening Statement.

Daily Reading

A team member reads aloud from a Twelve Step daily reader, then reads each of the following discussion points, allowing time for team sharing.

Report, Discuss, Plan

1. What went well in my recovery this past week? What could be improved? Do I want feedback?

2. What insights did I gain from my Twelve Step experiences? From last week's SFR assignment?

3. What new recovery behaviors will I practice this upcoming week? I will contact my accountability partner _____ times this week.

Learn Something New

When we identify harmful behavior patterns, we are preparing the ground for new seeds. Harvest time will bring a bounty of spiritual gifts. According to a parable on integrity and honesty, "If you plant honesty, you will reap trust. If you plant goodness, you will reap friends. If you plant humility, you will reap greatness. If you plant perseverance, you will reap victory. If you plant consideration, you will reap harmony. If you plant hard work, you will reap success. If you plant forgiveness, you will reap reconciliation. If you plant openness, you will reap intimacy. If you plant patience, you will reap improvements. If you plant faith, you will reap miracles."[107]

Steps Four and Five

Made a searching and fearless moral inventory of ourselves.

Admitted to God, to ourselves, and to another human being the exact nature of our wrongs.

We can experience a new freedom after completing Steps Four and Five, but only if we've been truly thorough in our inventory. Some people omit a particularly embarrassing incident from their Fifth Step, thinking erroneously that it will have been enough to write it in their Fourth Step. The relief we seek from these Steps will not be realized until we make an admission of powerlessness over the past and clear out all our baggage.

Working a Recovery Program

From a blog written by a member of AA, called *Mr. SponsorPants,* comes an honest account of the changes that come from working the Twelve Steps. "I am sharing about the storm on the surface because, if I don't, it gets worse. But rest assured, like the depths of the ocean, there is a core of peace which AA helped me to develop, and it is always there. Some would go further, saying it's a living connection with a God consciousness, and on some days I would more easily agree with them than others, but it is there regardless. . . . Find the seeds inside yourself and develop them, because from that place will come a connection to a power greater than yourself. From that place will come an ability to empathize with other people's struggles. . . . From that place will come the ability to maintain your physical sobriety . . . and then to grow into mental, emotional, and spiritual sobriety as well."[108]

Assignment

Completing Steps Four and Five is a rite of passage in Twelve Step programs. It's the single most important thing you can do to galvanize your recovery. Many people treat themselves to something special after completing this process. Reach out to others and celebrate this milestone.

Closing

The chairperson asks a team member to read the SFR Closing Statement.

Third Quarter

The next twelve weeks focus on issues common to the seventh, eighth, and ninth months of recovery. At this point, by following the directions, family and addict are likely to be starting to truly enjoy this journey. New and different things are happening, trust is being rebuilt, and recovery is beginning to bear fruit.

We expect that team members have completed Steps Four and Five by this point. Now it's time to get to the heart of recovery by working Steps Six, Seven, Eight, and Nine. It's easy to overlook these Steps, but they are transformational. It's said they separate the men from the boys, and the women from the girls. Actively work with your Twelve Step sponsor on these Steps while following the guidance of your SFR meetings.

WEEK 25: STRUCTURED FAMILY RECOVERY

Date: _____

Topic: Attitude

Opening

The chairperson asks a team member to read the SFR Opening Statement.

Daily Reading

A team member reads aloud from a Twelve Step daily reader, then reads each of the following discussion points, allowing time for team sharing.

Report, Discuss, Plan

1. What went well in my recovery this past week? What could be improved? Do I want feedback?

2. What insights did I gain from my Twelve Step experiences? From last week's SFR assignment?

3. What new recovery behaviors will I practice this upcoming week? I will contact my accountability partner _____ times this week.

Learn Something New

Attitude is a way of thinking and feeling that colors how we evaluate our relationships and circumstances. The Latin root words for *attitude—apto* and *acto*—mean "to do or to act." It was a clear connection between attitude and action. It wasn't until the mid-1800s that psychologists began using the word to mean "an internal state of preparation for action."[109] Today we know that when we witness someone else's positive behaviors, we are likely to behave in a similar manner. This leads to changes in attitude. The effective message for change is, "We're doing it and it works." It's easy to see why "Do what I say not what I do" has such a poor record of success.

Step Six

Were entirely ready to have God remove
all these defects of character.

This Step is about a new attitude. We admitted our defects, now we are asked to be entirely ready to let them all be removed from us. This Step doesn't ask us to remove our own character defects—something none of us has been able to manage—but to trust that a power greater than ourselves can and will remove them.

Working a Recovery Program

People working a Twelve Step program often say that AA could stand for "adjusting attitudes." The same could be said of Al-Anon and other Twelve Step groups. These programs work so well because members do exactly what social scientists say works best. First, they engage in the behaviors of recovery themselves. Second, they speak positively about the results they've achieved in recovery to others. Nobody speaks from on high, telling others to do what they, themselves, are not willing to do. Newcomers, witnessing the authenticity of behaviors in AA and other Twelve Step groups, are much more likely to choose these behaviors for themselves. This is how attitudes begin changing.

Assignment

What recovery behaviors are you exhibiting on a daily basis? Do your actions match your words? Talk about this with your sponsor and in a Twelve Step meeting. Journal your insights.

Closing

The chairperson asks a team member to read the SFR Closing Statement.

WEEK 26: STRUCTURED FAMILY RECOVERY

Date: _____

Topic: Readiness

Opening

The chairperson asks a team member to read the SFR Opening Statement.

Daily Reading

A team member reads aloud from a Twelve Step daily reader, then reads each of the following discussion points, allowing time for team sharing.

Report, Discuss, Plan

1. What went well in my recovery this past week? What could be improved? Do I want feedback?

2. What insights did I gain from my Twelve Step experiences? From last week's SFR assignment?

3. What new recovery behaviors will I practice this upcoming week? I will contact my accountability partner _____ times this week.

Learn Something New

A writer of poetry and literature, C. Joybell C., writes, "We can't be afraid of change. You may feel very secure in the pond that you are in, but if you never venture out of it, you will never know that there is such a thing as an ocean, a sea."[110] Becoming ready to change is a process of decision making. The brain starts scanning for evidence on why a change will benefit us. But if we rely only on the information at hand, never throwing ourselves out into the sea, we're likely to decide staying in the pond is just fine. We don't make great strides sitting around waiting to feel ready. We need to stand up and move our feet. By having completed Steps Four and Five, we have taken the action steps necessary to get us ready for Step Six.

Step Six

*Were entirely ready to have God remove
all these defects of character.*

Our readiness is usually a result of wanting to stop the pain. If our harmful patterns of behavior aren't causing us enough pain, or we don't identify them as the source of our pain, we might remain ambivalent. This is when we have to go back to our fearless and searching inventory. What kind of life are we willing to settle for right now? Is the pond still okay? Or have we had enough?

Working a Recovery Program

"When we tried to clean ourselves up with our own power and 'discipline' we kept ourselves agitated, confused, in denial, and worn out, and we were in almost constant emotional pain," writes J. Keith Miller in his book *A Hunger for Healing*. We think we can do this Step easily ourselves, that naming our character defects means we can just let them go. It's a form of denial about our true relationship with these behaviors. We've used them for a long while, we trust them, they're comfortable, they work for us in the short run (remember our propensity for immediate gratification in the near-term), and they feel good when we use them. It's going to take a power greater than ourselves to remove them. Our part is in the readiness.

Assignment

Discuss with your sponsor the character defect you will have the most difficulty letting go of and the one that will be easiest. Journal your insights.

Closing

The chairperson asks a team member to read the SFR Closing Statement.

WEEK 27: STRUCTURED FAMILY RECOVERY

Date: _____

Topic: Letting Go

Opening

The chairperson asks a team member to read the SFR Opening Statement.

Daily Reading

A team member reads aloud from a Twelve Step daily reader, then reads each of the following discussion points, allowing time for team sharing.

Report, Discuss, Plan

1. What went well in my recovery this past week? What could be improved? Do I want feedback?

2. What insights did I gain from my Twelve Step experiences? From last week's SFR assignment?

3. What new recovery behaviors will I practice this upcoming week? I will contact my accountability partner _____ times this week.

Learn Something New

Michelangelo, Italian sculptor and painter of the High Renaissance, upon finishing one of the most remarkable pieces of sculpture ever created, was asked how he did it. It is said that he replied, "I saw David in this block of marble, and I then chipped away everything that wasn't David." That block of marble represents us encased in the character defects caused by coping with the disease of addiction. In doing Step Six, we're ready to have our Higher Power chip away everything that isn't our best self, ready to live our best life in recovery.

Step Six

Were entirely ready to have God remove
all these defects of character.

What is our reluctance for letting go of defects of character? What is it about a particular pattern of behaviors that is so comforting to us, even when it blocks our spiritual growth? Do we believe we can continue relying on our defects without hurting ourselves or others?

Working a Recovery Program

We are often afraid of letting go of well-used character defects because we don't know what we'll have left. It's in working a recovery program that we are given the skills that replace old behaviors. We don't need to be afraid of letting go anymore. We are constantly developing new patterns that bring us a better way of living. Working an active recovery program provides a solution, which makes readiness a natural part of the process.

Assignment

Take fifteen minutes to journal a vision of who you will be without your old patterns of behavior.

Closing

The chairperson asks a team member to read the SFR Closing Statement.

WEEK 28: STRUCTURED FAMILY RECOVERY

Date: _____

Topic: Self-Acceptance

Opening

The chairperson asks a team member to read the SFR Opening Statement.

Daily Reading

A team member reads aloud from a Twelve Step daily reader, then reads each of the following discussion points, allowing time for team sharing.

Report, Discuss, Plan

1. What went well in my recovery this past week? What could be improved? Do I want feedback?

2. What insights did I gain from my Twelve Step experiences? From last week's SFR assignment?

3. What new recovery behaviors will I practice this upcoming week? I will contact my accountability partner _____ times this week.

Learn Something New

Moving through the Steps, from Four to Seven, is a quest to realize our best selves. In the past, we've had a tendency not to use the best of us in important ways. We put more faith into our trusted, but eventually ineffective, ways of responding to crisis, which brought out our defects. Now, we must take a good look at what is worth saving and then ask our Higher Power to help us chip away the rest. If Michelangelo hadn't seen David, why would he ever have begun chipping away at the marble?

Step Seven

Humbly asked Him to remove our shortcomings.

Approaching Step Seven humbly means we are accepting ourselves as we are, in this moment. By asking to have our shortcomings removed, we are trusting that our best selves, with all our imperfections, are enough.

Working a Recovery Program

A recovering friend said to me, "These two Steps, Six and Seven, gave me inner peace and a sense of beauty about myself. I was finally comfortable in my own skin." Step Seven tells us we can leave all the good stuff, meaning our true best selves, in place, while our Higher Power helps us remove everything that distracts from the good. God *as we understand Him* doesn't just come along and lop it all off with a single stroke. Defects of character are chipped away one day at a time. Our Higher Power comes to our assistance in many different forms through our program of recovery.

Assignment

Every morning for the next week, spend one minute with your eyes closed identifying one characteristic of your better self and how you will use it that day.

Closing

The chairperson asks a team member to read the SFR Closing Statement.

WEEK 29: STRUCTURED FAMILY RECOVERY

Date: _____

Topic: Service

Opening

The chairperson asks a team member to read the SFR Opening Statement.

Daily Reading

A team member reads aloud from a Twelve Step daily reader, then reads each of the following discussion points, allowing time for team sharing.

Report, Discuss, Plan

1. What went well in my recovery this past week? What could be improved? Do I want feedback?

2. What insights did I gain from my Twelve Step experiences? From last week's SFR assignment?

3. What new recovery behaviors will I practice this upcoming week? I will contact my accountability partner _____ times this week.

Learn Something New

In the words of Rabindranath Tagore, Nobel Laureate in Literature, "I slept and dreamt that life was joy. I awoke and saw that life was service. I acted and behold, service was joy." Service brings out the best in us. It's an external act of considering others before self. It is how we show gratitude for our recovery by giving back. In service, we gain a sense of belonging and feel the warmth of other people. Much of our positive spirituality comes through the outward journey of service.

Step Seven

Humbly asked Him to remove our shortcomings.

Our shortcomings separate us from others. When we humbly ask our Higher Power to remove these defects, we are accepting reality. By asking for help, we stop making unreasonable demands on ourselves. As an anonymous academic in recovery wrote, "Asking for help is the turning point. After that, the story changes tone, from anxiety to hope, from tragedy to laughter. That story is called recovery. And that is where it gets good."

Working a Recovery Program

In the Hazelden pamphlet *Steps 6 and 7: Ready, Willing and Able,* it's suggested we have a conversation with our Higher Power, "I am willing to let down the barriers between me and the rest of the world. Please remove all my defects and help me to become my best self. I am ready to go out and do Your work without the swords and shields I thought I needed."[111] Or we can use the Seventh Step Prayer from the Big Book of Alcoholics Anonymous: "My Creator, I am now willing that you should have all of me, good and bad. I pray that you now remove from me every single defect of character which stands in the way of my usefulness to you and my fellows."[112] This Step helps us develop ourselves more fully, both emotionally and spiritually.

Assignment

Discuss with your sponsor how you will complete your Seventh Step in a meaningful way.

Closing

The chairperson asks a team member to read the SFR Closing Statement.

WEEK 30: STRUCTURED FAMILY RECOVERY

Date: _____

Topic: Change

Opening

The chairperson asks a team member to read the SFR Opening Statement.

Daily Reading

A team member reads aloud from a Twelve Step daily reader, then reads each of the following discussion points, allowing time for team sharing.

Report, Discuss, Plan

1. What went well in my recovery this past week? What could be improved? Do I want feedback?

2. What insights did I gain from my Twelve Step experiences? From last week's SFR assignment?

3. What new recovery behaviors will I practice this upcoming week? I will contact my accountability partner _____ times this week.

Learn Something New

Everywhere, people resist change. Change occurs continually in the business world because of competition, yet many business leaders are always dealing with employees' resistance to change. It's one of the greatest contributors to loss of productivity and lowered quality of service. Change requires moving in the direction of the unknown, and we prefer to stay in the known, even when it's no longer relevant or effective in dealing with our current situation. Fear of change is common on a social level, too. We connect with people using our established patterns of behavior. It's how we're used to relating to each other. Anything else that falls outside of our comfort zone feels awkward and unnatural. For this reason, recovery asks us to take change in small steps.

Step Eight

Made a list of all persons we had harmed, and
became willing to make amends to them all.

This is the first Step that directly touches our personal relationships. We take a look around to see who we've harmed. We do this for two good reasons: 1) To consider how we can develop the best possible relationship with every person in our lives, and 2) To begin to end our emotional isolation. This is a *preparation* Step.

Working a Recovery Program

In AA and NA, members cannot deny that their disease has caused others harm. But in Al-Anon, it's harder to imagine the necessity of this Step. We say, "I haven't hurt anyone! I was the responsible one. I was the one who took the brunt of all the problems." But when we are defending ourselves from addiction in the family, we develop survival skills, and over time, they hurt us and others. Working with our sponsor and listening to others in Twelve Step meetings, our eyes are opened, and we begin to see. In Steps Four through Seven, we cleaned up past selves, now we are preparing to clean up our relationships. This is an act of integrity.

Assignment

Discuss Step Eight with your sponsor this week. Ask others in your Twelve Step meetings about their experiences with Step Eight. Journal your insights.

Closing

The chairperson asks a team member to read the SFR Closing Statement.

WEEK 31: STRUCTURED FAMILY RECOVERY

Date: _____

Topic: Progress

Opening

The chairperson asks a team member to read the SFR Opening Statement.

Daily Reading

A team member reads aloud from a Twelve Step daily reader, then reads each of the following discussion points, allowing time for team sharing.

Report, Discuss, Plan

1. What went well in my recovery this past week? What could be improved? Do I want feedback?

2. What insights did I gain from my Twelve Step experiences? From last week's SFR assignment?

3. What new recovery behaviors will I practice this upcoming week? I will contact my accountability partner _____ times this week.

Learn Something New

In the words of Ernest Hemingway, "There is nothing noble in being superior to your fellow man; true nobility is being superior to your former self." By now, in working our Twelve Step program and meeting weekly with our Structured Family Recovery team, we most assuredly are "superior to our former selves." How do we know? By the quality of our relationships. Take a look at your inventory, and notice the things you are not doing any more—and acknowledge how you're doing things differently now. Let's take a moment to smell the roses.

Step Eight

*Made a list of all persons we had harmed, and
became willing to make amends to them all.*

If everything we've done in recovery thus far has brought us to this point, Steps Eight and Nine represent a quantum leap forward in our relationships, with others and ourselves. Taking these Steps we become aware that we're people of worth. It's paradoxical. By becoming willing to make amends to all whom we've harmed—acknowledging our wrongs—we clear away the debris that prevents us from seeing what's right in our life. We live in the present with no regrets or fears about the past. It is a marvelous feeling.

Working a Recovery Program

We work Steps Eight and Nine with our Twelve Step sponsor. We need guidance on taking these Steps so we don't use them in a way that further injures others or ourselves. We also need help avoiding reluctance to "make amends to them all." Self-interest is a natural reaction to these Steps, which fuels avoidance. But with power we've gained from working the previous Steps, we are now coming from our better selves. We have already brought our best qualities to the world: willingness, thoroughness, courage, honesty, and acceptance. These qualities are all we need to make our list.

Assignment

Talk with your sponsor about the ways working a Twelve Step program has changed your relationships. This is the positive part of your relationship inventory, revealing the fruits of your efforts. It also helps you see the value of taking this next Step. Journal your insights.

Closing

The chairperson asks a team member to read the SFR Closing Statement.

WEEK 32: STRUCTURED FAMILY RECOVERY

Date: _____

Topic: Self-Awareness

Opening

The chairperson asks a team member to read the SFR Opening Statement.

Daily Reading

A team member reads aloud from a Twelve Step daily reader, then reads each of the following discussion points, allowing time for team sharing.

Report, Discuss, Plan

1. What went well in my recovery this past week? What could be improved? Do I want feedback?

2. What insights did I gain from my Twelve Step experiences? From last week's SFR assignment?

3. What new recovery behaviors will I practice this upcoming week? I will contact my accountability partner _____ times this week.

Learn Something New

Self-awareness is being conscious of the true condition of our existence. When we're living with addiction, we are so vigilant about what the alcoholic or addict is doing, we are no longer aware of ourselves. We even lose our grasp on just how bad things have become. Without self-awareness we cannot know our strengths or our limitations. Working the Twelve Steps wakes us up. We go through a series of Steps that help us look at ourselves and become aware of others in a new way. We may be bruised and battered—both alcoholic and family—but these Steps heal and strengthen us.

Step Eight

*Made a list of all persons we had harmed, and
became willing to make amends to them all.*

This Step gives us clear directions: make a list. But our lack of self-awareness can blind us to how we've harmed others. How do we begin to get ready if we can't see our part in a harm that has occurred? Here are some questions to ask: *How has my contempt for the addict hurt others? Have I turned people against each other by what I've said? Who have I taken my frustrations out on? How have my character defects harmed others, directly or indirectly? Have I withdrawn from others? In what ways have I neglected others, especially children? Where have I placed blame?* Living with addiction twists all of our behaviors; it's the true nature of the disease.

Working a Recovery Program

Working a Twelve Step program is a gift because it provides a place where everyone understands what it's like to live with the disease of addiction; where everyone is open and honest about their shortcomings and wrongdoings; where everyone takes action to thoroughly clean house; where everyone gives up blame, anger, and resentment, and knows how to accept and even laugh at the past. Those of us who have suffered under the tyranny of addiction are in the right place when we come to a Twelve Step meeting.

Assignment

Look back to your Fourth Step inventory to help you write your list for Step Eight. Do this with your sponsor's guidance.

Closing

The chairperson asks a team member to read the SFR Closing Statement.

WEEK 33: STRUCTURED FAMILY RECOVERY

Date: _____

Topic: Easy Does It

Opening

The chairperson asks a team member to read the SFR Opening Statement.

Daily Reading

A team member reads aloud from a Twelve Step daily reader, then reads each of the following discussion points, allowing time for team sharing.

Report, Discuss, Plan

1. What went well in my recovery this past week? What could be improved? Do I want feedback?

2. What insights did I gain from my Twelve Step experiences? From last week's SFR assignment?

3. What new recovery behaviors will I practice this upcoming week? I will contact my accountability partner _____ times this week.

Learn Something New

"Easy does it" is one of the most useful Twelve Step slogans. Many people may treat it scornfully as simplistic, but they overlook the power behind the words. The slogan means *relax*. First relax your muscles, then the expression on your face. Allow the corners of your mouth to lift in just a touch of a smile, and breathe in and out of your nose slowly. Notice the little space between your inhale and exhale. Some call it the "God space." Observe how your mind is following the example of your body, and it begins to relax, too. This one slogan has saved many a person from themselves, especially during those early months of recovery when working the Steps for the first time.

Step Eight

*Made a list of all persons we had harmed, and
became willing to make amends to them all.*

There are four common reasons people postpone taking this Step: fear, pride, procrastination, or the belief that we haven't harmed others. Whichever one we might be experiencing, our sponsor can help us examine our motives. Do we want to look good to others? Are we afraid our amends will be received poorly? Do we only see the ways we've been caught up in another's bad behaviors, without seeing our own role? When we are justifying or rationalizing, putting it off, or projecting into the future what might happen when we make amends, it's an indication we may just need to relax and remind ourselves, "Easy does it."

Working a Recovery Program

Most of us came to Step Four with trepidation but found it easier than we imagined. Now we are making another list that often proves *not* to be as difficult as we think. We will follow our sponsor's lead. We can even take this Step with a bit of excitement, thinking how good it will feel to finally have a thoroughly clean house.

Assignment

Talk with your sponsor about any trepidation you have about working this Step, and ask how he or she felt after completing Steps Eight and Nine. Then schedule a time to write your list.

Closing

The chairperson asks a team member to read the SFR Closing Statement.

WEEK 34: STRUCTURED FAMILY RECOVERY

Date: _____

Topic: Repairing the Past

Opening

The chairperson asks a team member to read the SFR Opening Statement.

Daily Reading

A team member reads aloud from a Twelve Step daily reader, then reads each of the following discussion points, allowing time for team sharing.

Report, Discuss, Plan

1. What went well in my recovery this past week? What could be improved? Do I want feedback?

2. What insights did I gain from my Twelve Step experiences? From last week's SFR assignment?

3. What new recovery behaviors will I practice this upcoming week? I will contact my accountability partner _____ times this week.

Learn Something New

Members of Al-Anon describe their experiences with Step Nine:

"My sponsor insisted I made amends to myself before approaching others."

"My sponsor guided me on how to make amends to each person on my list."

"It was very humbling. I hadn't realized that I'd played a part in the alcoholism."

"I couldn't make amends to someone on my list, so my sponsor had me make 'living amends' by changing my behavior."

"I was scared, but making amends made a huge difference in my life."

"Amends were about me getting my affairs in order not an attempt to seek forgiveness from others."

Step Nine

Made direct amends to such people wherever possible,
except when to do so would injure them or others.

Making amends is easier when we bring a love to the process that asks for nothing in return. The only expectation we have is for ourselves: Complete this Step under the guidance of a sponsor, move forward courageously, do no harm to anyone, be thorough, make amends to yourself, and keep it simple.

Working a Recovery Program

Working the previous eight Steps makes it possible to do Step Nine. We couldn't have done it any sooner, because we wouldn't have known what this Step required. Making amends isn't the same as saying empty words of apology. As is true of the rest of the program, it requires a change in behavior. We are cleaning up our side of the street and don't want to sully it in the months and years to come. Once we've completed Step Nine, we move into *living amends*: treating others the way we want to be treated.

Assignment

Sit down with your sponsor, go over your list, and decide the best way to proceed for each person you've listed. Ask yourself, "Am I leaving anyone off this list?"

Closing

The chairperson asks a team member to read the SFR Closing Statement.

WEEK 35: STRUCTURED FAMILY RECOVERY

Date: _____

Topic: Forgiveness

Opening
The chairperson asks a team member to read the SFR Opening Statement.

Daily Reading
A team member reads aloud from a Twelve Step daily reader, then reads each of the following discussion points, allowing time for team sharing.

Report, Discuss, Plan
1. What went well in my recovery this past week? What could be improved? Do I want feedback?

2. What insights did I gain from my Twelve Step experiences? From last week's SFR assignment?

3. What new recovery behaviors will I practice this upcoming week? I will contact my accountability partner _____ times this week.

Learn Something New
It's important to decide if we are still harboring anger, blame, or resentment toward anyone on our list. We need to work through these feelings before we make our amends. We are back to the topic of forgiveness. It's a skill important in all areas of life. In an article in *Forbes*, Amanda Neville writes how forgiveness can save, not a family, but a business: "Forgiveness is a process. It takes time and effort. Start by reflecting on what happened and try to see the other point of view. If you have a hard time seeing their side, try putting yourself in their shoes and write a letter to yourself outlining what happened. Think about how your choices and actions contributed to the situation. Evaluate the cost of holding on to your negative emotions versus letting go of them in the name of

forgiveness. The key is to reconnect with your empathy; with a more centered sense of reality; and with your attachment to your partner."[113]

Step Nine

Made direct amends to such people wherever possible,
except when to do so would injure them or others.

We are asked to make amends unless it will hurt that person or someone else. Determine with your sponsor if there is someone on your list you could harm. In these cases, we make creative amends, which provide other ways to clean up our part of the problem. Be sure your motives in avoiding direct amends are honest and not a case of avoidance.

Working a Recovery Program

If we struggle to forgive someone on our list, we must use the program to help us. Anger, blame, or resentments are treacherous for recovering people. Such emotions cause alcoholics to drink and addicts to use. These feelings can cause families to lose their emotional sobriety. Discuss the danger of hanging on to these negative emotions with your sponsor. It is in our best interest that we take necessary measures to overcome these lingering feelings.

Assignment

Go back to Steps One, Two, and Three to deal with any leftover anger, blame, or resentment. Ask your sponsor and members of your Twelve Step group how they've dealt with difficulties letting go of these feelings toward others. Journal your insights.

Closing

The chairperson asks a team member to read the SFR Closing Statement.

WEEK 36: STRUCTURED FAMILY RECOVERY

Date: _____

Topic: The Promises

Opening

The chairperson asks a team member to read the SFR Opening Statement.

Daily Reading

A team member reads aloud from a Twelve Step daily reader, then reads each of the following discussion points, allowing time for team sharing.

Report, Discuss, Plan

1. What went well in my recovery this past week? What could be improved? Do I want feedback?

2. What insights did I gain from my Twelve Step experiences? From last week's SFR assignment?

3. What new recovery behaviors will I practice this upcoming week? I will contact my accountability partner _____ times this week.

Learn Something New

We close each SFR meeting with *The Promises*. They are rightly titled *The Ninth Step Promises*, because it is after making amends—clearing out the rest of the debris—that all of the promises can materialize. Sitting in AA, NA, or Al-Anon meetings, you'll hear people who've *painstakingly* completed Steps One through Nine say these promises have come true for them, usually adding that they never believed it would happen and were quite amazed.

Step Nine

Made direct amends to such people wherever possible,
except when to do so would injure them or others.

When we make amends, we need to keep our expectations in check. If we move forward expecting certain things from people we are making amends to, we set ourselves up for disappointment. Their responses aren't our business. Our only job is to be honest about what we have done. We may hope to restore relationships, but we cannot control results. If someone remains angry, we know we did our best. These Steps have helped us grow along spiritual lines, but we must remember, not everyone has made spiritual progress to the point of being able to forgive some things, and they may have reasons why they can't at this time in their lives.

Working a Recovery Program

We didn't know what to expect when we attended our first Al-Anon, AA, or NA meeting, and may not have known why we needed to go. Now, after a relatively brief amount of time in the grand scheme of things, we are likely to have made significant spiritual progress *together as a family*. We have gotten better at keeping our commitments to one another and demonstrating trustworthiness. We are completing (or have completed) the last of the action Steps. It's a good time to take one minute to close our eyes in silent gratitude.

Assignment

Once you've completed your Ninth Step, sit down alone and turn to The Promises in this book or the Big Book and read them slowly to yourself. This is the legacy you've earned.

Closing

The chairperson asks a team member to read the SFR Closing Statement.

Fourth Quarter

The next twelve weeks focus on issues common to the tenth, eleventh, and twelfth months of recovery. As bad memories of active addiction begin to dim, this is a period when addict and family can begin to experience some complacency. Everyone on the team is in danger of becoming overconfident that the disease has been licked. It's more important than ever to continue following directions and work your recovery program.

This is also a time to begin planning again. The newly recovering person has been advised in treatment and by his sponsor not to make big changes in the first year of sobriety. Now approaching the one-year anniversary of sobriety, he may initiate beginning discussions about going back to school, career advancement, and any needed work on relationships.

We expect that team members have completed Steps Six, Seven, Eight, and Nine with their sponsors. By now, as a result of doing these Steps, we realize a positive spirituality is working in our lives. The team now comes to Steps Ten, Eleven, and Twelve. Step Ten is continuing to take a personal inventory on a daily basis. Step Eleven is, in essence, the whole program in one sentence, where we make our reliance on our Higher Power a daily practice. Step Twelve is the practice of helping others. Actively work with your Twelve Step sponsor on these Steps while following the guidance of your SFR meetings.

WEEK 37: STRUCTURED FAMILY RECOVERY

Date: _____

Topic: Trustworthiness

Opening
The chairperson asks a team member to read the SFR Opening Statement.

Daily Reading
A team member reads aloud from a Twelve Step daily reader, then reads each of the following discussion points, allowing time for team sharing.

Report, Discuss, Plan
1. What went well in my recovery this past week? What could be improved? Do I want feedback?

2. What insights did I gain from my Twelve Step experiences? From last week's SFR assignment?

3. What new recovery behaviors will I practice this upcoming week? I will contact my accountability partner _____ times this week.

Learn Something New
We are genetically wired to trust; it's tied to our survival and the need to cooperate with one another. Those we are most likely to trust are the people who share our DNA, and, to a degree, those who look most like us. Studies at the University of London show that we humans have a tendency to trust people who look more like us than those who don't.[114] In the online magazine *Evolution,* Dan Jones writes, "In the case of humans, it's possible that when people cooperate with us, treat us kindly or show us altruism, we tend to see them as more like family, and this influences the way we perceive their physical features."[115] This demonstrates the important role trust plays in our sense of who belongs to us. Is it any wonder it's often the first thing addicts are concerned about in

treatment: *How do I get my family to trust me again?* In other words, how do I belong to my family again?

Step Ten

*Continued to take personal inventory and
when we were wrong promptly admitted it.*

Step Ten is the trustworthiness Step. It is a daily inventory of our trustworthiness. *How did I do today? Did I trespass against someone or something? What amends do I need to make? How soon can I get it done?* If we do this every day, we are living as a trustworthy person. We don't have to be perfect, we just need to promptly admit it when we were wrong and then change that particular behavior, starting now. *Humbly asked Him to remove our shortcomings.*

Working a Recovery Program

We learn about what it means to be trustworthy from listening to others share their experience, strength, and hope. Not just the obvious stuff but the subtle little ways we're untrustworthy, which are easy to ignore or overlook. It's the stuff in the corners and under the bed. By taking a good Tenth Step on a daily basis, the house stays well scrubbed. We have peace of mind and clean relationships.

Assignment

Commit to faithfully working a Tenth Step. Identify your daily recovery trigger for your Tenth Step. Discuss with your sponsor and during a Twelve Step meeting. Journal your insights.

Closing

The chairperson asks a team member to read the SFR Closing Statement.

Date: _____

Topic: Inventory

Opening

The chairperson asks a team member to read the SFR Opening Statement.

Daily Reading

A team member reads aloud from a Twelve Step daily reader, then reads each of the following discussion points, allowing time for team sharing.

Report, Discuss, Plan

1. What went well in my recovery this past week? What could be improved? Do I want feedback?

2. What insights did I gain from my Twelve Step experiences? From last week's SFR assignment?

3. What new recovery behaviors will I practice this upcoming week? I will contact my accountability partner _____ times this week.

Learn Something New

Taking a personal inventory—or self-assessment—is an important personal activity that allows us to monitor our strengths and shortcomings. If we identify a shortcoming in our Fourth Step but don't take action, we can damage our sense of self-worth. Remember, taking an inventory is only the first step; the next step asks, "What do I need to do with this information?" As we learned in Steps Four through Nine, inventories are meant to give rise to positive actions and self-betterment. The same holds true for Step Ten.

Step Ten

*Continued to take personal inventory and
when we were wrong promptly admitted it.*

Using Step Ten to promptly admit we were wrong not only gives us an immediate opportunity to put things right, we give the people we hurt, angered, or disappointed an opportunity to forgive, cleaning up their reaction toward our transgression. Doing a Tenth Step opens doors for us both. As the American poet Emily Dickinson wrote, "Not knowing when the dawn will come, I open every door."

Working a Recovery Program

We depend on inventories because, with addiction in the family, we've been preoccupied with trying to manage and second-guess the disease. As it says in AA's *Twelve Steps and Twelve Traditions,* ". . . a great many of us have never really acquired the habit of accurate self-appraisal."[116] Working our recovery program with a daily Tenth Step changes the quality of how we live each day. We learn to depend on this Step to keep us looking forward.

Assignment

Ask members of your Twelve Step group to share how using Step Ten has changed how they live. Journal your insights.

Closing

The chairperson asks a team member to read the SFR Closing Statement.

Date: _____

Topic: Self-Righteousness

Opening

The chairperson asks a team member to read the SFR Opening Statement.

Daily Reading

A team member reads aloud from a Twelve Step daily reader, then reads each of the following discussion points, allowing time for team sharing.

Report, Discuss, Plan

1. What went well in my recovery this past week? What could be improved? Do I want feedback?

2. What insights did I gain from my Twelve Step experiences? From last week's SFR assignment?

3. What new recovery behaviors will I practice this upcoming week? I will contact my accountability partner _____ times this week.

Learn Something New

The power of spiritual inventories (what some call "soul inventories") is understood throughout world religions. For instance, Yom Kippur, the holiest day of the year among Jewish people, is a time for taking inventory of the previous year. Rabbi Ben A. Romer, writing for the *Richmond Times Dispatch*, says, "We can all too regularly be sure we are holding the higher moral ground. Too often we build our walls of assured righteousness, refusing to see the complicated lives of others. Too often we believe only our way is correct and if my way is right, yours is wrong. Perhaps there are several right ways?" Only after this soul checking, he says, is it possible for us to move forward humanly and spiritually.[117]

Step Ten

Continued to take personal inventory and
when we were wrong promptly admitted it.

We can use our Tenth Step inventory to monitor our tendencies to have to be right. Messages that we send to others that implicitly or explicitly say, "I know better; I'm right, you're not; you need to do it my way," are often symptoms of our controlling behaviors, our inability to trust other people, feelings of perfectionism, or fear of mistakes. Sometimes our insistence on being right can wrong others.

Working a Recovery Program

Recovering people often ask, "Would I rather be right or be happy?" The way we answer this question tells us much about ourselves and our relationships. A light sprinkle of self-righteousness, as author Stephen King says, "spread over all your scruples" can keep one from becoming milquetoast, but an overdose makes us insufferable. Working a program helps us create a balance. By taking even the most admirable characteristics too far in one direction or the other, we produce defects. We rely on the experiences and wisdom of other recovering people to help enlighten our thinking about balance. With this ever-increasing self-knowledge, our Tenth Step becomes a richer experience.

Assignment

In your Tenth Step, ask yourself if you are being true to the structure you built to support your recovery. By maintaining the structure, you will keep your balance during times that are rough or unpredictable. Use your Recovery Checklist to remind yourself of the components of your recovery structure.

Closing

The chairperson asks a team member to read the SFR Closing Statement.

WEEK 40: STRUCTURED FAMILY RECOVERY

Date: _____

Topic: Meditation

Opening

The chairperson asks a team member to read the SFR Opening Statement.

Daily Reading

A team member reads aloud from a Twelve Step daily reader, then reads each of the following discussion points, allowing time for team sharing.

Report, Discuss, Plan

1. What went well in my recovery this past week? What could be improved? Do I want feedback?

2. What insights did I gain from my Twelve Step experiences? From last week's SFR assignment?

3. What new recovery behaviors will I practice this upcoming week? I will contact my accountability partner _____ times this week.

Learn Something New

If you constantly stir a glass of muddy water, the sediment continues to swirl keeping the water cloudy and opaque; but by letting the water settle for a while, soon it clears. We can't stop our thoughts during meditation, but as author Deepak Chopra says, we find the quiet between thoughts. Begin by sitting up comfortably. Repeat a positive statement, such as, "My happiness is with me now in this moment." We remind ourselves that we are powerless over the past, and we cannot predict the future. We close our eyes, and breathe in and out slowly for a few moments, noticing that each inhale goes uphill and exhales go down the other side. This is a simple but effective meditation. We end the meditation by asking our Higher Power to guide our thoughts and behaviors, using Step Three.

Step Eleven

Sought through prayer and meditation to improve our conscious contact with God as we understood Him, *praying only for knowledge of His will for us and the power to carry that out.*

Whereas Step Ten asks us to review our day, Step Eleven asks us to begin each day by considering what we will make of it. This is our time to consider the day ahead. Through meditation or prayer, we ask our Higher Power to guide our thinking so we don't fall into destructive patterns. We're assured in the Big Book that if we do this daily, "Our thought-life will be placed on a much higher plane when our thinking is cleared of wrong motives."[118] We'll also have much less to be concerned with when doing our Tenth Step later.

Working a Recovery Program

Step Eleven harkens us back to Steps Two and Three, working in partnership with a power greater than ourselves. This Step encourages the good in us, helping us flower and grow. We maintain a positive spirituality by turning ourselves over to the care of our Higher Power every morning. As for prayer and what to pray for, the Greek philosopher Pythagoras wrote, "Do not pray for yourself: You do not know what will help you."

Assignment

Begin meditating or praying for a few minutes when you rise each morning. Discuss practicing Step Eleven with your sponsor.

Closing

The chairperson asks a team member to read the SFR Closing Statement.

WEEK 41: STRUCTURED FAMILY RECOVERY

Date: _____

Topic: Guidance

Opening

The chairperson asks a team member to read the SFR Opening Statement.

Daily Reading

A team member reads aloud from a Twelve Step daily reader, then reads each of the following discussion points, allowing time for team sharing.

Report, Discuss, Plan

1. What went well in my recovery this past week? What could be improved? Do I want feedback?

2. What insights did I gain from my Twelve Step experiences? From last week's SFR assignment?

3. What new recovery behaviors will I practice this upcoming week? I will contact my accountability partner _____ times this week.

Learn Something New

Known for her spiritual literary works, Saint Teresa of Avila is one of the most beloved and influential Christian saints. Her poem "Clarity Is Freedom" brings us to a deeper understanding of guidance. "I had tea yesterday with a great theologian, and he asked me, 'What is your experience of God's will?' I liked that question—for the distillation of thought hones thought in others. Clarity, I know, is freedom. What is my experience of God's will? Everyone is a traveler. Most all need lodging, food, and clothes. I let enter my mouth what will enrich me. I wear what will make my eyes content. I sleep where I will wake with the strength to deeply love all my mind can hold. What is God's will for a wing? Every bird knows that."[119]

Step Eleven

*Sought through prayer and meditation to improve our
conscious contact with God* as we understood Him, *praying only for
knowledge of His will for us and the power to carry that out.*

One definition of guidance is the act of setting and holding a course.
After coming this far in the Twelve Step program, we are working the
final three Steps that help us stay the course. They are called the maintenance Steps. We may be tempted to think, at this point, that we've arrived. But much like physical exercise, once you are in an optimal place,
you need to maintain it. For us in recovery, this requires ongoing guidance from those in the program and from our Higher Power.

Working a Recovery Program

The purpose of this Step is to make contact with our Higher Power and
embrace a higher purpose for our lives. Again, we are called to access a
power greater than ourselves to achieve what we could not achieve on
our own. We have witnessed a power at work in our Twelve Step groups.
Those of us who've worked these Steps with rigorous honesty find ourselves in a place we couldn't imagine just months ago. These are changes
that go far beyond the addict's sobriety. But every single one is necessary
for the continuation of sobriety, both physical and emotional.

Assignment

Discuss what guidance you need in this stage of your recovery with your
sponsor. How does Step Eleven bring you back to Steps Two and Three?
Journal your insights.

Closing

The chairperson asks a team member to read the SFR Closing Statement.

WEEK 42: STRUCTURED FAMILY RECOVERY

Date: _____

Topic: Conscious Contact

Opening

The chairperson asks a team member to read the SFR Opening Statement.

Daily Reading

A team member reads aloud from a Twelve Step daily reader, then reads each of the following discussion points, allowing time for team sharing.

Report, Discuss, Plan

1. What went well in my recovery this past week? What could be improved? Do I want feedback?

2. What insights did I gain from my Twelve Step experiences? From last week's SFR assignment?

3. What new recovery behaviors will I practice this upcoming week? I will contact my accountability partner _____ times this week.

Learn Something New

Hafiz, considered to be one of history's greatest lyricists and an inspiration to luminaries such as Emerson, Goethe, Brahms, and Nietzsche, penned these lines of poetry that speak to the need of conscious contact: "Just sit there right now. Don't do a thing. Just rest. For your separation from God is the hardest work in this world. Let me bring you trays of food and something that you like to drink. You can use my soft words as a cushion for your head."

Step Eleven

*Sought through prayer and meditation to improve our
conscious contact with God* as we understood Him, *praying only for
knowledge of His will for us and the power to carry that out.*

Recovering people often say that prayer is when you are talking to God; meditation is listening. Making conscious contact with our Higher Power moves us beyond our wants to higher aspirations and willingness to help others. We're being put in touch with our better selves. We're not asked to pray for what we can do for ourselves. This Step tells us to pray for the knowledge of what our Higher Power would have us do in these next twenty-four hours. It's a replacement for what we want to do. This is crucial for us all but especially for the recovering addict. It answers that question, *who is driving your bus?* We then ask for the power to carry out the will of God *as we understand Him.* As Søren Kierkegaard wrote, "The function of prayer is not to influence God, but rather to change the nature of the one who prays."

Working a Recovery Program

Step Eleven isn't used in isolation from the rest of our program. We need the people in recovery to "bring us trays of food and cushion our head," as we struggle to find this conscious contact. Step Eleven is about living our way into this higher place. Staying close to recovering people who have the wisdom to see what we cannot see helps us from veering off in another direction. Some people get on their knees—not necessarily in a religious fashion—to keep themselves humble enough to make a connection.

Assignment

When doing Step Eleven, keep it simple. Recalling the concept of "tiny tasks," take just two or three minutes every morning for prayer and meditation. Find a recovery trigger as a reminder, such as the moment you get out of bed, once you brush your teeth, or after your morning Twelve Step reading.

Closing

The chairperson asks a team member to read the SFR Closing Statement.

WEEK 43: STRUCTURED FAMILY RECOVERY

Date: _____

Topic: Spiritual Awakening

Opening

The chairperson asks a team member to read the SFR Opening Statement.

Daily Reading

A team member reads aloud from a Twelve Step daily reader, then reads each of the following discussion points, allowing time for team sharing.

Report, Discuss, Plan

1. What went well in my recovery this past week? What could be improved? Do I want feedback?

2. What insights did I gain from my Twelve Step experiences? From last week's SFR assignment?

3. What new recovery behaviors will I practice this upcoming week? I will contact my accountability partner _____ times this week.

Learn Something New

Rumi, born in the thirteenth century, is known as one of the greatest poets in history. His verse "The Silk Worm" seems an ode to spiritual awakening. "I stood before a silk worm one day. And that night my heart said to me, 'I can do things like that, I can spin skies, I can be woven into love that can bring warmth to people; I can be soft against a crying face, I can be wings that lift, and I can travel on my thousand feet throughout the earth, my sacks filled with the sacred.' And I replied to my heart, 'Dear, can you really do all those things?' And it just nodded 'Yes' in silence. So we began and will never cease."[120]

Step Eleven

*Sought through prayer and meditation to improve our
conscious contact with God* as we understood Him, *praying only for
knowledge of His will for us and the power to carry that out.*

A spiritual experience is often believed to be something ethereal, brought
on by mystical powers. Nothing could be further from what happens
in Twelve Step groups. The spiritual awakening we are talking about is
earned. We create a space for grace. These Twelve Steps move us toward our awakening. It's very real and practical in nature. What might
be thought of as mystical, or soul filling, may come as we work on these
Steps with a sponsor, practicing honesty, forgiveness, and service as we
work them. Thus our lives are different today. We started in such a dark,
hopeless place, but we aren't there any longer. Life is not meant to be
perfect, but we have a serenity we didn't have before.

Working a Recovery Program

The immensely thoughtful blog *AA Redux* posts: "A typical 'view of the
world' as seen by an alcoholic in the depths of his disease focused mainly
on only its most immediate, close by features. Being crazily 'self-absorbed'
as a result of the spiritual malady, the most obvious part of the world
seemed to center on the most recent threat. From that point of view, successful living seemed to have everything to do with surviving the latest
'attack' and very little to do with a more reasoned idea about living successfully on a planet with another six or seven billion people, the majority
of whom had no interest in 'attacking' us at all."[121] We family members can
also relate to this malady. This is what working a program of the Twelve
Steps has helped us leave behind. Our awakening is clear by comparison.

Assignment

Sit with your sponsor and look over the road you have traveled. Now at
Step Eleven, what are your fruits? How will this Step help you go further? Journal your insights.

Closing

The chairperson asks a team member to read the SFR Closing Statement.

WEEK 44: STRUCTURED FAMILY RECOVERY

Date: _____

Topic: Serenity

Opening

The chairperson asks a team member to read the SFR Opening Statement.

Daily Reading

A team member reads aloud from a Twelve Step daily reader, then reads each of the following discussion points, allowing time for team sharing.

Report, Discuss, Plan

1. What went well in my recovery this past week? What could be improved? Do I want feedback?

2. What insights did I gain from my Twelve Step experiences? From last week's SFR assignment?

3. What new recovery behaviors will I practice this upcoming week? I will contact my accountability partner _____ times this week.

Learn Something New

The Serenity Prayer tells us we must have serenity, courage, and wisdom. The Ninth Step Promises also speak of serenity, courage, and wisdom. Both family and addict may offer a litany of reasons why they want lasting sobriety, but in the end, whether we understand it or not, the goal of recovery is to achieve serenity. Once we've reached this inner peace, we have handled most everything we had the power to change. It's our serenity that allows us to accept the things we cannot change. To finally reach this place of inner peace required courage and wisdom so we could take the necessary steps to get there.

Step Twelve

Having had a spiritual awakening as a result of these steps,
we tried to carry this message to alcoholics, and to practice
these principles in all our affairs.

Step Twelve tells us serenity is already within us as a result of the spiritual awakening we've had working the Steps. Suddenly, it seemed to materialize. As a recovering friend of mine said, "It's as if I took a long deep breath, and there it was." Serenity is necessary for lasting sobriety. We desire inner peace, and if we don't find it, we will search for something to fill the void, slow the agitation. For the addict, it's another drink or drug.

Working a Recovery Program

After working a program of recovery for a couple of years or more, having largely put our lives back together, new outside issues begin to arise. A girlfriend leaves, there is friction with the boss, a beloved grandparent dies. Improved circumstances and relationships come with losses and difficulties, too. It's the internal benefits of recovery—the deep well of serenity—and our ability to reach out for help that carry us through. Spiritual maintenance is required so we don't relapse over life.

Assignment

How do Steps Ten, Eleven, and Twelve work together to maintain your spiritual condition on a daily basis? Discuss with your sponsor. Journal your insights.

Closing

The chairperson asks a team member to read the SFR Closing Statement.

WEEK 45: STRUCTURED FAMILY RECOVERY

Date: _____

Topic: Service

Opening

The chairperson asks a team member to read the SFR Opening Statement.

Daily Reading

A team member reads aloud from a Twelve Step daily reader, then reads each of the following discussion points, allowing time for team sharing.

Report, Discuss, Plan

1. What went well in my recovery this past week? What could be improved? Do I want feedback?

2. What insights did I gain from my Twelve Step experiences? From last week's SFR assignment?

3. What new recovery behaviors will I practice this upcoming week? I will contact my accountability partner _____ times this week.

Learn Something New

Service work in Twelve Step groups is a form of gratitude, a kind of giving that asks for no reward. We experience the program in an entirely new way when we begin to sponsor others. It also requires that we maintain our own recovery program, so in that way service also becomes accountability. But sweetest of all are the dear friendships that come from offering service to the newly recovering alcoholic, addict, or family member. These mutual bonds of sponsorship provide remarkable friendships, some lasting a lifetime.

Step Twelve

Having had a spiritual awakening as a result of these steps,
we tried to carry this message to alcoholics, and to practice
these principles in all our affairs.

Every word in Al-Anon's Twelve Steps is the same as in AA's Twelve
Steps except one: *alcoholics* became *others*. We recognize that when we
come to Step Twelve, we have already had a spiritual awakening. It is
at this time that we are ready to offer service to new members through
Twelve Step sponsorship. But first we must have that awakening, as we
define it. When we are asked to carry the message, we must have a message to carry.

Working a Recovery Program

Being asked to carry the message can be a startling notion at first. *AA
Redux* explains, "The fact is that *sobriety reveals an immense and unexpected decency in us!* What greater—or more complicated—reason is
needed to explain why we would be so determined to help others facing
the same malady we once suffered ourselves!"[122] Going from addiction
(including the family's role) to being a person qualified to help others
is a testament to the transformative effects of this program. As the song
"Amazing Grace" says, we were blind, but now we see.

Assignment

Discuss with your sponsor your readiness to offer your services in sponsorship to another.

Closing

The chairperson asks a team member to read the SFR Closing Statement.

WEEK 46: STRUCTURED FAMILY RECOVERY

Date: _____

Topic: In All Our Affairs

Opening

The chairperson asks a team member to read the SFR Opening Statement.

Daily Reading

A team member reads aloud from a Twelve Step daily reader, then reads each of the following discussion points, allowing time for team sharing.

Report, Discuss, Plan

1. What went well in my recovery this past week? What could be improved? Do I want feedback?

2. What insights did I gain from my Twelve Step experiences? From last week's SFR assignment?

3. What new recovery behaviors will I practice this upcoming week? I will contact my accountability partner _____ times this week.

Learn Something New

According to author and AA historian Bill Pittman, "The principles of Twelve Step recovery are the opposite of our character defects." As we work the Twelve Step program, it turns shortcomings into principles. Pittman offers examples: "   we work to change fear into faith, hate into love, egoism into humility, anxiety and worry into serenity, complacency into action, denial into acceptance, jealousy into trust, fantasizing into reality, selfishness into service, resentment into forgiveness, judgmentalism into tolerance, despair into hope, self-hate into self-respect, and loneliness into fellowship."[123] We live the Twelve Step principles as we are working our program.

Step Twelve

*Having had a spiritual awakening as a result of these steps,
we tried to carry this message to alcoholics, and to practice
these principles in all our affairs.*

In Twelve Step programs, we won't find a list of principles to somehow apply to our lives. We come to know these principles through our actions. They are infused within us because we worked to achieve them. Once this happens, practicing them in all our affairs is as automatic as a heartbeat.

Working a Recovery Program

By exhibiting great interest and sincerity toward the newcomer, we practice these principles. By following the Golden Rule (doing unto others as we would have them do unto us) in our communities, we practice these principles. By creating a loving and serene home life, we practice these principles. By demonstrating self-care, we practice these principles. By treating those in the workplace with dignity and respect, we practice these principles. Practicing these principles in all our affairs is our outward show of gratitude.

Assignment

Ask yourself, *How do I practice these principles in my home, work, social life, and community?* Discuss with your sponsor. Journal your insights.

Closing

The chairperson asks a team member to read the SFR Closing Statement.

WEEK 47: STRUCTURED FAMILY RECOVERY

Date: _____

Topic: Happy, Joyous, and Free

Opening

The chairperson asks a team member to read the SFR Opening Statement.

Daily Reading

A team member reads aloud from a Twelve Step daily reader, then reads each of the following discussion points, allowing time for team sharing.

Report, Discuss, Plan

1. What went well in my recovery this past week? What could be improved? Do I want feedback?

2. What insights did I gain from my Twelve Step experiences? From last week's SFR assignment?

3. What new recovery behaviors will I practice this upcoming week? I will contact my accountability partner _____ times this week.

Learn Something New

Sitting at dinner with a group of AAs, there was more raucous laughter and fun at our table than anywhere in the place. In recovery, as a friend of mine said, if we're not happy, joyous, and free, what's the point? Elizabeth Berg wrote in *The Art of Mending*, "There are random moments—tossing a salad, coming up the driveway to the house, ironing the seams flat on a quilt square, standing at the kitchen window and looking out at the delphiniums, hearing a burst of laughter from one of my children's rooms—when I feel a wavelike rush of joy. This is my true religion: arbitrary moments of nearly painful happiness for a life I feel privileged to lead." Having come to this place in recovery, most of us can find happiness almost anywhere.

The Twelve Steps

Working these marvelous Steps, painstakingly and with rigorous honesty, we come to know the gift. We understand those who have said that the Twelve Steps are among the greatest treasures the United States has given the world. But we cannot hang on to this treasure by *having done* the Steps. This is a living program. The Steps change and expand as we change and expand. We haven't reached a destination; the best is yet to come. Alice Munro, author and winner of the 2013 Nobel Prize in Literature, writes, "Few people, very few, have a treasure, and if you do you must hang onto it. You must not let yourself be waylaid, and have it taken from you."

Working a Recovery Program

Recovering people are some of the best people in the world. How could they not be? Our gift comes out of our desperation. After trying everything else, it brought us to this place. As Sister Molly Monahan writes in *Seeds of Grace*, "Thanks be to God for Alcoholics Anonymous." And we send thanks, too, for the Twelve Step program that serves those who love the alcoholics and addicts.

Assignment

Pay attention to the "arbitrary moments of nearly painful happiness" in your life, and take a moment to give thanks.

Closing

The chairperson asks a team member to read the SFR Closing Statement.

WEEK 48: STRUCTURED FAMILY RECOVERY

Date: _____

Topic: Family

Opening

The chairperson asks a team member to read the SFR Opening Statement.

Daily Reading

A team member reads aloud from a Twelve Step daily reader, then reads each of the following discussion points, allowing time for team sharing.

Report, Discuss, Plan

1. What went well in my recovery this past week? What could be improved? Do I want feedback?

2. What insights did I gain from my Twelve Step experiences? From last week's SFR assignment?

3. What new recovery behaviors will I practice this upcoming week? I will contact my accountability partner _____ times this week.

Learn Something New

Resilience was once thought to be a personality trait, but we now understand that it is a result of a process marked by change, activity, and progress. *Family resilience* is a term we use when the entire family develops traits that lead to successful changes in how they cope with significant adversity. In Structured Family Recovery, we have done that. We've used a framework that kept us active in Twelve Step recovery, resulting in the kind of change and progress that befits the nature of addiction. How we live this change, however, is in our relationship with ourselves and our family. We live it with our recovery community. We live it with our co-workers, our neighbors, our friends, and the clerk at the grocery store.

The Twelve Steps

There is much that is lovely and inspiring written on self-improvement and spiritual growth. But in the end, it is application of these ideas that counts. Beyond the enjoyment of the words and sentiments, how does it change us in a lasting way? Our brain is so easily fooled into believing that reading something today will change our tomorrows. It doesn't. The Twelve Steps require action from us. These Twelve Steps change us when we've taken action—rising to the challenge of doing the next right thing, knowing we learn by keeping at it, having patience to let things unfold as they are meant to, and trusting the process. But we are not done. The disease is never cured. So it's the love of recovery that ensures we hold on to this treasure. We keep it close as that good thing in our lives.

Working a Recovery Program

Where are we going now as a family? We've taken this journey through early recovery and can celebrate the commitment we've kept, and the new place we found in ourselves and each other. But we may be remembering that the addicted doctors—those recovery winners—didn't stop here. They keep going—meeting, talking, staying accountable to each other—but most of all, they keep recovery at the top of the list. The rest of their lives depend on it. So do ours. In the words of Abraham Lincoln, "I am a slow walker, but I never walk back."

Assignment

As a family, we decide how to keep recovery growing and expanding, but also how we keep this unique connection with each other. Will we make the time, perhaps once a month, more often if we need it, to keep our family recovery team united, walking forward together? Will we continue our Structured Family Recovery journey?

Closing

The chairperson asks a team member to read the SFR Closing Statement.

PART IV

Tools, Checklists, and Resources

THIS SECTION PROVIDES THE TOOLS needed for creating a Recovery Plan and resources to help families find additional guidance, education, and professional assistance.

Many of the tools found here, including the checklists, are also available as free downloadable PDFs at www .hazelden.org/web/go/ittakesafamily.

My Recovery Plan

All the family team members work on their individual recovery plans together, including the sober alcoholic or addict. The family doesn't begin until the addict has joined the SFR recovery team and is participating in Structured Family Recovery. Then they use the worksheets on the following pages.

If the addict has refused to participate in Structured Family Recovery, however, the family continues. Moving forward with recovery behavior is crucial at this point. In doing so, the family is modeling prosocial behaviors that the addicted person is likely to follow eventually. If the family follows an uncooperative addict's lead—negative social behavior—then the entire family collapses back into the ways of addiction. Consulting with an SFR counselor to discuss next steps to take with your reluctant addicted loved one can be helpful.

To begin your recovery plan, first write your Recovery Goal. Discuss this with others, and take some time to think about it. Once you've completed your goal, write a Recovery Commitment Statement. (See the next two headings in this section.) Share both in an SFR meeting.

Second, reread these sections in this book's chapter 11: "Begin with a Team," "How Do I Talk to My Addict?" and "How Do I Talk to My Family?" Most of what occurs between family members is determined by how we talk to one another. Changes in patterns of engagement have a tremendous impact on how we feel about one another. If your family has difficulty changing negative patterns of communicating, consult with an SFR counselor or a counselor who specializes in addiction and families to begin breaking the pattern.

Third, complete the appropriate worksheet that focuses on relapse warning signs. There is one for the family (Family Relapse Warning Signs) and another for the addict (Addiction Relapse Warning Signs).

This process isn't about relapse but about creating self-awareness that supports physical and emotional sobriety. Share your results in an SRF meeting, and record relapse signs in your recovery plan.

Fourth, complete the Eight Essential Elements worksheet. This requires open communication with one another, asking for feedback and thoughtful responses. Teamwork is what makes this effective at producing lasting sobriety. Each person's individual responses to these Eight Essential Elements creates a direction for the entire family recovery team. Everyone knows the expectations.

The first of the Eight Essential Elements helps us determine our negative and positive consequences. What negative consequences do you expect for yourself if you relapse or exhibit relapse behavior? What are the positive consequences for recovery behaviors? Some of these will be natural consequences that automatically follow our behavior. Other consequences are responses from our family. Some consequences are choices we make for ourselves today—they are coming from our *better selves* (our healthy thinking) talking to our *future selves* (healthy or unhealthy thinking). We are setting up self-accountability, clear expectations, and a plan that allow us to let go of some of our nervousness around relapse.

To complete a list of our negative and positive consequences, we must get input from others. We need to know how they will support our recovery. We also need to know exactly how they will not support our disease. This is a loving process. We do not expect relapse to happen. We are confident that by engaging with each other as a recovery team, doing something radically different as a family, and following the lead of the recovery winners, we will never see a relapse. But part of success is about being prepared, having specific expectations, and putting relapse on notice. Because our brains grab on to the negative more intensely than the positive, use the ratio one to five. For every negative, list five positive recovery consequences.

Following are the benefits of clearly listing the consequences.

1. We do not fall into random "punishing" reactions.
   Instead, we act based on clear, predetermined choices.

2. We each choose our own consequences and tell others
   on the team what we'd like them to do.

3. Our team members add consequences, too. If we relapse, they must not support the disease (family or addict) and need to take care of themselves.

4. These decisions create accountability. If I relapse, I know the price I am going to pay. But if I am in recovery, I know it comes with many happy things.

5. We don't forget about positive consequences.

Remember, families relapse, too. Emotional insobriety and enabling behaviors are a danger to sobriety and shouldn't be taken lightly. So family members determine the consequences of sabotaging behaviors by asking for the addict's input and input from the rest of the team. Relapse is serious business; consequences are created to keep us sober.

Complete the remaining seven Essential Elements. If you need recommendations for the second, Frequent Random Drug Testing and Monitoring, you will find information in the resource section.

Fifth, complete the Relapse Agreement. This should be as specific as possible. Each family member and the addict complete a relapse agreement with feedback from others. (Some questions don't apply to family members, so skip them.) This is very important for the Red Light, Yellow Light, Green Light decision-making process.

Completing the section A Conversation with My Future Self is key In doing so, we are actively participating in any future problem we might have using our *better selves,* not leaving ourselves victim to the voice of addiction. I can't stress enough that, although we are talking about relapse, this is about creating lasting sobriety.

Sign your completed recovery plan. Share it with the team. Ask for feedback. This is a group project with the goal of building great lives and a great family. Addiction is a disease, not a moral failing, so let's not take decisions as personal judgment. Respond as if we were talking about diabetes or coronary disease. *What do I need to get well, stay well, and live a great life? Nothing else will do!*

If your team needs help completing your recovery plans, engage with an SFR counselor, if you haven't already. You can work together over the short term to complete the process or engage in a longer relationship.

By beginning a relationship with the SFR counselor, you have someone to reach out to in the future if the need arises.

My Recovery Goal

Discuss your Recovery Goal with your SFR team members, your sponsor, members of your Twelve Step group, and your SFR counselor. Before writing your goal, spend some time reading recovery literature and your daily reader. Take time to reflect, and then write your goal in three sentences or less.

Recovery Commitment Statement

The purpose of the Recovery Commitment Statement is to create clear communication and cooperation in the recovery process with a goal of maintaining lasting sobriety and healing the family. As a member of the SFR team, make the following commitment to your addicted loved one, the members of your family, and yourself. Also make this commitment to future generations of your family and other people who will be positively affected by the decisions you make today. Write your commitment statement below and sign it. Once you've done so, share it with your team and your SFR counselor.

_____

_____

_____

_____

_____

_____

Family Relapse Warning Signs

The following are common relapse warning signs for family members. The list is adapted and expanded from the work of Terence T. Gorski.[124] Check all that apply. You do not have to be experiencing these signs at the moment, but recognize them as requiring attention to prevent them from becoming relapse triggers.

- ☐ I allow my daily activities to interrupt my recovery schedule, including my Al-Anon meeting, daily readings, time with my sponsor, service work, or working the Twelve Steps.

- ☐ Temporary issues, such as an illness, keep me away from recovery activities, but I do not return once I am well or otherwise unburdened.

- ☐ I've stopped enjoying or doing the little things I do for myself.

- ☐ I've let my appearance or hygiene deteriorate.

- ☐ I have an inability to set appropriate limits with others, especially children. I'm either too lenient or too rigid.

- ☐ I'm overwhelmed by personal responsibilities and cannot prioritize.

- ☐ I increasingly have difficulties making decisions related to daily living.

- ☐ I'm obsessive in needing to take on all responsibility and, even then, feel like I am not doing enough.

- ☐ I go to bed too late and get up too early to get sufficient sleep. I suffer from insomnia or fitful sleep.

- ☐ I mentally ruminate over old resentments, feeling increasingly angry.

- ☐ I've returned to old controlling behaviors, trying to control not only the addict but other people, places, and things.

☐ When anyone points out the unhealthiness of my behaviors, I become defensive.

☐ I'm magnifying problems from the present or past.
I fall into self-pity, complaining to others about all that is wrong in my life.

☐ I worry constantly about money, or I'm overspending, using shopping as an escape.

☐ I'm not eating enough or eating too much.

☐ I engage in the blame game, making others the scapegoat for all my problems, avoiding self-responsibility.

☐ I'm nervous or worry chronically. I may not know the source of my worries, but instead feel a free-floating anxiety.

☐ I've lost faith in a Higher Power or feel angry toward my Higher Power.

☐ My attendance at Al-Anon is sporadic; I always come up with excuses not to go.

☐ My mind is always racing and I cannot calm down.
I'm constantly thinking of everything that is undone.

☐ I cannot solve problems. I'm always getting stuck and can't seem to move forward with decisions. I feel frustrated and unable to figure out the right thing to do.

☐ I feel a general sense of being out of sorts, but I don't know what's wrong.

☐ I'm overly emotional with no understanding of why, either crying or raging.

☐ I lose control over my temper with spouse, children, or other family members.

☐ I have extreme mood swings without warning; feelings are exaggerated.

- ☐ I have deep feelings of loneliness or isolation. I've stopped reaching out to friends or family.

- ☐ I suffer from tunnel vision. I cannot see others' points of view. I insist on being right.

- ☐ I've had an onset or increase of panic attacks or depression. Feelings snowball and create a dread of the next episode of panic or depression.

- ☐ I use dishonesty to manage my world. I create lots of little lies to control others or hide what's going on with me or my alcoholic.

- ☐ I suffer from physical maladies with no obvious causes: headaches, body aches, hives, stomach pains, hair loss, dizziness, diarrhea or constipation, frequent colds, tingling or numbness, rapid heartbeat, nausea.

- ☐ I medicate with tranquilizers, alcohol, or other drugs.

- ☐ I lack energy and sleep excessively.

- ☐ I feel hopelessness and helplessness. I don't believe anyone can understand or help me.

- ☐ I have an apathetic "whatever" attitude.

Addiction Relapse Warning Signs

The following list addresses common relapse warning signs for alcoholics and addicts. It is adapted and expanded from the work of Terence T. Gorski.[125] Check all that apply. You do not have to be experiencing these signs at the moment, but recognize them as requiring attention to prevent them from becoming relapse triggers.

- ☐ I doubt my ability to stay sober but keep this a secret.
- ☐ I'm afraid, but I deny it.
- ☐ I've decided I can be abstinent without recovery.
- ☐ I am overconfident in my recovery.
- ☐ I avoid talking about problems or my recovery.
- ☐ My life is out of balance. (I work too much or too little. I get too much exercise or very little or none. I overeat or don't eat enough.)
- ☐ I overreact to stressful situations.
- ☐ I am isolating physically or emotionally.
- ☐ I feel depressed or anxious.
- ☐ I am making unrealistic plans.
- ☐ I ruminate about the past.
- ☐ I never do anything to have fun.
- ☐ I can't relate to people in my recovery program.
- ☐ I am easily angered or irritated.
- ☐ I am blaming others for my problems or the past.
- ☐ I have a chaotic daily schedule.
- ☐ I lack structure in my days.
- ☐ I live with people who drink or use other drugs.

- ☐ I medicate with tranquilizers, alcohol, or other drugs.
- ☐ I lack energy and sleep excessively.
- ☐ I openly reject help from others.
- ☐ I resent the people closest to me.
- ☐ I am apathetic; I don't care what happens.
- ☐ I don't want to take responsibility; I expect others to take care of me.
- ☐ I think about drinking and drugging, or experience cravings, but don't share this in my recovery circles.
- ☐ I am experiencing a great deal of self-pity.
- ☐ I am consciously lying to others.
- ☐ I am experiencing anger and resentments that I keep to myself.
- ☐ I am hanging around drinking or using friends and "wet places."
- ☐ I believe I could drink or drug again and control it this time.
- ☐ I think about seeing a doctor to get a prescription for mood-altering drugs.
- ☐ I don't believe I'll ever have fun sober.
- ☐ I don't take positive action to improve my circumstances.
- ☐ I skip meetings and feel resentful if anyone mentions it to me.
- ☐ I unrealistically think I should be happy all the time.
- ☐ I drive by places where I used to buy liquor or drugs.
- ☐ I am still seeing the doctor who prescribed me my drugs.
- ☐ I haven't emptied my house of alcohol or other drugs.
- ☐ I don't talk to my sponsor, and I'm not working the Steps.
- ☐ I sit in the back of meetings and don't participate.

☐   I don't get to know anyone in recovery.

☐   I get to meetings late and leave early.

☐   I overreact emotionally.

☐   I act happy, as if everything is great, but I feel miserable.

☐   I am thinking I could use a different substance than my drug of choice, and I wouldn't have a problem.

☐   I feel like I am bouncing from one crisis to another.

☐   I think I'm more fun to be around when I'm drinking or high.

☐   I don't think I can date or be romantic without getting slightly buzzed.

☐   I don't believe I'll ever be able to rebuild my life.

☐   I feel hopeless.

☐   I am thinking about using tranquilizers or sleeping pills.

☐   I think I'm too young or too old for recovery.

☐   I have no confidence in myself.

My Top Relapse Warning Signs

After completing your Addiction Relapse Warning Signs Checklist, list your top ten relapse signs below. Discuss with your sponsor a plan to deal with each one. Provide copies to your SFR family recovery team, chairperson, SFR counselor, and Twelve Step sponsor.

1. Relapse sign: _____

   Plan to address it: _____

2. Relapse sign: _____

   Plan to address it: _____

3. Relapse sign: _____

   Plan to address it: _____

4. Relapse sign: _____

    Plan to address it: _____

5. Relapse sign: _____

    Plan to address it: _____

6. Relapse sign: _____

    Plan to address it: _____

7. Relapse sign: _____

    Plan to address it: _____

8. Relapse sign: _____

    Plan to address it: _____

9. Relapse sign: _____

    Plan to address it: _____

10. Relapse sign: _____

    Plan to address it: _____

Notes: _____

_____

_____

_____

_____

_____

_____

The Eight Essential Elements

Thoroughly complete all that apply to you, asking your SFR team for feedback. Provide copies to your SFR counselor and chairperson as well as your Twelve Step sponsor.

Positive Rewards and Negative Consequences

Negative consequences related to addiction behaviors:

_____

_____

_____

_____

_____

_____

Positive consequences for recovery behaviors:

_____

_____

_____

_____

_____

_____

Frequent Random Drug Testing and Monitoring

The company I will use: _____

The monitoring services being provided: _____

The people who will receive reports: _____

Notes: _____

_____

_____

_____

_____

Twelve Step Program and the Abstinence Standard

I am committed to attending Twelve Step meetings.	☐ yes	☐ no
I am committed to abstinence from all mood-altering substances, including alcohol, illicit drugs, and prescription drugs.	☐ yes	☐ no
I am following the aftercare plans developed by treatment professionals.	☐ yes	☐ no

Notes: _____

_____

_____

_____

_____

Viable Role Models and Recovery Mentors

I will identify someone in AA or Al-Anon to be
my sponsor.   ☐ yes   ☐ no

I will use the alumni association from my treatment
program to find someone in recovery in my home area.   ☐ yes   ☐ no

I will call friends or family members who are in
recovery and ask them to go to some meetings with me.   ☐ yes   ☐ no

I will use a professional Twelve Step Recovery Mentor.   ☐ yes   ☐ no

Notes: _____

_____

_____

_____

_____

_____

_____

_____

_____

_____

_____

_____

_____

_____

Modified Lifestyle

These are the people, places, things, activities, and behaviors I will remove from my life:

_____

_____

_____

_____

These are the people, places, things, activities, and behaviors I will add to my life:

_____

_____

_____

_____

Notes: _____

_____

_____

_____

_____

_____

_____

Active and Sustained Monitoring

I commit to Structured Family Recovery with my
family team for a minimum of forty-eight meetings.   ☐ yes   ☐ no

At the end of the forty-eight weeks, as a family team
we will evaluate our recovery needs.   ☐ yes   ☐ no

I will commit to sustained random drug screens
for a minimum of twelve months, but with serious
consideration of extending this more closely to
match the Physician Health Program for doctors.   ☐ yes   ☐ no

If I have one or more relapses in the first
twelve months, I will definitely extend drug
screening for another twelve months.   ☐ yes   ☐ no

Notes: _____

_____

_____

_____

_____

_____

_____

_____

_____

_____

_____

Active Management of Relapse

If I relapse (physical or emotional), I expect my
family recovery team to use my relapse agreement
to intervene and help me.   ☐ yes ☐ no

If I relapse, I will work with my recovery team or an
addictions professional to determine the right level
of care to restart my recovery.   ☐ yes ☐ no

I will reconsider the support I need going forward
to ensure lasting sobriety.   ☐ yes ☐ no

I will engage my Twelve Step sponsor in my
ongoing recovery plans.   ☐ yes ☐ no

If I have an Al-Anon relapse (emotional insobriety,
enabling behaviors, or recovery sabotage), I will
look for appropriate individual counseling with a
specialist in addiction and family issues.   ☐ yes ☐ no

If I have an Al-Anon relapse, I will talk to my
Twelve Step sponsor to discuss the number of
Al-Anon meetings I need to go to per week.   ☐ yes ☐ no

I will work with the family recovery team, my sponsor,
or an SFR counselor to put into place an appropriate level
of accountability, recovery alliances, and increased
monitoring that will sustain my ongoing recovery.   ☐ yes ☐ no

Notes: _____ _____

_____

_____

_____

_____

A Continuing Care Approach

I understand addiction is a chronic disease
with no cure.   ☐ yes   ☐ no

I understand that lifelong recovery is achieved
by managing the chronic nature of addiction
through Twelve Step recovery and other support
systems, as needed.   ☐ yes   ☐ no

Al-Anon is also an ongoing recovery program,
maintaining the best spiritual health and capacity
of families to engage the alcoholic or addict in
a healthy, happy relationship.   ☐ yes   ☐ no

I understand that physicians sustain this level of
support for five years, which is credited with their
high and lasting rates of sobriety.   ☐ yes   ☐ no

Notes: _____

_____

_____

_____

_____

_____

_____

_____

_____

_____

Relapse Agreement

This agreement is meant to protect your recovery. It is also an opportunity for you to inform your recovery team how to respond in case you experience a relapse crisis. Always complete the Relapse Agreement with the feedback of your team and Twelve Step sponsor. Some find working with an SFR counselor to be especially helpful when completing this. Answer questions as a family member or addict, as appropriate to your specific Twelve Step program.

1. If anyone on my family recovery team is concerned that my recovery program is inconsistent or is in danger, please do the following:

   ☐ Review my relapse warning signs.

   ☐ Identify the warning signs you are observing.

   ☐ Talk to the SFR chairperson or SFR counselor.

   ☐ Have the SFR chairperson or SFR counselor talk with me.

   ☐ Have _____ talk to me.

   ☐ Ask me to share at an SFR meeting and ask for feedback.

   ☐ With my team, create a plan for more recovery structure.

   ☐ With the SFR counselor, create a plan for more recovery structure.

   ☐ With my Twelve Step sponsor, create a plan for more recovery structure.

   ☐ Other: _____

2. If anyone on my family recovery team believes I am in a relapse, using alcohol or other drugs, please do the following:

☐ Consult with SFR counselor or addiction professional.

☐ Put together the following people as an intervention team:

_____

_____

_____

☐ Have the intervention team review my relapse agreement with me and help me implement it.

☐ Contact my Twelve Step sponsor. Phone: _____

☐ Have _____ and _____ talk to me.

☐ Determine the professional help I need to appropriately address relapse.

☐ With the SFR counselor, create a plan for more recovery structure after receiving professional help.

☐ With my sponsor, create a plan for more recovery structure.

If I have a full-blown relapse, I agree to detox plus one of the following:

☐ Intensive outpatient or day treatment.

☐ Inpatient or residential treatment.

☐ A halfway house or professionally monitored sober house.

☐ I will follow all aftercare recommendations.

☐ I will also do everything listed under a "slip" below.

☐ Other: _____

If I have a one- or two-day slip, not requiring detox:

☐ I will get honest with my family recovery team.

☐ I will get honest with my Twelve Step sponsor.

☐ I will be honest with the members of my home group.

☐ I will pick up a white chip.

☐ I will go to ninety meetings in ninety days.

☐ I will talk with my sponsor daily.

☐ I will use my accountability person, SFR checklists, and recovery triggers to keep me on track.

☐ Other: _____

If I have an Al-Anon relapse:

☐ I will get honest with my family recovery team.

☐ I will get honest with my Twelve Step sponsor.

☐ I will get honest with the members of my home group.

☐ I will increase Al-Anon meetings and working with my sponsor.

☐ I will discuss my need for some individual professional guidance from the SFR counselor or another therapist.

☐ I will use my accountability person, SFR checklists, and recovery triggers to keep me on track.

☐ Other: _____

A Conversation with My Future Self

In the future, if I am exhibiting relapse signs or am in a relapse and I am unwilling to honor the promises I made in my relapse agreement, or I am in denial of my need for help, I am writing myself a message here. Please ask me to read the following to myself and to our SFR team.

Rapid Relapse Response: Present this statement to the SFR team or use it as an example for writing a personalized Rapid Relapse Response statement.

"I ask my family to act as quickly as possible if I am in danger of relapse or in relapse. I may be difficult to deal with while I am in such a bad place, but do not let me persuade you not to help me. The sooner you help me, the less damage is done by this insidious and powerful disease. Regardless of what I may say or do, remember, I love you."

Provide copies of this Recovery Plan and Relapse Agreement to:

☐ The SFR chairperson

☐ The SFR counselor

☐ My Twelve Step sponsor:

_____

☐ The following professionals:

_____

_____

_____

☐ The following SFR team members:

_____

_____

_____

☐ Other:

_____

_____

Signed: _____

Date: _____

Structured Family Recovery
Checklists

All SFR checklists are located in this chapter, making them easy to reference. Each is designed as a "Read–Do" checklist: Read the checklist, and then do what it says. These checklists reduce the steps to their simplest form by organizing information for the purpose of taking action. They are perfect when doing something new and unfamiliar.

Checklists prevent common mistakes and omissions. They act as triggers for what actions we need to take—we read and do. Checklists keep it simple, preventing us from complicating things and making it harder than it needs to be. Checklists prevent patterns from our past that have caused failures.

The following checklists are a reflection of what you've learned reading this book, not an outline of every detail. Our brains turn off when we see complex, lengthy checklists. So, short and simple is the rule. When we need more information about any particular step, we use the book or talk to our SFR counselor, chairperson, or teammates. Checklists are simply reminders.

The brain can work against us. Our natural-born faith in ourselves often trips us up. We believe we'll remember things we don't and trust that the motivation we feel in the moment will extend to next week or the week after. But it often doesn't. We may feel gung-ho today but be totally uninterested later. Our brains give us the benefit of the doubt when we really don't deserve it. Checklists help us avoid the disconnect between what we believe we will do and what we really do.

Checklists also help us avoid cutting corners, another thing our brains are famous for. "Things will work out fine. Don't worry about skipping a few steps." We are prone to underestimating what it takes to do the job, which can lead us down the road to relapse. Following check-lists helps us avoid starting down this path. These checklists will help keep your SFR team on track:

- SFR Overview Checklist

- Daily Recovery Checklist

- SFR Chairperson Checklist

- SFR Secretary Checklist

- Red Light, Yellow Light, Green Light Decision-Making Checklist

- Recovery Plan Checklist

Structured Family Recovery Overview Checklist

☐ Read the book *It Takes a Family*.

☐ Here family members begin SFR meetings and attend Al-Anon before inviting the recovering person.

☐ Select an SFR counselor or chairperson, or both.

☐ Select a team secretary, who may delegate to other teammates.

☐ Review the SFR meeting format and make preparations before meetings.

☐ Use checklists as a simple way to stay on track.

☐ Practice optimism and the spirituality of kindness.

☐ Add fun to recovery.

☐ Review the "Red Light, Yellow Light, Green Light" method of decision making.

☐ Explore guidelines for developing a Recovery Plan: 1) refer to the resources section in part IV of this book; 2) work with the SFR counselor and/or chairperson to begin work; 3) begin only after the newly recovering addict has joined the SFR team.

Daily Recovery Checklist

Reminders:

- **Twelve Step meetings for the family are Al-Anon, Nar-Anon, Adult Children of Alcoholics, and Families Anonymous.** Families begin by attending at least one meeting per week. Select a home group; this is the group you always attend.

- **Twelve Step meetings for the alcoholic or addict are Alcoholics Anonymous or Narcotics Anonymous.** Follow recommendations from the treatment staff or Twelve Step sponsor for weekly meeting attendance. Ninety meetings in ninety days are often recommended. Select a home group.

- **Choose a sponsor promptly.** It is with a sponsor that you will work the Twelve Steps and find a Twelve Step service position.

- **Fellowship is socializing or calling another person from your Twelve Step meetings.** A sponsor can help initiate fellowship.

Photocopy checklist for repeated use.

Daily Recovery Checklist

	MON.	TUES.	WED.	THURS.	FRI.	SAT.	SUN.
Twelve Step Meeting and Home Group							
Daily Reading							
Twelve Step Sponsor							
Service Work							
Step Work							
Fellowship							
SFR Meeting							
SFR Assignment							
Accountability Partner							
Recovery Trigger							

SFR Chairperson Checklist

Reminders:

- ☐ **Chairperson moderates,** starting and ending meetings on time.

- ☐ **Daily Reading is selected prior to the SFR meeting.** At the close of each meeting, a teammate is selected to choose and read next week's Daily Reading. The teammate will use the index of a daily reader to choose a topic that corresponds with the topic for the upcoming SFR meeting. Readings rotate weekly between Al-Anon and AA daily readers.

- ☐ **Special topics are:** 1) conversations about inviting the alcoholic to join the team; 2) discussions and action steps for creating Recovery Plans; 3) pressing issues as determined appropriate by Red, Yellow, Green Light decision making; 4) housekeeping issues.

- ☐ **If the chairperson cannot attend an SFR meeting,** he or she will select a teammate to act as chairperson for that meeting.

- ☐ **If you are working with an SFR counselor,** he or she will assume some of these responsibilities.

Photocopy checklist for repeated use.

SFR Chairperson Checklist

	WEEK ___	WEEK ___	WEEK ___	WEEK ___	WEEK ___	WEEK ___	WEEK ___
Select teammate for:							
• Opening Statement							
• Closing Statement							
Opening statement							
Daily reading on meeting topic							
Moderate meeting:							
• Report, Discuss, Plan							
• Learning Something New							
• Step Work							
Fellowship							
Working a recovery program							
Special topic							
Closing statement							
Select reader for next daily reading							

SFR Secretary Checklist

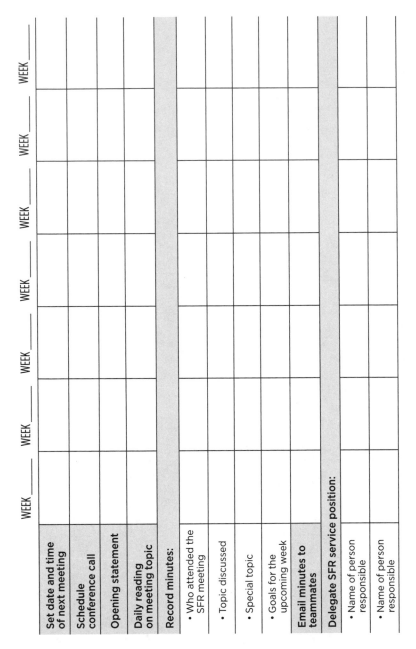

	WEEK___	WEEK___	WEEK___	WEEK___	WEEK___	WEEK___	WEEK___	WEEK___
Set date and time of next meeting								
Schedule conference call								
Opening statement								
Daily reading on meeting topic								
Record minutes:								
• Who attended the SFR meeting								
• Topic discussed								
• Special topic								
• Goals for the upcoming week								
Email minutes to teammates								
Delegate SFR service position:								
• Name of person responsible								
• Name of person responsible								

Photocopy checklist for repeated use.

Red Light, Yellow Light, Green Light Decision-Making Checklist

☐ No surprises: We don't drop bombs in the middle of SFR meetings.

☐ We bring concerns to SFR counselor or team chairperson before a meeting.

☐ We ask: "Is this concern directly or indirectly related to relapse warning signs or symptoms?"

☐ Decisions are made upon reviewing the concern and its appropriateness for SFR.

☐ Red Light: A concern may be legitimate, but it's not appropriate for an SFR meeting.

☐ Yellow Light: A concern may be legitimate, but we're not sure if it is or isn't appropriate for an SFR meeting. We give ourselves more time to contemplate.

☐ Green Light: A concern is legitimate and is appropriate for an SFR meeting.

☐ We follow the guidelines in our Recovery Plans when approaching teammates who are demonstrating relapse symptoms or who have relapsed.

☐ We demonstrate flexibility, giving teammates reasonable time to make better recovery decisions, unless they are in imminent danger. We then act quickly, engaging professional services as needed.

Photocopy checklist for repeated use.

Recovery Plan Checklist

Reminders:

- Recovery Plan worksheet and instructions are found in the resources section of this book. Photocopy pages to use as you work on your plan.

- Family and addict work on Recovery Plans at the same time. This is a team activity. Go back to the book to refresh your memory on suggestions for completing the Recovery Plan and on the Eight Essential Elements.

- Share your Recovery Plan. Hold a special SFR meeting to give everyone an opportunity to share their plans with the team. Ask for team feedback. SFR counselor or team chairperson moderates.

- Get help if you need it. Even families who are now working with a professional sometimes engage an SFR counselor to guide them through creating Recovery Plans. Make this decision as a team.

- Give your team chairperson and/or SFR counselor a signed copy of your Recovery Plan. You might also give a copy to your Twelve Step sponsor. If someone is concerned about relapse signs in a teammate, contact the team chairperson or SFR counselor and consult the Recovery Plan to guide your actions.

- SFR secretary uses this checklist to keep track of team members' progress. Each individual uses this checklist to track his or her own progress.

Photocopy checklist for repeated use.

Recovery Plan Checklist

	NAME ____	NAME ____	NAME ____	NAME ____	NAME ____	NAME ____	NAME ____	NAME ____
Write My Recovery Goal								
Write Recovery Commitment Statement								
Complete Relapse Warning Signs Worksheet								
Complete Eight Essential Elements Worksheet								
Complete Relapse Agreement								
Write Rapid Relapse Response								
Share Recovery Plan with My Team								
Invite Team to Give Me Feedback								
Give a Copy to Team Chairperson								
Give a Copy to SFR Counselor								

Resources

Lovefirst.net

This website is dedicated to families helping the people they love. The site has continued to grow with information for anyone who is concerned about an addicted loved one or friend or colleague. Below is a small sampling of its resources.

Structured Family Recovery Counselors. The website maintains information on Structured Family Recovery. It also retains a list of addiction therapists who are certified SFR counselors, and clinical interventionists who are also certified SFR counselors.

Intervention. If your loved one has not yet received treatment and is not willing to go to treatment, you will find an extended amount of information on family intervention, including a free intervention video workshop, checklists, articles, and frequently asked questions.

Random Drug Testing and Monitoring. Under "Mentoring" on the lovefirst.net menu, you'll find information about drug testing and monitoring as well as the types of monitoring services that offer a high level of support.

Books

There are many books that families and addicts will find helpful. Some are featured on lovefirst.net; all titles listed here are recommend.

Aging and Addiction: Helping Older Adults Overcome Alcohol or Medication Dependence by Debra Jay and Carol Colleran (Hazelden, 2002). Written for families, this is the definitive guide for dealing with an older parent, relative, or friend with a substance addiction.

Another Chance: Hope and Health for the Alcoholic Family by Sharon Wegscheider-Cruse (Science and Behavior Books, 1981, 1989). This classic describes the impact addiction has on family members and the specific roles they unwittingly play within the family system.

Courage to Change: One Day at a Time in Al-Anon II (Al-Anon Family Group Headquarters, 1992). Daily reader for people who have been affected by someone else's addiction.

Daily Reflections: A Book of Reflections by A.A. Members for A.A. Members (AA World Services, 2014). A collection of daily readings for a calendar year.

Today's Gift: Daily Meditations for Families (Hazelden, 1985). This is the classic meditation book designed to strengthen family bonds and nurture relationships and spirituality.

Intervention: How to Help Someone Who Doesn't Want Help by Vernon E. Johnson (Hazelden, 1986). This classic text describes the disease of addiction, provides the reader with an introduction on intervention, and instructs families in how to get help for themselves.

Love First: A Family's Guide to Intervention by Debra Jay and Jeff Jay (Hazelden, 2000, 2008). This is the standard-setting book on intervention, used by tens of thousands of people around the world.

No More Letting Go: The Spirituality of Taking Action Against Alcoholism and Drug Addiction by Debra Jay (Bantam, 2006). Offers a spiritual and practical lifeline to families, arguing that addiction is everybody's business—not just the addict's—and addiction doesn't have the right to trump the welfare of the family.

Not God: A History of Alcoholics Anonymous by Ernest Kurtz (Hazelden, 1991). The most complete history of AA ever written, including anecdotes and excerpts from the diaries, correspondence, and memoirs of AA's early figures.

The Selfish Brain: Learning from Addiction by Robert L. DuPont, MD (Hazelden, 2000). From the basics of brain chemistry to the workings of particular drugs such as alcohol, tobacco, marijuana, cocaine, and heroin, this book explains how various treatments and approaches lead to recovery and whole, healthy lives.

Recovery Now: A Basic Text for Today (Hazelden, 2013). This is an accessible basic text written in today's language for anyone guided by the Twelve Steps in recovering from addiction to alcohol and other drugs.

Everything Changes: Help for Families of Newly Recovering Alcoholics by Beverly Conyers (Hazelden, 2009). A basic guide for the family members of addicts who have just come home from treatment or are newly recovering in an outpatient program or Twelve Step program. Outlines the changes that addicts and family members go through and offers practical advice on self-care for everyone as they find their mutual paths to recovery.

Twelve Step Sponsorship: How It Works by Hamilton B. (Hazelden, 1996). A clear step-by-step guide on the principles and practices of sponsorship including sections on finding and choosing a sponsor as well as being an effective sponsor.

Codependent No More: How to Stop Controlling Others and Start Caring for Yourself by Melody Beattie (Hazelden, 1986, 1992). The *New York Times* bestselling book that defined codependency and gave people across the world a way to overcome it.

Treatment Centers

If your loved one is still drinking or drugging, go to lovefirst.net for an extensive list of treatment centers as well as low-cost programs. We have referred patients to many treatment centers and feel comfortable recommending those on our list, but treatment centers change in philosophy and ownership, so always do your homework. There are many treatment centers not listed that also do good work. Be vigilant, and ask thoughtful questions to be sure the treatment center you choose is right for your loved one.

Here are a few examples.

Betty Ford Center: 888-454-1458 / bettyfordcenter.org
This premiere chemical dependency treatment center for adults, with excellent family and children's programs in Rancho Mirage, California, offers an intensive assessment program, pain management, and relapse prevention. Its services include a special executive track and also a new program for young adults. The Betty Ford Center is now part of the Hazelden Betty Ford Foundation.

Caron Foundation: 800-854-6023 / caron.org
With multiple locations and high-quality services based in Wernersville, Pennsylvania, the Caron Foundation offers programs for older adults, baby boomers, adults, young adults, adolescents, and family education.

Cirque Lodge: 877-997-3422 / cirquelodge.com
Clinically advanced treatment is provided in two different settings: The Lodge is nestled in the mountains of Sundance, Utah, and provides an intimate treatment environment in luxurious surroundings. The Studio, located in Orem, Utah, is also high quality but more competitively priced. The family-owned facility includes a first-class clinical staff.

Crossroads Centre Antigua: 888-452-0091 / crossroadsantigua.org
Eric Clapton's beautiful residential treatment center located in Antigua, West Indies, offers reasonably priced, world-class treatment in a wonderful location. There are also renewal programs for those already in recovery and a family program.

Hazelden Betty Ford Foundation: 800-257-7810 / hazelden.org
Since 1949, Hazelden has been the originator of modern alcoholism treatment. Its specializations include inpatient and outpatient services, dual diagnosis, adolescent, young adults, impaired physicians and legal professionals, women's program, extended care, family programs, and more. An online bookstore carries all Hazelden publications. Its treatment centers are located in Minnesota, New York, Oregon, Florida, and California.

La Hacienda: 800-749-6160 / lahacienda.com
A high-quality residential program in the Texas hill country, La Hacienda offers adult programs, a collegiate program, a program with a Christian perspective, outpatient services, and a family program.

Pavillion: 828-694-2300 / Pavillion.org
Located in a beautiful country setting near Lake Lure in western North Carolina, Pavillion offers longer treatment stays with a one-to-six counselor-patient ratio. With primary residential treatment, extended care, and specialized programs for professionals and young adults, Pavillion also provides sober living for men. Its family program helps family members start their own recovery.

Pine Grove: 888-574-4673 / pinegrovetreatment.com
Moderately priced residential programs are available from forty-five to ninety days, including a women's program (treating both addiction and eating disorders), men's program, programs for older adults, sex addiction treatment, and outpatient services Based in Hattiesburg, Mississippi, Pine Grove also offers a family program, an addiction evaluation program, and intensive workshops.

Low-Cost Treatment Centers
Those that offer lower-cost treatment include:

Dawn Farm: (734) 485-8725 / dawnfarm.org
Located in a lovely country setting in Ann Arbor, Michigan, with gardens and farm animals, this residential recovery program has offered stays up to 120 days since 1973. Dawn Farm also provides outpatient treatment and transitional housing. It's very involved with the local AA community and produces one of the best blogs on addiction, "Addiction & Recovery News."

New Found Life: 800-635-9899 / newfoundlife.com
This family-run, high-quality residential treatment center near the ocean in Long Beach, California, offers extended care, residential continuing care, and a family program featuring notable guest speakers. It's very involved with the local AA community.

The Retreat: 866-928-3434 / theretreat.org
Located in a beautiful wooded setting in Wayzata, Minnesota (a suburb of Minneapolis), the Retreat is an impeccable residential, AA-immersion recovery program with veteran staff. It also offers an evening outpatient program, an older adult day program, family program, and weekend retreats. It has an active alumni organization and is highly involved in the AA community.

If you do not have funds for treatment, contact the Salvation Army. They offer no-cost, long-term treatment at locations throughout the country in their Harbor Lights Centers. To help families who have nowhere to turn to get their loved ones help, make a donation earmarked for the alcohol and drug treatment programs at salvationarmyusa.org/usn /harbor-lights.

Twelve Step Resources

Alcoholics Anonymous World Services: aa.org. Use this site to find AA meetings around the world and much more.

Narcotics Anonymous World Services: na.org. Use this site to find NA meetings around the world and much more.

Al-Anon Family Groups: al-anon.alateen.org. Use this site to find Al-Anon meetings around the world, meetings for teens, and much more.

Families Anonymous Recovery Fellowship: familiesanonymous.org. Use this site to find FA in the United States and twelve other countries, and much more.

Nar-Anon Family Groups: nar-anon.org. Use this site to find Nar-Anon meetings around the world, meetings for teens, and much more.

Blogs

Addiction and Recovery News. This blog began as a way to provide the staff of Dawn Farm with the most up-to-date information and critical analysis of scientific research and commentary in the popular media. It has grown into one of the most widely followed blogs on addiction and recovery issues. Visit addictionandrecoverynews.wordpress.com.

AA Redux. This blog features some of the most thoughtful writing on AA and the Twelve Steps. Families can apply it to their Al-Anon program. Its goal is to write about the role of a sponsor, but it is so much more. The writing team is composed of three generations of AA sponsor–sponsee relationships. Visit www.aaredux.com.

Collegiate Recovery Programs

College-based programs that support recovery are growing rapidly throughout colleges and universities. Here are some helpful resources.

Association of Recovery in Higher Education. This nonprofit is dedicated to "changing the trajectory of recovery students' lives." The site lists colleges and universities that offer programs and offer suggestions for how to start a program: collegiaterecovery.org.

Augsburg College StepUP Program. This highly recommended program at Augsburg College in Minneapolis is well established, with excellent outcomes in both GPA and recovery success. The website provides results of outcome studies: augsburg.edu/stepup.

Tribeca Twelve. Hazelden's collegiate recovery residence is for young adults 18 to 29. The sober residence offers hope, help, and healing in Manhattan's Tribeca neighborhood, with access to Hazelden resources as well as colleges and universities throughout the New York metro area. Visit hazelden.org/web/public/new_york_recovery_housing_tribeca.page.

University of Michigan Collegiate Recovery Program. This program offers a supportive recovery community for students with an exemplary understanding of addiction and recovery: uhs.umich.edu/recovery# meetings.

The Twelve Steps of Alcoholics Anonymous and Al-Anon*

1. We admitted we were powerless over alcohol—that our lives had become unmanageable.

2. Came to believe that a Power greater than ourselves could restore us to sanity.

3. Made a decision to turn our will and our lives over to the care of God *as we understood Him.*

4. Made a searching and fearless moral inventory of ourselves.

5. Admitted to God, to ourselves, and to another human being the exact nature of our wrongs.

6. Were entirely ready to have God remove all these defects of character.

7. Humbly asked Him to remove our shortcomings.

8. Made a list of all persons we had harmed, and became willing to make amends to them all.

9. Made direct amends to such people wherever possible, except when to do so would injure them or others.

10. Continued to take personal inventory and when we were wrong promptly admitted it.

11. Sought through prayer and meditation to improve our conscious contact with God *as we understood Him,* praying only for knowledge of His will for us and the power to carry that out.

12. Having had a spiritual awakening as the result of these steps, we tried to carry this message to alcoholics (others*), and to practice these principles in all our affairs.[126]

The Twelve Traditions of Alcoholics Anonymous

1. Our common welfare should come first; personal recovery depends upon A.A. unity.

2. For our group purpose there is but one ultimate authority—a loving God as He may express Himself in our group conscience. Our leaders are but trusted servants; they do not govern.

3. The only requirement for A.A. membership is a desire to stop drinking.

4. Each group should be autonomous except in matters affecting other groups or A.A. as a whole.

5. Each group has but one primary purpose—to carry its message to the alcoholic who still suffers.

6. An A.A. group ought never endorse, finance, or lend the A.A. name to any related facility or outside enterprise, lest problems of money, property, and prestige divert us from our primary purpose.

7. Every A.A. group ought to be fully self-supporting, declining outside contributions.

8. Alcoholics Anonymous should remain forever nonprofessional, but our service centers may employ special workers.

9. A.A., as such, ought never be organized; but we may create service boards or committees directly responsible to those they serve.

10. Alcoholics Anonymous has no opinion on outside issues; hence the A.A. name ought never be drawn into public controversy.

11. Our public relations policy is based on attraction rather than promotion; we need always maintain personal anonymity at the level of press, radio, and films.

12. Anonymity is the spiritual foundation of all our traditions, ever reminding us to place principles before personalities.[127]

Notes

Introduction: We Come Home Together

1. Jim Collins, *Good to Great: Why Some Companies Make the Leap . . . And Others Don't* (New York: HarperBusiness, 2001), 170.

2. Erma Bombeck, "Erma Bombeck Quotes," GoodReads, www.goodreads .com/quotes/209784-the-family-we-were-a-strange-little-band-of-characters (accessed June 21, 2014).

Chapter 1: The Missing Element

3. Since research on outcomes for the general population post-treatment are few and validity varies, a statistical range of 50 to 90 percent is commonly used. No one statistic can claim accuracy in reporting relapse rates. To complicate matters, levels of support and time in treatment vary widely, as do the environments addicted persons return to after treatment. If you would like to research this further, here are some beginning points: R.L. Hubbard, M.E. Marsden, E. Cavanaugh, and J.V. Rachal, *Drug Use After Drug Treatment,* background paper prepared for the IOM/NAS Committee on a National Strategy for HIV/AIDS, April 1986; Rudolf H. Moos, John W. Finney, and Ruth C. Cronkite, *Alcoholism Treatment: Context, Process, and Outcome* (New York: Oxford University Press, 1990); J.W. Finney and R.H. Moos, "The long-term course of treated alcoholism: I. Mortality, remission, and relapse rates and comparisons with community controls," *Journal of Studies on Alcohol* 52 (1991): 44–54; K. Humphrey, R. H. Moos, and C. Cohen, "Social and community resources and long-term recovery from treated and untreated alcoholism," *Journal of Studies on Alcohol* 58:3 (1997): 231–238; D. C. Walsh, R. W. Hingson, D. M. Merrigan, S. M. Levenson, et al., "A randomized trial of treatment options for alcohol-abusing workers," *New England Journal of Medicine* 325 (1991): 775–782; and Polich and Braiker, 1991. Another helpful article: Omar Manejwala, "How Often Do Long-Term Sober Alcoholics and Addicts Relapse?" *Psychology Today,* February 14, 2014.

4. Eric Topol, *The Creative Destruction of Medicine: How the Digital Revolution Will Create Better Health Care* (New York: Basic Books, 2013).

5. Robert L. DuPont, A. T. McLellan, W. L. White, et al., "Setting the standard for recovery: Physicians' Health Programs," *Journal of Substance Abuse Treatment* 36:2 (March 2009), 159–171.

6. Stephen King, "Frey's Lies." *Entertainment Weekly,* February 1, 2007.

7. Marie T. Brown and Jennifer K. Bussell, "Medical Adherence: WHO Cares?" *Mayo Clinic Proceedings* 86:4 (April 2011), 304–314.

Chapter 2: Stick with the Winners

8. Douglas R. Scott II, "The Direct Medical Costs of Healthcare-Associated Infections in U.S. Hospitals and the Benefits of Prevention." Division of Healthcare Quality Promotion, National Center for Preparedness, Detection, and Control of Infectious Diseases, Coordinating Center for Infectious Diseases, Centers for Disease Control and Prevention, March 2009, www.cdc.gov/hai /pdfs/hai/scott_costpaper.pdf (accessed June 21, 2014).

9. National Institute of Justice, "'Swift and Certain' Sanctions in Probation Are Highly Effective: Evaluation of the HOPE Program," National Institute of Justice, February 2, 2012, www.nij.gov/topics/corrections/community/drug -offenders/Pages/hawaii-hope.aspx (accessed June 21, 2014).

10. Robert L. DuPont, A. T. McLellan, W. L. White, et al., "Setting the standard for recovery: Physicians' Health Programs," *Journal of Substance Abuse Treatment* 36:2 (March 2009), 159–171.

Chapter 3: How It All Started

11. Molly Monahan, *Seeds of Grace: A Nun's Reflection on the Spirituality of Alcoholics Anonymous* (New York: Riverhead Books, 2001).

12. This originated with Bill Wilson. It was used in "A Newcomer Asks" (New York: Alcoholics Anonymous World Services, 1980).

13. Alcoholics Anonymous, *Alcoholics Anonymous, 4th Edition* (New York: Alcoholics Anonymous World Services, 2000), xvii.

14. William G. Borchert, *The Lois Wilson Story: When Love Is Not Enough* (Center City, Minnesota: Hazelden, 2005), x.

15. Al-Anon Family Group Headquarters, Inc., *Al-Anon Faces Alcoholism, 2nd Edition* (New York: Al-Anon Family Group Headquarters, Inc., 1984), 98.

Chapter 5: A Misunderstood Disease

16. Lucius Annaeus Seneca, *Letters from a Stoic,* Robin Campbell, trans. (London: Penguin Books, 1969).

17. "Inebriety as a Disease," *Scientific American,* January 27, 1877.

18. T. L. Wright, "The Property of Alcohol Which Allures the Neurotic to Drink," *Scientific American Supplement,* 474, January 31, 1885.

19. American Association for the Study and Cure of Inebriety, "The Disease of Inebriety: From Alcohol, Opium and Other Narcotic Drugs, Its Etiology, Pathology, Treatment and Medivo-Legal Relations" (New York: E. B. Treat, 1893).

20. Isaiah De Zouche, "On Inebriety and the Duty of the State with Regard to Inebriates" (Dunedin, New Zealand: Joseph Brajthwaite, 1885).

21. Dale Mitchel, *Silkworth: The Little Doctor Who Loved Drunks* (Center City, Minnesota: Hazelden, 2002).

22. Gretchen Voss, "Disease and Diet: Outsmart Your DNA Destiny," *Women's Health,* January 19, 2012.

23. Since researchers cannot decisively determine exactly the ratio between the genetics of addiction and environmental factors (such as the drinking culture one inhabits), a statistical range of 50 to 65 percent is commonly used. If you would like to research the genetics of addiction further, including twin and adoption studies and animal studies, here are some beginning points: Matt McGue, *Behavioral Genetics Models of Alcoholism and Drinking* (New York: Guildford Press, 1999); A. C. Heath, K. K. Bucholz, P. A. Madden, S. H. Dinwiddie, et al., "Genetic and environmental contributions to alcohol dependence risk in a national twin sample: Consistency of findings in women and men," National Institute on Alcohol Abuse and Alcoholism, 1997; Danielle M. Dick and Arpana Agrawal, "The Genetics of Alcohol and Other Drug Dependence," National Institute on Alcohol Abuse and Alcoholism, 2008; R. L. Bell, Z. A. Rodd, L. Lumeng, J. M. Murphy, and W. J. McBride, "The alcohol-preferring P rat and animal models of excessive alcohol drinking," National Institute on Alcohol Abuse and Alcoholism, 2006; and T. K. Li, L. Lumeng, W. J. McBride, and J. M. Murphy, "An experimental approach to understanding the genetic and neurobiological basis of alcoholism," *Transactions of the American Clinical and Climatological Association* 104 (1993): 61–73. Additionally, refer to: Howard J. Edenberg, "The Collaborative Study on the Genetics of Alcoholism," *Alcohol Health and Research World,* 1995; and National Institute on Drug Abuse, "Genetics: The Blueprint of Health and Disease," *Topics in Brief: Genetics of Addiction,* 2008. For twins research in the United States, see C. A. Prescott and K. S. Kendler, "Genetic and Environmental Contributions to Alcohol Abuse and Dependence in a Population-Based Sample of Male Twins," *American Journal of*

Psychiatry 156 (1999), 34–40. The statement that alcoholism is one of the most complex genetic diseases to study came from a 1999 conversation the author had with Robert W. Karp, director of the Genetics Program, National Institute on Alcohol Abuse and Alcoholism, National Institutes of Health from 1991 to 2001.

24. Nelson Mandela, untitled speech (Healing and Reconciliation Service, Johannesburg, South Africa, December 6, 2000).

25. Harry Haroutunian, *Being Sober: A Step-by-Step Guide to Getting to, Getting through, and Living in Recovery* (New York: Rodale Books, 2013).

26. Mark Muraven and Roy F. Baumeister, "Self-Regulation and Depletion of Limited Resources: Does Self-Control Resemble Muscle?" *Psychological Bulletin* 126: 2 (2000), 247–259.

27. Ibid.

28. *Alcoholics Anonymous*, 553.

Chapter 6: Motivation Isn't the Answer

29. C. Ayyad and T. Andersen, "Long-term efficacy of dietary treatment of obesity: A systematic review of studies published between 1931 and 1999," *Obesity Reviews* 1 (2000), 113–119.

30. Jeni Cross, "Three Myths of Behavior Change: What You Think You Know That You Don't," TEDxCSU, 2013, www.youtube.com/watch?v=l5d8G W6GdR0 (accessed June 22, 2014).

31. Jessica M. Nolan, P. Wesley Shultz, and Robert B. Scaldini, et al., "Normative Social Influence Is Underdetected," *Personality and Social Psychology Bulletin* 34 (July 2008), 913–923.

32. *Alcoholics Anonymous*, 568.

Chapter 7: A Closer Look at Relapse

33. *A Day at a Time: Daily Reflections for Recovering People* (Center City, Minnesota: Hazelden, 1987).

34. These statistics have been commonly used since Dr. Silkworth's success rate of about 2 percent while working with alcoholics prior to the formation of Alcoholics Anonymous. Since research in this area is limited, varies in validity, and findings may have limitations, it is difficult to know exact numbers. Research sometimes combines alcoholics with alcohol abusers (substance use disorder) and often doesn't report switched addictions (switching to another type of intoxicant). If you would like to research this further, here is a beginning point: Rudolf H. Moos and Bernice S. Moos, "Rates and predictors of relapse

after natural and treated remission from alcohol use disorder," *Addiction* 101: 2 (February 2006): 212–222.

35. *Twelve Steps and Twelve Traditions* (New York: Alcoholics Anonymous World Services, 2002), 58.

36. Elizabeth Landau, "Alcoholics Anonymous as a Spiritual Experience," The Chart, CNN Health, December 14, 2010, http://thechart.blogs.cnn.com /2010/12/14/alcoholics-anonymous-as-a-spiritual-experience (accessed June 22, 2014).

37. Buddy T., "Spouse's Attitude Can Affect Alcoholic's Relapse," About. com, http://alcoholism.about.com/library/weekly/aa020101a.htm (accessed June 22, 2014).

Chapter 8: Tiny Tasks

38. B. J. Fogg, "Fogg Method: 3 Steps to Changing Behavior," B. J. Fogg, www.foggmethod.com (accessed June 22, 2014).

39. B. J. Fogg, "Forget Big Change, Start with a Tiny Habit," TEDxFremont, www.youtube.com/watch?v=AdKUJxjn-R8 (accessed June 22, 2014).

40. National Institute on Drug Abuse, "Shatter the Myths: General Questions About Drug Abuse," National Institute on Drug Abuse, http://drugfacts week.drugabuse.gov/chat/chatfaqs_topics/general_questions.php (accessed June 22, 2014).

41. *Alcoholics Anonymous,* 60.

42. *Courage to Change: One Day at a Time in Al-Anon II* (New York: Al-Anon Family Group Headquarters, Inc., June 1992).

43. Robert Smith, "Dr. Bob's Farewell Talk" Alcoholics Anonymous, www .aa.org/pages/en_US/dr-bobs-farewell-talk (accessed June 22, 2014).

44. Jeni Cross, "Three Myths of Behavior Change: What You Think You Know That You Don't," TEDxCSU, 2013, www.youtube.com/watch?v=l5d8GW 6GdR0 (accessed June 22, 2014).

45. *Alcoholics Anonymous,* 83–84.

46. Joseph Martin, "The Promises of AA," www.youtube.com/watch?v =vvDmSV8yktM (accessed June 22, 2014).

Chapter 9: A New Look at Enabling Addiction

47. Robert Brault, *Round Up the Usual Subjects: Thoughts on Just About Everything* (self-published, CreateSpace Independent Publishing Platform, 2014).

48. Toni Morrison, interview by Bob Swaim, *Wired for Books,* September 15, 1987, www.wiredforbooks.org/tonimorrison (accessed June 22, 2014).

49. Leo Buscaglia, *Love* (Greenwich, Connecticut: Fawcett, 1972).

Chapter 10: Families Pay a High Price

50. Robert M. Sapolsky, *Why Zebras Don't Get Ulcers, Third Edition* (New York: Holt Paperbacks, 2004).

51. John J. Medina, *Brain Rules: 12 Principles for Surviving and Thriving at Work, Home, and School* (Seattle: Pear Press, 2014).

52. Jonah Lehrer, "The Reinvention of the Self," *SEED Magazine,* February/March 2006, 58–67.

53. Amy Arnesten, "Creative Minds: Making Sense of Stress and the Brain," National Institutes of Health, March 18, 2014, http://directorsblog.nih .gov/2014/03/18/creative-minds-making-sense-of-stress-and-the-brain (accessed June 22, 2014).

54. National Sleep Foundation, www.sleepfoundation.org.

55. Jeffrey Iliff, "How our brains wash away the gunk during sleep," Brain Institute, Oregon Health and Science University, 2002, www.ohsu.edu/blogs /brain/2013/10/30/how-our-brains-wash-away-the-gunk-during-sleep (accessed June 22, 2014).

56. Christopher Peterson, Steven F. Maier, and Martin E.P. Seligman, *Learned Helplessness: A Theory for the Age of Personal Control* (New York: Oxford University Press, 1995).

57. Douglas A. Bernstein, *Essentials of Psychology* (Stamford, Connecticut: Cengage Learning, 2013).

58. Sonia J. Lupien, Bruce S. McEwen, Megan R. Gunnar, and Christine Heim, "Effects of Stress Throughout the Lifespan on the Brain, Behaviour and Cognition," *Nature Reviews Neuroscience* 10 (June 2009), 434–445.

59. Ibid.

60. Center on the Developing Child, "Key Concepts: Toxic Stress," Harvard University, http://developingchild.harvard.edu/index.php/key_concepts/toxic_ stress_response (accessed June 22, 2014).

61. Bruce D. Perry, Ronnie A. Pollard, Toi L. Blakely, William L. Baker, Domenico Vigilante, "Childhood Trauma, the Neurobiology of Adaptation, and 'Use-Dependent' Development of the Brain: How 'States' Become 'Traits,'" *Infant Mental Health Journal* 16:4 (Winter 1995), 271–291.

62. Jerry Moe, written specifically for inclusion in *It Takes a Family,* 2014.

63. Joseph Califano Jr., "No Safe Haven: Children of Substance Abusing Parents," The National Center on Addiction and Substance Abuse at Columbia University, January 1999, www.casacolumbia.org/addiction-research/reports /no-safe-haven-children-substance-abusing-parents (accessed June 22, 2014).

64. Sis Wenger, "The Challenge: Drawn By Anger . . . Motivated By Hope," National Association for Children of Alcoholics, Summer 2008, www.nacoa .org/pdfs/Summer_08_comment.pdf (accessed June 22, 2014).

65. Molly Monahan, *Seeds of Grace: A Nun's Reflection on the Spirituality of Alcoholics Anonymous* (New York: Riverhead Books, 2001).

66. Jerry Moe, written specifically for inclusion in *It Takes a Family,* 2014.

Chapter 11: It Takes a Family

67. David R. Mace, "Family Strengths," Encyclopedia.com., www.encyclo pedia.com/doc/1G2-3406900165.html (accessed June 22, 2014).

68. Robert L. DuPont, A. T. McLellan, W. L. White, et al., "Setting the standard for recovery: Physicians' Health Programs," *Journal of Substance Abuse Treatment* 36:2 (March 2009), 159–171.

69. Bruce Feiler, *The Secrets of Happy Families: Improve Your Mornings, Rethink Family Dinner, Fight Smarter, Go Out and Play, and Much More* (New York: William Morrow, 2013).

Chapter 12: Twelve Step Meetings

70. *Al-Anon/Alateen Service Manual* (Virginia Beach, Virginia: Al-Anon Family Group Headquarters, Inc., 1992).

71. *Al-Anon/Alateen Service Manual,* "Suggested Al-Anon Welcome."

72. *Al Anon/Alateen Service Manual,* "Al-Anon/Alateen Closing."

73. Carol W., "My sponsor's unconditional love was the turning point," *The Forum,* December 2012, www.al-anon.org/forum-magazines-stories/item /539-my-sponsor's-unconditional-love-was-the-turning-point (accessed June 22, 2014).

74. Erica Dhawan, "7 Tips for Making the Most of Your Sponsor," *Forbes,* February 19, 2013.

75. "AA Preamble," *AA Grapevine, Inc.,* June 1947.

76. *Questions and Answers on Sponsorship* (New York: Alcoholics Anonymous World Services, Inc., 1983).

77. Ibid.

78. "The Unity Declaration," Alcoholics Anonymous World Services, Inc.,

www.aa.org/pages/en_US/frequently-asked-questions-about-aa-history#doce (accessed June 22, 2014).

79. *Questions and Answers on Sponsorship.*

Chapter 13: Putting Structured Family Recovery into Place

80. Randy Mayeux, "Two Great Dilemmas: Ignorance and Ineptitude– Insights from Atul Gawande's *The Checklist Manifesto*," *First Friday Book Synopsis*, February 23, 2010, http://ffbsccn.wordpress.com/2010/02/23/two-great -dilemmas-ignorance-and-ineptitude-insight-from-atul-gawandes-the-checklist -manifesto/ (accessed June 22, 2014).

81. Atul Gawande, *The Checklist Manifesto: How to Get Things Right* (New York: Picador, 2011).

82. Martin E. P. Seligman, *Learned Optimism: How to Change Your Mind and Your Life* (New York: Vintage, 2006).

83. Kevin McCauley, *Pleasure Unwoven: A Personal Journey about Addiction* (DVD), The Institute for Addiction Study, 2010.

84. Tom Landry, LibraryofQuotes.com, 2013, www.libraryofquotes.com /quotes/author/Tom/Landry (accessed June 22, 2014).

Chapter 14: The Heart Triumphs

85. David Brooks, "Other People's Views," *New York Times*, February 6, 2014, www.nytimes.com/2014/02/07/opinion/brooks-other-peoples-views.html ?partner=rssnyt&emc=rss&_r=1 (accessed June 22, 2014).

86. Naomi Shihab Nye, "Kindness," in *Words Under the Words: Selected Poems* (Portland, Oregon: Eighth Mountain Press, 1994). Used with permission.

87. Alina Tugend, "Praise Is Fleeting, but Brickbats We Recall," *New York Times*, March 23, 2012, www.nytimes.com/2012/03/24/your-money/why-people -remember-negative-events-more-than-positive-ones.html?pagewanted=1& .tsrc=sun&partner=yahoofinance (accessed June 22, 2014).

88. George Vaillant, *Spiritual Evolution: A Scientific Defense of Faith* (New York: Harmony, 2009).

89. Eric Mosley, "Crowdsource Your Performance Reviews," HBR Blog Network, *Harvard Business Review*, June 15, 2012, http://blogs.hbr.org/2012/06 /crowdsource-your-performance-r/ (accessed June 22, 2014).

90. Mark Muraven and Roy F. Baumeister, "Self-Regulation and Depletion of Limited Resources: Does Self-Control Resemble Muscle?" *Psychological Bulletin* 126:2 (2000), 247–259.

91. Alina Tugend, "Praise Is Fleeting."

92. The National Institute for Play, www.nifplay.org (accessed June 22, 2014).

93. Eric Clapton, *Clapton: The Autobiography* (New York: Three Rivers Press, 2008).

94. *A Brief History of A.A.* (New York: Alcoholics Anonymous World Services, Inc., 1957).

95. William G. Borchert, "Books and Movies," http://williamborchert.com /photos.html (accessed June 23, 2014).

Epilogue: The Hero's Journey

96. Joseph Campbell, *The Hero with a Thousand Faces, 3rd Edition* (Novato, California: New World Library, 2008).

Structured Family Recovery Weekly Meetings

97. *Alcoholics Anonymous*, 83–84.

98. Terence T. Gorski and Merlene Miller, *Staying Sober: A Guide for Relapse Prevention, 1st Edition* (Independence Press, 1986).

99. John J. McCloy, "Thoughts on the Business of Life," *Forbes*, http:// thoughts.forbes.com/thoughts/john-j-mccloy (accessed June 23, 2014).

100. Bridgette Boudreau, "What I Learned from 12-Step Slogans," *The Wild Life* Blog, March 5, 2009, http://bridgetteboudreau.com/2009/03/05/what -i-learned-from-aa-slogans (accessed June 22, 2014).

101. Audrey Barrick, "Most Americans Still Believe in God; Nonbelief Rises," *The Christian Post*, June 3, 2011, www.christianpost.com/news/most -americans-still-believe-in-god-nonbelief-rises-50791 (accessed June 22, 2014).

102. *Twelve Steps and Twelve Traditions*, 34.

103. *Alcoholics Anonymous*, 75.

104. George Mann and Dick Rice, *Touch Life Gently–Step Four*, The Retreat, Wayzata, Minnesota, 1987, www.youtube.com/watch?v=zR3W8N_H5O4 (accessed June 22, 2014).

105. *Alcoholics Anonymous*, 62.

106. "A Guide to the Twelve Steps of Alcoholics Anonymous" (Akron, Ohio: Akron Area Intergroup Council of Alcoholics Anonymous, 1941/2007).

107. "Planting and Reaping," HumanityAndLove.com, www.humanityand love.com/amazing_facts/Planting_and_Reaping.htm (accessed June 23, 2014.

108. *Mr. SponsorPants: An AA Sponsor Blog*, October 19, 2010, http://mrsponsorpants.typepad.com/mr_sponsorpants/2010/10/questions-via-email-if-you-are-sober-a-long-time-and-still-have-a-hard-time-whats-the-point.html (accessed June 23, 2014).

109. Lewis Aiken, *Attitudes and Related Psychosocial Constructs: Theories, Assessment, and Research* (Thousand Oaks, California: Sage Publications, 2002).

110. C. Joybell C., *Vade Mecum: (n) a needed thing carried around everywhere; a useful handbook or guidebook always kept on one's person; lit. "go with me"* (self-published, CreateSpace Independent Publishing Platform, 2013).

111. Hazelden, *Steps 6 and 7: Ready, Willing and Able* (Center City, Minnesota: Hazelden, 1992).

112. *Alcoholics Anonymous*, 76.

113. Amanda Neville, "How Forgiveness Can Save Your Business," *Forbes*, June 21, 2013, www.forbes.com/sites/amandaneville/2013/06/21/how-forgiveness-can-save-your-business (accessed June 23, 2014).

114. University of Royal Holloway London, "Study shows trustworthy people perceived to look similar to ourselves," *Science Daily*, November 7, 2013, www.sciencedaily.com/releases/2013/11/131107094406.htm (accessed June 22, 2014).

115. Dan Jones, "Trustworthy People Are Seen as More Similar to Ourselves," *Evolution: This View of Life*, January 11, 2014, www.thisviewoflife.com/index.php/magazine/articles/trustworthy-people-are-seen-as-more-similar-to-ourselves (accessed June 23, 2014).

116. *Twelve Steps and Twelve Traditions*, 192.

117. Rabbi Ben A. Romer, "Yom Kippur: The Time of the Year for Soul Inventory," *Richmond Times Dispatch*, September 27, 2009, www.timesdispatch.com/news/yom-kippur-the-time-of-year-for-soul-inventory/article_cfa6554f-bc32-5c31-8bda-c86702af6045.html (accessed June 22, 2014).

118. *Alcoholics Anonymous*, 86.

119. Various authors, *Love Poems from God: Sacred Voices from the East and West*, Daniel Ladinsky, trans. (New York: Penguin Books, 2002).

120. Ibid.

121. Anonymous, "Sponsorship in the 21st Century," *AA Redux*, www.aaredux.com (accessed June 23, 2014).

122. Ibid.

123. Bill Pittman, *Practice These Principles* and *What Is the Oxford Group?* (Center City, Minnesota: Hazelden, 1997), xi.

Tools, Checklists and Resources

124. Used with permission of Terence T. Gorski.

125. Used with permission of Terence T. Gorski.

126. The Twelve Steps of Alcoholics Anonymous and Al-Anon are taken from *Alcoholics Anonymous, 4th Edition*, 59–60. Reprinted with permission. Alcoholics Anonymous is for recovery from alcoholism, and Twelve Step programs patterned after AA address other problems.

127. The Twelve Traditions of Alcoholics Anonymous are taken from *Twelve Steps and Twelve Traditions*, 129–87. Reprinted with permission. Alcoholics Anonymous is for recovery from alcoholism, and Twelve Step programs patterned after AA address other problems.

About the Author

Debra Jay is the co-author with Jeff Jay of Hazelden's bestselling *Love First* and is a certified addiction counselor and interventionist. She is also the author of *No More Letting Go* (Bantam, 2002) and numerous journal and magazine articles on addiction. She has appeared on *Oprah* several times and *Doctor Oz,* among other TV shows, and is an in-demand keynote speaker and trainer at behavioral health conferences and treatment centers internationally.

Also of Interest

Love First
A Family's Guide to Intervention
Jeff Jay and Debra Jay
This standard-setting book has helped tens of thousands of families, friends, and professionals create a loving and effective plan for helping those who suffer from addiction. The second edition offers updated tools and techniques to help loved ones heal.
Order No. 7395; ebook EB7395

Everything Changes
Help for Families of Newly Recovering Addicts
Beverly Conyers
Easing fears and uncertainty, this book helps readers navigate the often tumultuous early months of a loved one's recovery.
Order No. 3807; ebook EB3807

Recovering My Kid
Parenting Young Adults in Treatment and Beyond
Joseph Lee, MD
A renowned expert explains the nature of youth addiction and treatment and how families can create a safe and supportive environment to promote recovery.
Order No. 4693; ebook EB4693

For more information or to order these or other resources from Hazelden Publishing, call **800-343-4499** or visit **hazelden.org/bookstore.**